Understanding Organizational Behavior

Understanding Organizational Behavior

Helen Stevenson

Willford Press
www.willfordpress.com

Published by Willford Press,
118-35 Queens Blvd., Suite 400,
Forest Hills, NY 11375, USA

ISBN: 978-1-68285-992-6

Cataloging-in-Publication Data

Understanding organizational behavior / Helen Stevenson.
p. cm.
Includes bibliographical references and index.
ISBN 978-1-68285-992-6
1. Organizational behavior. 2. Management. 3. Organization.
4. Psychology, Industrial. I. Stevenson, Helen.
HD58.7 .U53 2021
302.35--dc23

For information on all Willford Press publications
visit our website at www.willfordpress.com

WILLFORD PRESS

Contents

Preface

The study of human behavior within organizational settings is referred to as organizational behavior. It also studies the interface between human behavior and the organization. The study of organizational behavior is broadly classified into a few categories such as micro-level, meso-level and macro-level. The individuals in organizations fall under micro-level, the work groups are studied under meso-level and the study of the ways in which an organization behaves comes under macro-level. A number of methods are used for research in the field of organizational behavior such as quantitative methods and qualitative methods. Quantitative methods include statistical methods such as correlation, meta-analysis, multilevel modeling, multiple regression and structural equation modeling. Some of the methods which fall under the category of qualitative research are ethnography, case studies, historical methods and interviews. This textbook provides comprehensive insights into the field of organizational behavior. Some of the diverse topics covered herein address the varied branches that fall under this category. This book will provide extensive knowledge to the readers.

To facilitate a deeper understanding of the contents of this book a short introduction of every chapter is written below:

Chapter 1- The study within an organization which focuses on the performance of an individual as well as groups is known as organizational behavior. This is an introductory chapter which will introduce briefly all the significant aspects of organizational behavior such as its characteristics, features, challenges and opprtunities.

Chapter 2- Some of the attributes of individual behavior are personality, attitude, motivation and perception. There are different theories on personality such as type theory, trait theories and psychoanalytic theory. This chapter has been carefully written to provide an easy understanding of the varied attributes of individual behavior.

Chapter 3- People forms groups in order to interact and achieve particular objectives. The different types of communication which take place within organizations and groups are downward communication, upward communication, horizontal communication and diagonal communication. This chapter discusses in detail these theories related to group dynamics and team behavior.

Chapter 4- Leadership in a group involves creating a vision and then influencing, motivating and transforming others in order to achieve that vision. Some of the different processes which are associated with leadership are assessment of the organization or business, development of strategy and integrated management of business performance. All these diverse principles of leadership have been carefully analyzed in this chapter.

Chapter 5- The system which details the manner in which specific activities of an organization are directed and divided is known as organizational structure. The process through which the different elements of an organization are arranged into an efficient structure is known as departmentalization. The topics elaborated in this chapter will help in gaining a better perspective about the different aspects of organizational structure and systems.

I would like to share the credit of this book with my editorial team who worked tirelessly on this book. I owe the completion of this book to the never-ending support of my family, who supported me throughout the project.

Helen Stevenson

1

Introduction to Organizational Behavior

The study within an organization which focuses on the performance of an individual as well as groups is known as organizational behavior. This is an introductory chapter which will introduce briefly all the significant aspects of organizational behavior such as its characteristics, features, challenges and opprtunities.

Organizational behavior (OB) is the academic study of the ways people act within groups. Its principles are applied primarily in attempts to make businesses operate more effectively.

The study of organizational behavior includes areas of research dedicated to improving job performance, increasing job satisfaction, promoting innovation, and encouraging leadership. Each has its own recommended actions, such as reorganizing groups, modifying compensation structures, or changing methods of performance evaluation.

The study of organizational behavior has its roots in the late 1920s, when the Western Electric Company launched a now-famous series of studies of the behavior of workers at its Hawthorne Works plant in Cicero, Illinois.

Researchers there set out to determine whether workers could be made to be more productive if their environment was upgraded with better lighting and other design improvements. To their surprise, the researchers found that the environment was less important than social factors. It was more important, for example, that people got along with their co-workers and felt their bosses appreciated them.

Those initial findings inspired a series of wide-ranging studies between 1924 and 1933. They included the effects on productivity of work breaks, isolation, and lighting, among many other factors.

The best known of the results is called the Hawthorne Effect, which describes the way test subjects' behavior may change when they know they are being observed. Researchers are taught to consider whether and to what degree the Hawthorne Effect is skewing their findings on human behavior.

Organizational behavior was not fully recognized by the American Psychological Association as a field of academic study until the 1970s. However, the Hawthorne research is credited for validating organizational behavior as a legitimate field of study, and it's the foundation of the human resources profession as we now know it.

Goals of Organizational Behavior Study

The leaders of the Hawthorne study had a couple of radical notions. They thought they could use the techniques of scientific observation to increase an employee's amount and quality of work. And, they did not look at workers as interchangeable resources. Workers, they thought, were unique in terms of their psychology and potential fit within a company.

Over the following years, the concept of organizational behavior widened. Beginning with World War II, researchers began focusing on logistics and management science. Studies by the Carnegie School of Home Economics in the 1950s and 1960s solidified these rationalist approaches to decision-making.

Today, those and other studies have evolved into modern theories of business structure and decision-making.

The new frontiers of organizational behavior are the cultural components of organizations, such as how race, class, and gender roles affect group building and productivity. These studies take into account the ways in which identity and background inform decision-making.

Real World Examples of Organizational Behavior

Findings from organizational behavior research are used by executives and human relations professionals to better understand a business's culture, how that culture helps or hinders productivity and employee retention, and how to evaluate candidates' skills and personality during the hiring process.

Organizational behavior theories inform real-world evaluation and management of groups of people. There are a number of components:

- Personality plays a large role in the way a person interacts with groups and produces work. Understanding a candidate's personality, either through tests or through conversation, helps determine whether they are a good fit for an organization.
- Leadership, what it looks like and where it comes from, is a rich topic of debate and study within the field of organizational behaviour. Leadership can be broad, focused, centralized or de-centralized, decision-oriented, intrinsic in a person's personality, or simply a result of a position of authority.
- Power, authority, and politics all operate inter-dependently in a workplace. Understanding the appropriate ways these elements are exhibited and used, as agreed upon by workplace rules and ethical guidelines, are key components to running a cohesive business.

Characteristics and Nature of Organizational Behavior

Characteristics of Organisational Behavior

1. Behavioural Approach to Management:

Organisational behaviour is that part of whole management which represents the behavioural approach to management. Organisational behaviour has emerged as a distinct field of study because of the importance of human behaviour in organisations.

2. Cause and Effect Relationship:

Human behaviour is generally taken in terms of cause and effect relationship and not in philosophical terms. It helps in predicting the behaviour of individuals. It provides generalizations that managers can use to anticipate the effect of certain activities on human behaviour.

3. Organisational Behaviour is a Branch of Social Sciences:

Organisational behaviour is heavily influenced by several other social sciences viz. psychology, sociology and anthropology. It draws a rich array of research from these disciplines.

4. Three Levels of Analysis:

Organisational behaviour encompasses the study of three levels of analysis namely individual behaviour, inter-individual behaviour and the behaviour of organisations themselves. The field of organisational behaviour embraces all these levels as being complementary to each other.

5. A Science as well as an Art:

Organisational behaviour is a science as well as an art. The systematic knowledge about human behaviour is a science and the application of behavioural knowledge and skills is an art. Organisational behaviour is not an exact science because it cannot exactly predict the behaviour of people in organisations. At best a manager can generalize to a limited extent and in many cases, he has to act on the basis of partial information.

6. A Body of Theory, Research and Application:

Organisational behaviour consists of a body of theory, research and application which helps in understanding the human behaviour in organisation. All these techniques help the managers to solve human problems in organisations.

7. Beneficial to both Organisation and Individuals:

Organisational behaviour creates an atmosphere whereby both organisation and individuals are benefitted by each other. A reasonable climate is created so that employees may get much needed satisfaction and the organisation may attain its objectives.

8. Rational Thinking:

Organisational behaviour provides a rational thinking about people and their behaviour. The major objective of organisational behaviour is to explain and predict human behaviour in organisations, so that result yielding situations can be created.

Nature of Organisational Behavior

Organisational behaviour in the study of human behaviour in the organisations. Whenever an individual joins an organisation he brings with him unique set of personal characteristics, experiences from other organisations and a personal background. At the first stage organisational behaviour must look at the unique perspective that each individual brings to the work setting.

The second stage of organisational behaviour is to study the dynamics of how the incoming individuals interact with the broader organisation. No individual can work in isolation. He comes into contact with other individuals and the organisation in a variety of ways. The individual who joins a new organisation has to come into contact with the co-workers, managers, formal policies and procedures of the organisation etc.

Over the time, he is affected by his work experience and the organisation as well as his personal experiences and maturity. On the other hand, the organisation is also affected by the presence or absence of the individual. Thus, it is essential that OB must study the ways in which the individuals and organisation interact with each other.

The organisational behaviour must be studied from the perspective of the organisation itself because an organisation exists before a particular individual joins in and continues to exist after he or she has left the organisation. Thus, OB is the study of human behaviour in the organisation, the individual-organisation interaction and the organisation itself. And these factors are influenced by the external environment in which the individuals and the organisation exist.

Thus, we can say that we cannot study individual behaviour completely without learning something about the organisation. On the other hand, we cannot study the organisations without studying the behaviour of the individuals working in it. This is because the organisation influences and is influenced by the people working in it. Moreover, both the individuals and the organisation are influenced by the external environment. Thus, the field of organisational behaviour is a complex field. It seeks to throw light on the entire canvas of human factor in the organisations which will include the causes and effects of such behaviour.

Features of Organizational Behavior

Organizational Behavior is the study and application of knowledge about how people, individuals, and groups act in organizations. It does this by taking a system approach.

That is, it interprets people-organization relationships in terms of the whole person, the whole group, the whole organization, and the whole social system.

Its purpose is to build better relationships by achieving human objectives, organizational objectives, and social objectives.

Organizational Behavior:

- A Separate Field of Study and not a Discipline Only.
- An Interdisciplinary Approach.
- Applied Science.
- A Normative Science.
- A Humanistic and Optimistic Approach.
- A Total System Approach.

Objectives of Organizational Behavior

The organizations in which people work have an effect on their thoughts, feelings, and actions. These thoughts, feelings, and actions, in turn, affect the organization itself.

Organizational behavior studies the mechanisms governing these interactions, seeking to identify and foster behaviors conducive to the survival and effectiveness of the organization.

- Job Satisfaction.
- Finding the Right People.
- Organizational Culture.
- Leadership and Conflict Resolution.
- Understanding the Employees Better.
- Understand how to Develop Good Leaders.
- Develop a Good Team.
- Higher Productivity.

Fundamental Concepts of Organizational Behavior

Organization Behavior is based on a few fundamental concepts which revolve around the nature of people and organizations.

- Individual Differences.
- Perception.
- A whole Person.
- Motivated Behavior.
- The desire for Involvement.
- The value of the Person.
- Human Dignity.
- Organizations are Social System.
- Mutuality of Interest.
- Holistic Concept.

Main Challenges and Opportunities of Organizational Behavior

Challenges and opportunities of organizational behavior are massive and rapidly changing for improving productivity and meeting business goals.

- Improving Peoples' Skills.
- Improving Quality and Productivity.
- Total Quality Management (TQM).
- Managing Workforce Diversity.
- Responding to Globalization.
- Empowering People.
- Coping with Temporariness.
- Stimulating Innovation and Change.
- Emergence of E-Organisation & E-Commerce.
- Improving Ethical Behavior.
- Improving Customer Service.

- Helping Employees Balance Work-Life Conflicts.
- Flattening World.

Limitations of Organizational Behavior

Recognize the limitations of organizational behavior. Organizational Behavior will not abolish conflict and frustration; it can only reduce them. It is a way to improve, not an absolute answer to problems.

Furthermore, it is but part of the whole cloth of an organization.

We can discuss organizational behavior as a separate subject, but to apply it, we must tie it to the whole reality. Improved organizational behavior will not solve unemployment.

Organizational Behavior will not make up for our deficiencies, cannot substitute for poor planning, inept organizing, or inadequate controls. It is only one of the many systems operating within a larger social system.

Major limitations of OB are

- Behavioral Bias.
- The Law of Diminishing Returns.
- Unethical Manipulation of People.

Behavioral Bias

Behavioral Bias is a condition which is a reflection of tunnel vision, in which people have narrow viewpoints as if they were looking through a tunnel.

They see only the tiny view at the other end of the tunnel while missing the broader landscape.

Following the behavioral bias, people who lack system understanding may develop a behavioral bias, which leads them to develop a narrow viewpoint that emphasizes employee satisfaction while overlooking the broader system of the organization in relation to all its stakeholders.

It should be clear that the concern for employees can be so greatly overdone that the original purpose of bringing people together, which is "productivity organizational outputs for society" could be lost.

An effective organizational behavior should help accomplish organizational purposes. It should not replace them.

The person who does not consider the needs of people as consumers of organizational output while fighting for employee needs is not applying the ideas of organizational behavior correctly.

It is a mistake to make an assumption that the objective of organizational behavior is as simple as to create a satisfied employee-base, as that goal will not automatically turn into new products and stellar customer service.

It is also a fact that the person who pushes production outputs without regard for employee needs is also not applying organizational behavior in the right fashion.

The most effective OB dwells, acknowledges and appreciates a social system that consists of many types of human needs that are served in many ways.

Behavioral bias can be so misapplied in a way that it can be harmful to employees as well as the organization as a whole. Some individuals, despite having good intentions, so overwhelm others with the care that the recipients of such care become dependent and unproductive.

They find excuses for failure rather than take responsibility for progress. They do not possess a high degree of self-respect and self-discipline.

The Law of Diminishing Returns

Overemphasis on an organizational behavior, the practice may produce negative results, as indicated by the law of diminishing returns. It places an overemphasis on an OB practice may produce negative results.

It is a limiting factor in organizational behavior in the same way that it is in economics. In economics, the law of diminishing return refers to a declining amount of extra outputs when more of a desirable input is added to an economic situation.

After a certain point, the output from each unit of added input tends to become smaller. The added output eventually may reach zero and even continue to decline when more units of input are added.

The law of diminishing returns in organizational behavior works in a similar way.

According to the law of diminishing returns, at some point, increases of a desirable practice produce declining returns, finally resulting in zero returns, and then follows negative returns as more increases are added. More of a good thing is not necessarily good.

The concept means that for any situation there is an optimum level of a desirable practice, such as recognition or participation.

When that point is exceeded, there is a decline in returns realized. To put it differently, the fact that a practice is desirable does not necessarily imply that more of the same practice is more desirable.

Unethical Manipulation of People

A significant concern about organizational behavior is that its knowledge and techniques can be used to manipulate people unethically as well as to help them develop their potential.

People who lack respect for the basic dignity of the human being could learn organizational behavior ideas and use them for selfish ends.

They could use what they know about motivation or communication in the manipulation of people without regard for human welfare. People who lack ethical values could use people in unethical ways.

Importance of Organizational Behavior

During their careers, most people have worked for a company where people didn't get along, where no one knew what the expectations were, or where the boss failed to promote teamwork. The company most likely lacked a strong OB model.

Organizational behavior can help employees navigate a business's culture as well as help managers better understand how that culture helps or hinders employee productivity and retention. OB can also help managers evaluate a potential job candidate's skills and personality during the hiring process, allowing human resources to find the best fit for departments within the company. While there is never one exact way to assess these things, OB theory offers a set of guidelines to help organizations create a positive and vibrant internal culture.

One of the main goals of OB is to understand what motivates employees. How organizations measure job satisfaction varies, but most common metrics include a fair and equitable reward system, compelling work, enjoyable working conditions and good supervisors. By understanding what motivates employees, managers can adjust their policies to increase job satisfaction, thereby increasing productivity.

OB not only helps employees understand themselves better, it also offers a roadmap for managers to improve all aspects of their organizations:

- Improve job performance.
- Increase job satisfaction.
- Promote innovation.
- Encourage leadership.
- Improve customer service.

- Encourage ethical behavior.
- Create a positive work environment.

Depending on the challenges and desired outcomes, managers may use different tactics such as reorganizing workgroups, changing performance evaluations or modifying compensation structures. Understanding what motivates employees also plays a large part in how managers adjust company procedures or policies.

Not only does organizational behavior provide a roadmap for human resources and supervisors to manage more effectively, it also helps employees navigate an organization's culture.

When a strong model of OB is in place, employees can understand themselves better and know how they can best flourish inside an organization. And managers are better able to predict how employees might react under differing circumstances and adjust accordingly.

Creating a culture where relationships are cooperative, employees feel valued and companies flourish is at the heart of organizational behavior.

Contributing Disciplines to Organization Behavior Field

There are some important disciplines in the organizational behavior field which developed it extensively.

Due to an increase in organizational complexity, various types of knowledge are required and help in many ways.

Organizational Behavior
1. Political sciences
2. Anthropology
3. Economics
4. Social psychology
5. Sociology
6. Psychology

Contributing Disciplines to the Organization Behavior Field are given below:

- Psychology.
- Sociology.

- Social Psychology.
- Economics.
- Anthropology.
- Political Sciences.

Psychology

Psychology has perhaps the first influence on the field of organizational behavior because it is a science of behavior. A psychologist studies almost all aspects of behavior.

Psychology deals with studying human behavior that seeks to explain and sometimes change the behavior'of humans and other animals.

Psychologists are primarily interested in predicting the behavior of individuals to a great extent by observing the dynamics of personal factors.

Those who have contributed and continued to add to the knowledge of OB are teaching theorists, personality theorists, counseling psychologists and primary, industrial and organizational psychologist.

Some of the numerous areas of interest within the disciplines of psychology are given below:

- General Psychology,
- Experimental Psychology,
- Clinical Psychology,
- Consumer Psychology,
- Personality and Social Psychology,
- Industrial Psychology,
- Counseling Psychology,
- Educational Psychology, and
- Consulting Psychology.

Understanding Psychological principles and its models help significantly in gaining the knowledge of determinants of individual behavior such as:

- The learning process,
- Motivation techniques,

- Personality determinants and development,
- Perceptual process and its implications,
- Training process,
- Leadership effectiveness,
- Job satisfaction,
- Individual decision making,
- Performance appraisal,
- Attitude measurement,
- Employee selection,
- Job design and work stress.

Sociology

The major focus of sociologists is on studying the social systems in which individuals fill their roles. The focus is on group dynamics.

They have made their greatest contribution to OB through their study of group behavior in organization, particularly formal and sophisticated organizations.

Sociological concepts, theories, models, and techniques help significantly to understand better the group dynamics, organizational culture, formal organization theory and structure, corporate technology, bureaucracy, communications, power, conflict, and intergroup behavior.

Psychologists are primarily interested in focusing their attention on the individual behavior.

Key Concepts of Sociology

Most sociologists today identify the discipline by using one of the three statements:

- Sociology deals with human interaction arid this communication are the key influencing factor among people in social settings.
- Sociology is a study of plural behavior. Two or more interacting individuals constitute a plurality pattern of behaviour.
- Sociology is the systematic study of social systems.

A social system is an operational social unit that is structured to serve a purpose.

It consists of two or more persons of different status with various roles playing a part in a pattern that is sustained by a physical and cultural base.

When analyzing organizing as a social system, the following elements exist:

- People or actors.
- Acts or Behavior.
- Ends or Goals.
- Norms, rules, or regulation controlling conduct or behavior.
- Beliefs held by people as actors.
- Status and status relationships.
- Authority or power to influence other actors.
- Role expectations, role performances, and role relationships.

Therefore, organizations are viewed by sociologies as consists of a variety of people with different roles, status, and degree of authority.

The organization attempts to achieve certain generalized and specific objectives.

To attain some of the abstract ends such as the development of company loyalty, the organization's leaders appeal to the shared cultural base.

Social Psychology

It has been defined as the scientific investigation of how the thoughts, feelings, and behavior of individuals are influenced by the actual, imagined or implied the presence of others.

It deals with how people are affected by other individuals who are physically present or who are imagined to be present or even whose presence is implied.

In general, sociology focuses on how groups, organizations, social categories, and societies are organized, how they function, how they change.

The unit of analysis is the group as a whole rather than the individuals who compose the group.

Social Psychology deals with many of the same phenomena but seeks to explain whole individual human interaction and human cognition influences culture and is influenced by culture.

The unit of analysis is the individual within the group.

In reality, some forms of sociology are closely related to social psychology.

Social Psychologists study an enormous range of topics including conformity, persuasion, power, influence, obedience, prejudice, discrimination, stereotyping, sexism and racism, small groups, social categories, inter-group behavior, crowd behavior, social conflict, social change, decision making, etc.

Among them, the most important topics relevant to the organizational behavior field are behavioral change, attitude change, communication, group process and group decision making. Social psychologists making significant contributions.

Social psychologists making significant contributions to measuring, understanding and improving attitudes, communication patterns how groups can satisfy individual needs and group decision-making process.

Anthropology

The main aim of anthropology is to acquire a better understanding of the relationship between the human being and the environment. Adaptations to surroundings constitute culture. The manner in which people view their surroundings is a part of the culture.

Culture includes those ideas shared by groups of individuals and languages by which these ideas are communicated. In essence, culture is a system of learned behavior.

Their work on culture and environment has helped us to understand differences in fundamental values, attitudes, and behavior among people in different countries and within different organizations.

Much of our current understandings of organizational culture, environments, and differences between national cultures are the results of the work of anthropologists or those using their methodologies.

The world is the laboratory of anthropologists, and human beings must be studied in the natural habitat. Understanding the importance of studying man in natural settings over time enables one to grasp the range of anthropology.

Familiarity within some of the cultural differences of employees can lead to a greater managerial objectivity and depth in the interpretation of behavior and performance.

Anthropologists contribute to study some aspects of organizational settings – similar values, comparative attitudes, cross-cultural analysis between or among the employees.

Political Sciences

Contributions of political scientist are significant to the understanding of behavior in organizations. Political scientists study the behavior of individuals and groups within a political environment.

They contribute to understanding the dynamics of power centers, structuring of conflict and conflict resolutions tactics, allocation of power and how people manipulate power for individual self-interest.

In a business field, organizations wanted to attain supremacy in their field and indulge in politicking activities to gain maximum advantages by following certain tasks like Machiavellianism, coalition formation, malpractices, etc.

The knowledge of political science can be utilized in the study the behavior of employees, executives at micro as well as macro level.

Economics

Economics contributes organizational behavior to a great extent in designing the organizational structure. Transaction cost economics influence the organization and its structure.

Transaction costs economics implies costs components to make an exchange on the market.

This transaction cost economics examines the extent to which the organization structure and size of an organization varies in response to attempts to avoid market failures through minimizing production and transaction costs within the constraints of human and environmental factors.

Costs of transactions include both costs of market transactions and internal coordination.

A transaction occurs when a good or service is transferred across a 'technologically separable barrier" Transaction costs arise for many reasons.

So we can assume that there are various types of disciplines which involve organizational behavior. They, directly and indirectly, influence the overall activities of OB.

Absolutes in Organizational Behavior

There are few, if any, simple and universal principles that explain organizational behavior. There are laws in the physical sciences–chemistry, astronomy, physics–that are consistent and apply in a wide range of situations. They allow scientists to generalize about the pull of gravity or to confidently send astronauts into space to repair satellites .But as one noted behavioral researchers aptly concluded, God gave all the easy problems to the physicists. Human's beings are complex. Because they are not alike, our ability to make simple, accurate, and sweeping generalizations is limited. Two people often act very differently in the same situation ,and the same person's behavior changes in different situations .For instances, not everyone is motivated by money, and you behave differently at church on Sunday than you did at the beer party the night before.

That doesn't mean, of course, that we can't offer reasonably accurate explanations of human behavior or make valid predictions. It does mean, however, that OB concepts must reflect situational, or contingency, conditions. We can say that x leads to you, but only under conditions specified in z(the contingency variables).The science of OB has developed by using general concepts and then altering their application to the particular situation .So, for example, OB scholars would avoid stating that effective leader should always seek the ideas of their followers before making a decision. Rather, we shall find that in some situations a participative style is clearly superior, but, in other situations, an autocratic decision style is more effective .In other words, the effectiveness of a particular leadership style is contingent upon the situation in which it is used.

Management and Organization Behavior

Companies of the same industry are being affected by the same environmental factors. Some companies attract a number of customers while some other companies repel them. Employees refer to be identified with some companies while they prefer to be unemployed in case of some other companies. Why do companies perform differently when they operate under the same environmental conditions, serve the same customer, and use the same raw material and technology and employ the people with similar skills? The answer for this question, invariably, is management practices. Thus 'Management' makes remarkable difference between the companies regarding their performance in terms of productivity, products, sales, profitability, service to the customer, employee welfare etc.

- Definition of management- Mary Parker defines the term management as "the art of getting things done through others."
- Ivancerich, Donnelly and Gibson, defines the term management as "the process undertaken by one or more persons to coordinate the activities of other persons to achieve results not attainable by any one person acting alone."
- John A. Pearce and Richard B. Robinson included all kinds of resources in their definition on management. According to them, "Management is the process of optimizing human, material and financial contribution for the achievement of organizational goals."

The analysis of the above definitions provides the following aspects of management.

- The purpose of management is to formulate effective (right) organizational strategies and to achieve them efficiently (productively) based on the missions objectives and goals.
- Management deals with both internal and external environment.

- Management is concerned with all kinds of resources viz., human, financial, material machines, technology and technical know- how.
- Management functions include: planning, organizing, directing and controlling.
- Managers should possess varied skills in order to play a variety of roles.
- It applies to managers at all levels in an organization.
- Management is applicable to all kind of organizations i.e., both profit and non-profit oriented organizations.
- Management vs. Administration.
- Management is an art and a science in order to create a surplus.
- Management need to be a profession to achieve goals continuously with an incremental efficiency.

Management deals with internal and external environment:

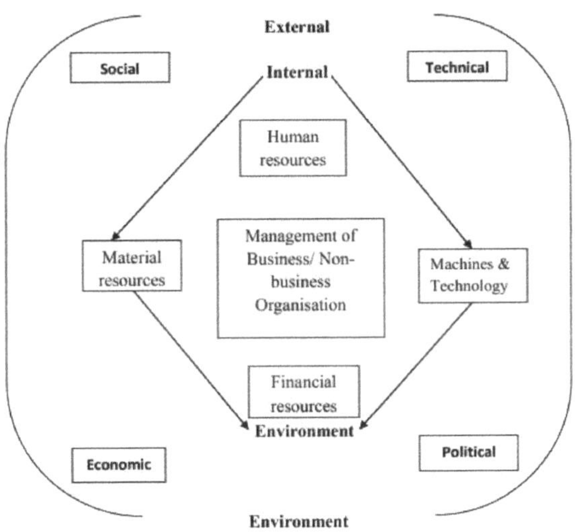

Management: Science or an Art

We should know what is science and what is a before discussing whether management is a science or an art?

Science: Science is a body of knowledge developed systematically, based on observation, measurement, and experimentation and drawing inferences based on data. The knowledge can be verified through cause- effect relationship. The knowledge provides principles, theory and laws. Management satisfies the characteristics of science like.

Art: Art understands how a particular activity can be done. Art can be acquired by conscious effort and practice. Management is getting things done by and through other people. They have to continuously analyze the environment and formulate the plans and strategies. They have to modify the strategies based on environmental changes. The principles of management cannot be implemented as learn, in the real world. They are to be applied after making necessary modifications based on the real life situations.

Nature of Management

Nature of Management	
Management as a Continuous Process	Management as a Discipline
Management as a Career	Art as well as Science
Goal Oriented	Guidance
Management is a Human Activity	Management Signifies Authority
Management is Universal	Co-ordination is the soul of Management
Management is Dynamic	Management is essentially a Leadership Activity
Management is Decision Making	Management is Profession

Scope of Management	
Activity Point of View	Functional Areas of Management
Management is an Inter Disciplinary Approach	Universality of Management
Essential of Management	Modern Management is an Agent of Change

Functions of Management

As indicated earlier, management is the process of planning, organizing, staffing, directing and controlling the efforts of organization members in utilizing all resources to achieve organizational goals, objectives and mission. Management is a process as it operates the activities systematically.

Process of Management

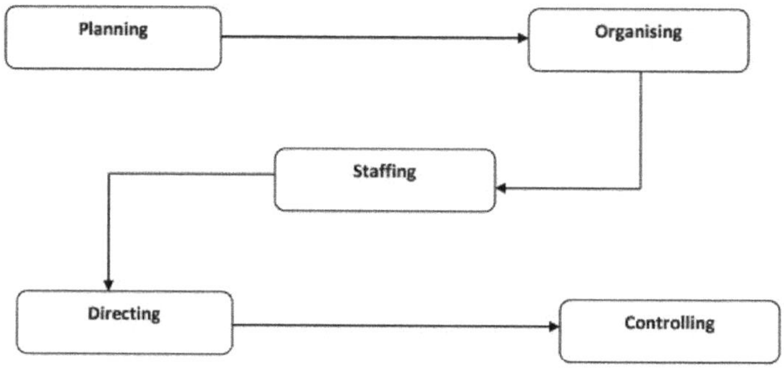

Planning

- Planning consists of the activities involved in choosing courses of action to achieve organizational objectives.
- It is deciding in advance what to do, when to do, how to do and who will do it, in order to achieve these objectives.
- Both long- term and short- term plans are necessary to achieve goals.

Organizing

- Organizing involves the grouping of jobs into framework for coordination and direction.
- Formal organizations may be portrayed by use of an organisation chart.
- Organizations are structured based on product, function, geography, customer and project.
- The matrix structure has evolved as a result of complex environments, markets and technology.

Staffing

- Staffing is planning, organizing, directing and controlling of procurement, development, compensation, integration and maintenance of people for the purpose of contributing to individual, organizational and social goals.
- This process requires the performance of the functions like job analysis, human resources planning, recruitment, selection, induction, placement, training, execute development, wage and salary administration, leadership, teamwork, motivation, grievance procedure, disciplinary procedure etc.

Directing

- The important function of management at any level is directing the people by motivating, commanding, leading and activating them.
- The willing and effective cooperation of employees for the attainment of organizational goals is possible through direction.
- Tapping the maximum potentialities of the people is possible through and command.
- Thus, direction is an important managerial function in securing employee's contribution.

Controlling

- After planning, organizing, staffing and directing the various activities, the performance is to be verified in order to know whether the activities are performed in conformity with the plans and objectives or not.
- Controlling also involves checking, verifying and comparing of actual performance with the plans, identification of deviations, if any and correcting of identified deviations.
- Thus, actions and operations are adjusted to predetermined plans and standards through control.
- The purpose of control is to ensure the effective operation of an organisation by focusing on all resources- human, material, finance and machines.

Management Levels

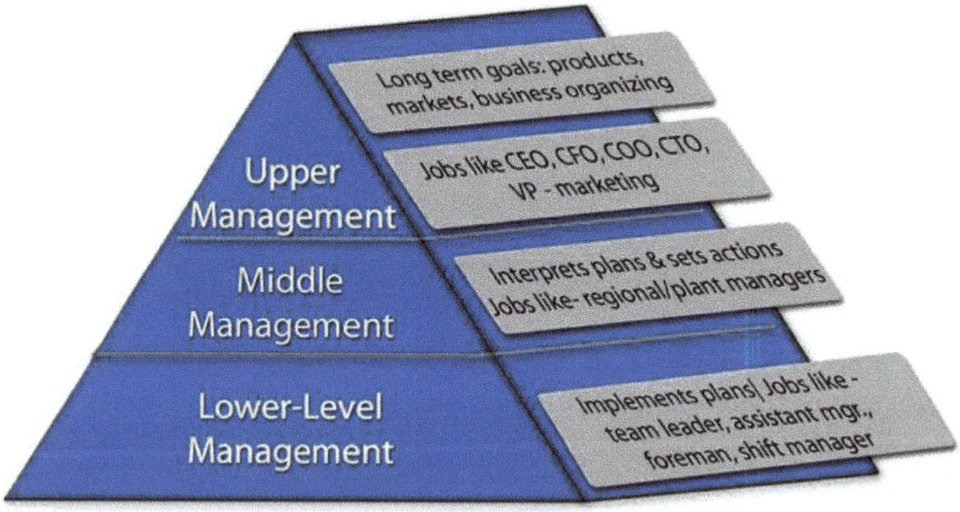

Top Level Managements

Top level management are the senior level executives of the company including the Managing director or President Vice- Presidents, General managers, Chief managers of company, ect. Top level management particularly the managing director or President of the company is responsible for the overall management and performance of the company. Top level management formulates objectives, policies and corporate level strategies of the company.

Middle level managers

Middle level managers are responsible for coordination of the activities of various departments. Middle managers include managers of various departments, marketing, finance, human resource and research and development departments. These managers are responsible for the success or failure of their departments. Middle level managers formulate the objectives, goals and strategies of their departments based on those of the organisation.

Lower Level Managers

Lower level managers are responsible for the work of the operating staff working with them. Lower level managers are also called first- Line or First- Line or junior managers. They direct, lead, motivate and coordinate the activities of the operating employees. These managers mostly supervise the operating perform their work. As such, the lower level managers are also called 'Supervisors'.

Principles of Management

Henry Fayol started his career as a mining engineer in 1860 in a collier company in France. In 1866, he was appointed as the manager of the collieries and remained in this position for 22 years. In 1888, when the company's financial position was critical, he was appointed as the General Manager.

Fayol felt that the activities of business could be dividing into six groups.

1. Technical
2. Commercial
3. Financial
4. Security
5. Accounting
6. Managerial.

Fayol's Principles of Management

In addition, Fayol listed out fourteen principles of management. They are:

1. Division of labour - The more people specialize, the more efficiently they can perform their work. This principle is epitomized by the modern assembly line.
2. Authority - Managers must give orders so that they can get things done. While their formal authority gives them the right to command, managers will not always compel obedience unless they have personal authority (such as relevant expertise) as well.
3. Discipline - Members in an organization need to respect the rules and agreements that govern the organization. To Fayol, discipline results from good leadership at all levels of the organization, fair agreements.

4. Unity of command - Each employee must receive instructions from only one person. Fayol belied that when an employee reported to more than one manager, conflicts in instructions and confusion of authority would ultimately result.
5. Unity of direction - Those operations within the organization that have the same objective should be directed by only one manager using one plan.
6. Subordination of individual interest to the common goal - In any undertaking, the interests of employees should not take precedence over the interests of the organization. As a whole.
7. Remuneration - Compensation for work done should be fair to both employees and employers.
8. Centralization - Decreasing the role of subordinates in decision making is centralization, increasing their roles is decentralization.
9. The hierarchy - The lines of authority in an organization are often represented today by the neat boxes and lines of the organization chart that runs in order of rank from the top management to the lowest level of the enterprise.
10. Order - Materials and people should be in the right place at the right time. People in particular, should be in the jobs or positions in which they are most suited.
11. Equity - Manager should be both friendly and fair to their subordinates.
12. Stability of staff - A high employee turnover rate undermines the efficient functioning of an organization.
13. Initiative - Subordinates should be given the freedom to conceive and carry out their plans, even though some mistakes may result.
14. Esprit de corps - Promoting team spirit will give the organization a sense of unity.

Taylor's Scientific Management

The concept of scientific management was introduced by Fredric Winslow Taylor in USA in the beginning of 20th century.

"Scientific management is concerned with knowing exactly what you want men to do and then see in that they do it in the best and cheapest way".

Elements and Tools of Scientific Management

1. Separation of planning and doing - Taylor emphasized the separation of planning aspect from actual doing of the work. Before Taylor's scientific management, a work used to plan about how he had to work and what instruments were necessary for that. The worker was put under the supervision of a supervisor commonly known as gang boss.

2. Functional foremanship - Separation of planning from doing resulted into development of supervision system which could take planning work adequately besides keeping supervisions on workers.

3. Job analysis - Job analysis is undertaken to find out the one best way of doing the thing. The best way of doing a job is one which requires the last movements, consequently less time and cost. The best way of doing the thing can be determined by taking up time motion fatigue studies.

4. Standardization - As far as possible, standardization should be maintained in respect of instruments and tools, period of work, amount of work, work conditions, cost of production cet.

5. Scientific selection and Training of workers - Taylor has suggested that workers should be selected on scientific basis taking into account their education, work experience, aptitude, physical strength.

6. Financial incentives - Financial incentives can motivate workers to put in their maximum efforts. If provisions exist to earn higher wages by putting in extra effort, workers will be motivated to earn more.

7. Economy - While applying scientific management, not only scientific & technical aspects should be considered but adequate consideration should be given to economy & profit. For this purpose, techniques of cost estimates and control should be adopted.

8. Mental revolution - scientific management depends on the mutual co-operation between management and workers. For this co-operation, there should be mental change in both parties from conflict to co-operation.

Principles of Scientific Management

1. Science, but not rule of the thumb - Scientific management organized knowledge should be applied which will replace rule of thumb. While the use of scientific method denotes precision in determining any aspect of work.

2. Group hormony - Group hormony suggests that there should be mutual given and takes situation and proper understanding so that group as a whole contributes to the maximum.

3. Cooperation - scientific management involves achieving co-operation rather than chaotic individualism. Scientific management is based on mutual confidence, cooperation and good will. Co-operation between management and workers can be developed through mutual understanding and a change in thinking.

4. Maximum output - Scientific management involves continuous increase in production and productivity instead of restricted production either by management or by worker.

5. Development of workers - In scientific management, all workers should be developed to the fullest extent possible for their own and for the company's prosperity.

Systems Approach to Management

A system is a set of interrelated but separate parts working towards a common purpose. The arrangement of elements must be orderly and there must be proper communication facilitating interaction between the elements and finally this interaction should lead to achieve a common goal.

Key concepts of Systems Approach

1. Subsystem - Systems are those parts which make up the whole system. Each system in turn may be a subsystem of a still larger system. Thus, a department is a subsystem of a factory, which is a subsystem of a firm, which is a subsystem of industry.
2. Synergy - Synergy is a situation in which the whole is greater than the sum of its parts. In organizational terms, synergy means those departments that interact co-operatively are more productivity than they would be.
3. Open system - It is a system that interacts with its environment. All organizations interact with their environment, but the extent to which they do so varies.
4. Closed system - It is a system that does not interact with its environment.
5. System boundary - It is the boundary that separates each system from its environment. It is rigid in a closed system while flexible in an open system.

Flows

A System has flows of information, materials, and energy. These enter the system from the environment as in puts like raw materials.

Challenges and Opportunities of Organizational Behavior

Challenges and opportunities of organizational behavior are massive and rapidly changing for improving productivity and meeting business goals.

Although the problems with organizations and the solutions over the ages have not really changed, the emphasis and surrounding environmental context certainly have changed.

Although the resulting lean and mean organizations offered some short-run benefits in terms of lowered costs and improved productivity, if they continued to do business, as usual, they would not be able to meet current or future challenges.

As a Harvard Business Review article argues, "These are scary times for managers".

The singular reason given for these frightening times – the increasing danger of disruptive change.

The nature of work is changing so rapidly that rigid job structures impede the work to be done now, and that may drastically change the following year, month, or even week.

Main Challenges and Opportunities of Organizational Behavior

1. Improving Peoples' Skills.
2. Improving Quality and Productivity.
3. Total Quality Management (TQM).
4. Managing Workforce Diversity.
5. Responding to Globalization.
6. Empowering People.
7. Coping with Temporariness.
8. Stimulating Innovation and Change.
9. Emergence of E-Organisation & E-Commerce.
10. Improving Ethical Behavior.
11. Improving Customer Service.
12. Helping Employees Balance Work-Life Conflicts.
13. Flattening World.

Improving People's Skills

Technological changes, structural changes, environmental changes are accelerated at a faster rate in the business field.

Unless employees and executives are equipped to possess the required skills to adapt those changes, the targeted goals cannot be achieved in time.

These two different categories of skills – managerial skills and technical skills.

Some of the managerial skills include listening skills, motivating skills, planning and organizing skills, leading skills, problem-solving skill, decision-making skills etc.

These skills can be enhanced by organizing a series of training and development programs, career development programs, induction, and socialization etc.

Improving Quality and Productivity

Quality is the extent to which the customers or users believe the product or service surpasses their needs and expectations.

For example, a customer who purchases an automobile has a certain expectation, one of which is that the automobile engine will start when it is turned on.

If the engine fails to start, the customer's expectations will not have been met and the customer will perceive the quality of the car as poor. The key dimensions of quality as follows:

- Performance: Primary rating characteristics of a product such as signal coverage, audio quality, display quality etc.
- Features: Secondary characteristics, added features, such as calculators, and alarm clock features in hand phone.
- Conformance: Meeting specifications or industry standards, workmanship of the degree to which a product's design or operating characteristics match pre-established standards.
- Reliability: The probability of a product's falling within t a specified period of time.
- Durability: It is a measure of product's life having both economic and technical dimension.
- Services: Resolution of problem and complaints, ease of repair.
- Response: Human to human interfaces, such as the courtesy of the dealer.
- Aesthetics: Sensory characteristics such exterior finish.
- Reputations: Past performance and other intangibles, such as being ranked first.

More and more managers are confronting to meet the challenges to fulfill the specific requirements of customers.

In order to improve quality and productivity, they are implementing programs like total quality management and reengineering programs that require extensive employee involvement.

Total Quality Management (TQM)

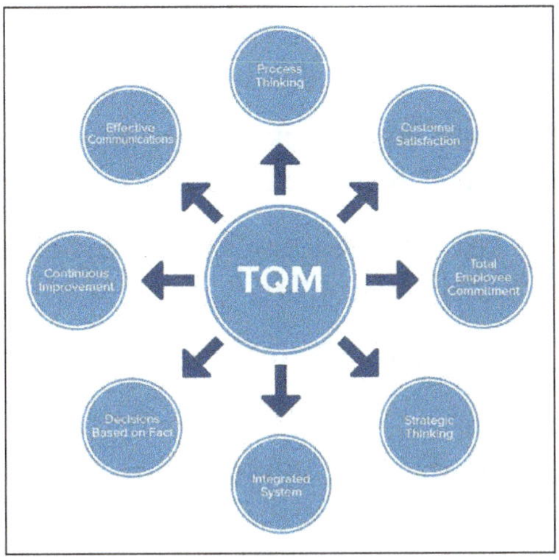

It is a philosophy of management that is driven by the constant attainment of customer satisfaction through the continuous improvement of all organizational process.

Components of TQM

(a) An intense focus on the customer,

(b) Concern for continual improvement,

(c) Improvement in the quality of everything the organization does,

(d) Accurate measurement and,

(e) Empowerment of employees.

Managing Workforce Diversity

This refers to employing different categories of employees who are heterogeneous in terms of gender, race, ethnicity, relation, community, physically disadvantaged, elderly people etc.

The primary reason to employ heterogeneous category of employees is to tap the talents and potentialities, harnessing the innovativeness, obtaining synergetic effect among the divorce workforce.

In general, employees wanted to retain their individual and cultural identity, values and life styles even though they are working in the same organization with common rules and regulations.

The major challenge for organizations is to become more accommodating to diverse groups of people by addressing their different life styles, family needs, and work styles.

Responding to Globalization

Today's business is mostly market driven; wherever the demands exist irrespective of distance, locations, climatic Conditions, the business.

Operations are expanded to gain their market share and to remain in the top rank etc. Business operations are no longer restricted to a particular locality or region.

Company's products or services are spreading across the nations using mass communication, the internet, faster transportation etc.

More than 95% of Nokia (Now Microsoft) hand phones are being sold outside of their home country Finland.

Japanese cars are being sold in different parts of the globe. Sri Lankan tea is exported to many cities around the globe.

Garment products of Bangladesh are exporting in USA and EU countries. Executives of Multinational Corporation are very mobile and move from one subsidiary to another more frequently.

Empowering People

The main issue is delegating more power and responsibility to the lower level cadre of employees and assigning more freedom to make choices about their schedules, operations, procedures and the method of solving their work-related problems.

Encouraging the employees to participate in work related decision will sizable enhance their commitment to work.

Empowerment is defined as putting employees in charge of what they do by eliciting some sort of ownership in them.

Managers are doing considerably further by allowing employees full control of their work.

Movement implies constant change. An increasing number of organizations are using self-managed teams, where workers operate largely without a boss.

Due to the implementation of empowerment concepts across all the levels, the relationship between managers and the employees is reshaped.

Managers will act as coaches, advisors, sponsors, facilitators and help their subordinates to do their task with minimal guidance.

Coping with Temporariness

In recent times, the product life cycles are slimming, the methods of operations are improving, and fashions are changing very fast. In those days, the managers needed to introduce major change programs once or twice a decade.

Today, change is an on-going activity for most managers.

The concept of continuous improvement implies constant change.

In yesteryears, there used to be a long period of stability and occasionally interrupted by a short period of change, but at present, the change process is an on-going activity due to competitiveness in developing new products and services with better features.

Everyone in the organization faces today is one of permanent temporariness. The actual jobs that workers perform are in a permanent state of flux.

So, workers need to continually update their knowledge and skills to perform new job requirements.

Stimulating Innovation and Change

Today's successful organizations must foster innovation and be proficient in the art of change; otherwise, they will become candidates for extinction in due course of time and vanished from their field of business.

Victory will go to those organizations that maintain flexibility, continually improve their quality, and beat the competition to the market place with a constant stream of innovative products and services.

For example, Compaq succeeded by creating more powerful personal computers for the same or less money than EBNM or Apple, and by putting their products to market quicker than the bigger competitors.

Amazon.com is putting a lot of independent bookstores out of business as it proves you can successfully sell books from an Internet website.

Emergence of E-Organisation and E-Commerce

It refers to the business operations involving the electronic mode of transactions. It encompasses presenting products on websites and filling the order.

The vast majority of articles and media attention given to using the Internet in business are directed at online shopping.

In this process, the marketing and selling of goods and services are being carried out over the Internet.

In e- commerce, the following activities are being taken place quite often – the tremendous numbers of people who are shopping on the Internet, business houses are setting up websites where they can sell goods, conducting the following transactions such as getting paid and fulfilling orders.

It is a dramatic change in the way a company relates to its customers. At present e-commerce is exploding. Globally, e-commerce spending was increasing at a tremendous rate.

Improving Ethical Behavior

The complexity in business operations is forcing the workforce to face ethical dilemmas, where they are required to define right and wrong conduct in order to complete their assigned activities.

For example:

- Should the employees of chemical company blow the whistle if they uncover the discharging its untreated effluents into the river are polluting its water resources?
- Do managers give an inflated performance evaluation to an employee they like, knowing that such an evaluation could save that employee's job?

The ground rules governing the constituents of good ethical behavior has not been clearly defined, Differentiating right things from wrong behavior has become more blurred.

Following unethical practices have become a common practice such as successful executives who use insider information for personal financial gain, employees in competitor business participating in massive cover-ups of defective products etc.

Improving Customer Service

OB can contribute to improving an organizational performance by showing drat how employees' attitude and behavior are associated with customer satisfaction.

In that case, service should be the first production oriented by using technological opportunities like a computer, the internet etc.

To improve the customer service need to provide sales service and also the after sales service.

Helping Employees Balance Work-Life Conflicts

The typical employee in the 1960s or 1970s showed up at the work place Monday through Friday and did his or her job 8 or 9-hour chunk of time.

The workplace and hours were clearly specified. That's no longer true for a large segment of today's workforce.

Employees are increasingly complaining that the line between work and non-work time has become blurred, creating personal conflict and stress.

A number of forces have contributed to blurring the lines between employees' work life and personal life.

- First, the creation of global organizations means their world never sleeps. At any time and on any day, for instance, thousands of General Electric employees are working somewhere.
- Second, the communication technology allows employees to do their work at home, in their cars, or on the beach in Cox's Bazar.
- This lets many people in technical and professional jobs do their work anytime and from any place.
- Third, organizations are asking employees to put in longer hours.
- Finally, fewer families have only a single breadwinner. Today's married employee is typically part of a dual-career couple. This makes it increasingly difficult for married employees to find the time to full fill commitments to home, spouse, children, parents, and friends.

Today's married employee is typically part of a dual-career couple.

This makes it increasingly difficult for married employees to find the time to fulfill commitments to home, spouse, children, parents, and friends.

Employees are increasingly recognizing that work is squeezing out personal lives and they're not happy about it.

For example, recent studies suggest that employees want jobs that give them flexibility in their work schedules so they can better manage work/life conflicts.

In addition, the next generation of employees is likely to show similar concerns.

A majority of college and university students say that attaining a balance between personal life and work is a primary career goal. They want a life as well as a job.

Flattening World

Thomas Friedman makes the point that the Internet has "flattened" the world and created an environment in which there is a more level playing field in terms of access to information.

This access to information has led to an increase in innovation, as knowledge can be shared instantly across time zones and cultures.

It has also created intense competition, as the speed of business is growing faster and faster all the time.

Don Tapscott notes that mass collaboration has changed the way work gets done, how products are created, and the ability of people to work together without ever meeting.

References

- Organizational-behavior: investopedia.com, Retrieved 12 February, 2019
- Organizational-behaviour-definition-characteristics-and-nature, organizational-behaviour, organization: yourarticlelibrary.com, Retrieved 14 June, 2019
- Organizational-behavior: iedunote.com, Retrieved 11 April, 2019
- Limitations-of-organizational-behavior: iedunote.com, Retrieved 13 January, 2019
- What-is-organizational-behavior: usi.edu, Retrieved 3 July, 2019
- Contributing-disciplines-to-organization-behavior-field: iedunote.com, Retrieved 12 August, 2019
- Absolutes-in-organizational-behavior: hrknowledge.blogspot.com, Retrieved 9 May, 2019
- Challenges-opportunities-organizational-behavior: iedunote.com, Retrieved 19 March, 2019

2

Important Attributes of Individual Behavior

Some of the attributes of individual behavior are personality, attitude, motivation and perception. There are different theories on personality such as type theory, trait theories and psychoanalytic theory. This chapter has been carefully written to provide an easy understanding of the varied attributes of individual behavior.

Attitude, Personality and Values

The term personality often figures in discussions on one's job prospects, achievements, marriage and on other similar occasions. In all these events, personality is understood in its narrow sense as implying one's charm, popularity, dress and other physical attractiveness. Perceiving personality in this narrow sense will not help much in understanding an individual's behaviours in an organization.

Theories on Personality

There are several theories but more prominent among them are:

Type Theory

Type theories place personalities into clearly identifiable categories. Classification into types is the beginning of most sciences-types of rocks, kinds of plants and so on. Thus, it is not surprising that the first student of human nature try to classify kinds of people. In type theories relationship was sought to be established between features of face or body and personality. Classification of personalities on body basis is subjective. Type theories are simple and popular but carry no substances. The second basis to type personalities is psychological factors. One of the Freud's pupils, the Swiss psychologists Carl Jung, divided all personalities into introverts and extroverts. These terms are normally associated with an individual's sociability and interpersonal orientation. Extroverts are gregarious, sociable individuals, while introverts are shy, quiet and retiring.

Thus, type theories, body or psychological, though appealing as they provide a simple way of looking at personality, fail to reveal all complexities of personality.

Trait Theories

Trait theories is another way of understanding personality. A personality trait is understood as an enduring attribute of a person that appears consistently in a variety of situations. A trait of an individual is abstracted from his behaviour and serves an useful — "unit of analysis" to understand personality.

Trait theorists assume that a personality can be described by its position on a number of continuous dimensions or scales, each of which represents a trait. Thus, we could rate an individual on a scale of intelligence, emotional stability, aggressiveness, creativeness or any of a number of other dimensions.

It is important to remember that traits are reactions, not something a person possesses. One does not possesse shyness, he feels and acts shy under some circumstances. In many ways, the trait theory is a multiple model of type theory.

The search for personality, social, physical or intellectual attributes that describes leaders from non-leaders goes back to 1930s. Research efforts in leadership traits resulted in a number of dead ends. A review of different studies identified that, leadership traits were common in five out of twenty cases. The research was carried out to find out a set of traits that would differentiate leaders from followers but the research failed. The overall cumulative finding from research conclude that, some traits increase the likelihood of becoming leaders but none of the traits will guarantee a success.

Psychologists working in an area of trail theory are concerned with:

1. Determining the basic traits that provide a meaningful description of personality.
2. Finding some way to measure them. There are two ways of assessing personality traits:
    i. The person describes himself by answering questions about his attitudes, feelings and behaviours.
    ii. Someone else evaluates the person's traits from what he knows about the individual.

With the first method, a personality inventory is most often used, whereas the second, usually involves a rating scale. A personality inventory is essentially a questionnaire in which the person reports the reactions or feelings in certain situations.

A rating scale is a device for recording judgement about traits. A rating scale is filled up by someone else by what he knows about the individual or by studying his behaviour in certain situations.

Evaluation of Trait Theory

Trait theory is an improvement over type theories. The type theories unrealistically, attempt to place personalities into discrete, discontinuous categories. The trait theory, on the other hand, gives recognition to the continuity of personalities. The theory has also contributed to personality ratings and factor analysis techniques to behavioural science.

However, there are several problems with the trait approach. Terms are different to define, there are contradictions and the scientific reliability of the results is open to considerable challenge. A major objection to trait theories is that, they are very descriptive rather than analytical and are a long way from being comprehensive theories of personality. Further, some trait theories tend to focus on isolated traits without specifying how these traits are organised within the personality. Finally, traits are abstracted from behaviour. But we cannot use the same traits to explain behaviour.

Trait theory with Examples

Theories, which consider personal qualities and characteristics that differentiate leaders from non-leaders, for example. Margaret Thatcher, former Prime Minister of Great Britain was always known for her leadership. She was described as confident, iron-willed, determined and decisive. These terms are traits and people using them are trait willed, determined and decisive. These terms are traits and people using them are trait Theorist supporters. The media is a strong supporter of trait theories of leadership; say focusing on personal qualities and characteristics. The media identifies people like Margaret Thatcher, Nelson Mandela. New York mayor Rudolph Gintiani, Virgin group's CEO- Richard Branson as charismatic enthusiastic. Traits in different leaders and non-leaders are ambitions and energy, the desire to live, honesty and integrity, self-confidence, intelligence and job relevant knowledge. Recent research shows that high self-monitors that is they are highly flexible to adjust to indifferent situations and are more likely to immerge as leaders. When leaders like Steve Jobs of Apple computer were described as charismatic or enthusiastic, these adjectives reflected the trait theory of leadership that seeks to identify specific personal qualities and characteristics of leaders to explain their success. Effective leaders behave in unique manner. For example: Titan International CEO Marry Tailor and Siebel System CEO Tom Siebel have led their companies in very critical periods in a very successful manner. Their leadership style consists of tough talking, intense and autocratic.

The difference between trait and behavioural theories in terms of applications lies in their underlying assumptions. Trait theories are valid. The leaders are born and not made by the specific behaviour identified leader. The leadership could be taught and designed as to implant behavioural patterns in individuals who desire to be leaders.

Drawbacks of Trait Theory

The trait theory has certain limitations. First and foremost, there are no universal traits that will give leadership in all situations, while trait appears to predict leadership on relative situations. Secondly, trait predicts behaviour more in weak situations rather than in strong situations. Strong situations are there when the behaviour norms are strong incentives for specific type of behaviour and clear expectations as to which behaviour is rewarded and which is punished. Some strong situations create the opportunities for leaders to express. Organizations with strong cultures fit in the description of strong situation but here power of trait to predict leadership is limited. The third drawback is the inability to separate cause from effect. For example: Does self-confidence create leadership or does success as a leader build self-confidence. Finally, trait helps in predicting the appearance of leadership than distinguish between effective and ineffective leaders.

The major movement away from trait began as early as 1940's. 1960 emphasized research in the behavioural theories.

This theory differs from that of trait theory. This theory is based on the in-depth study of individual personalities.

Siemund Freud is credited with psychoanalytic theory. Freud, acknowledged as one of the intellectual giants in the history of modern thought, developed.

i. The first comprehensive personality theory.

ii. A method for treating neurotic ills.

iii. An extensive body of clinical observations based on his therapeutic experience and self-analysis.

Freud saw personality as composed of three structures:

i. The ID: Refers exclusively to the innate component of personality. The id is the mental agency containing everything inherited, present at birth, and fixed in the individual's constitution especially instincts. It is raw, animalistic, unrecognized knows no laws, obeys no rules and remains basic to the individual throughout life. The id, according to Freud, employs to rid the personality of tension, reflex actions and primary process. Primary process refers to attempts of an individual to form a mental image of the object that will remove the tension.

ii. The ego: Mental images do not satisfy needs. The starving man cannot satisfy hunger by eating images. Reality must be considered. This is the role of the ego. The ego develops out of the id because of the necessity for dealing with the real world.

iii. The super ego: In order for a person to function constructively in society, he should acquire a system of values, norms, ethics and attitudes which are reasonably compatible with that society. The superego, represents the internalized representation of the values and morals of society as taught to the child by the parents and others. The super ego judges whether an action is right or wrong according to the standards of society. The id seeks pleasure, the ego tests reality and the superego strives for perfection.

Sometimes, the three components of personality are at odds: the ego postpones gratification that the id wants right away and the superego battles with both the ego and the id, because behaviour often falls short of the moral code it represents. But more often in the normal person the three work as a team, producing integrated behaviour.

Evaluation of Psychoanalytic Theory

This theory has had an enormous impact on psychological and philosophical conceptions of people.

Freud's emphasis on the conscience has been partially supported by some of the current research findings of cognitive psychologists. This work has revealed that, mental processes about which people are unaware have all important impact on thinking and actions.

The importance of this theory is underscored by the fact that it has spawned a significant and enduring method of treating psychological disturbances.

Freud's psychoanalytic theory has been criticize as it has been praised. One criticism against the theory is that the approach is not based on empirically verifiable facts. The psychoanalytic elements are largely hypothetical constructs and are not measurable, observable items, susceptible to scientific analysis and verification.

Some critics point out that Freud's theory of personality is based almost entirely upon his observations of emotionally disturbed individuals. It may not represent an appropriate description of the normal, healthy personality. Freud assumed that all human events (actions, thoughts, feelings, aspirations) are lawful and determined by powerful instinctual forces i.e. aggression. Thus, human beings are seen as essentially mechanistic, they are governed by the same natural laws that apply to the behaviour of other organisms. In his approach, there is no room for concepts such as free will, choice, personal responsibility, spontaneity and self-determination.

Social Learning Theory

Much of human behaviour is either learned or modified by learning. Through learning, one acquires knowledge, language attitudes, values, fears, personality traits and self-insight. Therefore, a study of the process of learning throws more light on understanding human activities.

The social learning theorists on personality regard the situation as an important determinant of behaviour. The social learning theory focuses on behaviour patterns and cognitive activities in relation to the specific conditions that evoke, maintain or modify them. The emphasis is what an individual does in a given situation. Some of the personal variables like that determine what an individual will do in a particular situation include:

i. Competencies: Intellectual abilities, social skills and other abilities.

ii. Cognitive Strategies: Habitual ways of selectively attending to information and organizing it into meaningful units.

iii. Outcome expectations: Expectations about the consequences of different behaviours and the meaning of certain stimuli.

iv. Self-regulatory systems and plans: Individual differences in self-imposed goals, rules guiding behaviour, self-imposed rewards for success or punishment for failure and ability to plan and execute steps leading to a goal will lead to differences in behaviour. All of the above variables interact with conditions of the particular situation to determine what an individual will do in that situation.

The social learning theorists also believe in reciprocal behaviour patterns. Situation is no doubt capable of evoking, maintaining or modifying the behaviour patterns of individuals. An individual in turn, is able to mould conditions of a situation. Our behaviour reflects the 'situations' of life as well as being influenced by them, the relationship is reciprocal. By selectively attended to what is happening, we can prevent certain conditions from imposing on us. And by our actions we can partly create the conditions that imposing, changes in behaviour towards others are usually followed by reciprocal changes in the behaviour of others.

Evaluation of Social Learning Theory

Social learning theory has made a major contribution to both clinical psychological and personality theory. It has led us to look more closely at the situation that can be used to modify behaviour. Careful applications of learning principles has proved very successful in changing maladaptive behaviour.

Social learning theorists have been criticized for over emphasizing the importance of situational factors in behaviour to the neglect of individual differences. They show little interest.

An individual is regarded as flexible, malleable and passive victim of external stimuli — the permanent of environmental fate. Environmental conditions are held to be superior to human nature.

The Humanistic Approach

The humanistic approach to the study of personality includes number of theories, although different in some respects, share a common emphasis on man's potential for self-direction and freedom of choice. They are concerned with the 'self' and the individual subjective experiences. The theories stress man's positive nature — his push towards growth and self-actualizations. Their emphasis is also on the "here and now" rather than on events in early childhood that may have shaped the individual's personality.

Carl Rogers and Abraham Maslow are credited with the humanistic theory of personality. Their views on personality are explained below:

Rogers Self Theory

Rogers approach to personality is described as phenomenological. Phenomenology is the study of individuals subjective experience, feelings and private concepts as well as his views of the world and self. For Rogers, behaviour is utterly dependent upon how one perceives the world — that is, behaviour is the result of immediate events as they are actually perceived and interpreted by the individual. Such an approach to personality emphasises the self and its characteristics.

Rogers ideas of human nature grew out of his experiences in working with emotionally disturbed people. Roger has concluded that the inner most nature of human nature is essentially purposive, forward moving, constructive, realistic and quite trustworthy. He regards the person as an active force of energy, oriented towards future goals and self-directed purpose rather than a created pushed and pulled by forces beyond his control.

Rogers agrees that people occasionally express all kinds of bitter and antisocial actions, but he argues that at such times they are not behaving in concert with their inner natures. Thus, people are functioning as fully human beings, when they are free to experience and to satisfy their inner nature, they show themselves to be positive and rational creatures who can be trusted to live in harmony with themselves and others. Roger has profound (almost religious) sense of respect for human nature. He — that human organism has a natural tendency to move in the direction of differentiation, self-responsibility, co-operation, and maturity. Self-actualization, according to Rogers, is the basic motivating force representing the inherent tendency of the organism to develop all its capabilities in ways which serve to maintain or enhance the person.

Maslow's Self-actualization Theory

Abraham Maslow is regarded as the spiritual father of humanism in American psychology. Humanistic psychology of Maslow radically differ from psychoanalytic and learning or behaviouristic theories. Humanistic psychology of Maslow, on the other hand, postulates man as self actualiser. By self-accusation, Maslow meant the development of full individuality, with all parts of personality in harmony.

Maslow's humanistic psychology is steeped in European existential philosophy and psychology as developed by thinkers and writers as Kierkegard, Camus, Binswanger and Boss.

Existential philosophy is concerned with man as an individual and each person alone is responsible for his own existence. Contrary to popular belief, he is never static. He is always in the process of becoming something different. He tries to use his potentials to become a useful member of society and to lead a truly authentic and fruitful life. This drive of a man which is inherent in him, is called selfactualisation. Existential philosophy also stresses human consciousness, subjective feelings and moods and personal experiences as they relate to one's existence in the world of other people. This outlook may be called "here-and-now" perspective. Existentialists and humanist alike emphasis subjective experience as the primary phenomenon in the study of human nature. Both theoretical explanations and over-behaviour are secondary to experience itself and its meaning to the experiencing person.

Thus, central to the humanistic approach are:

i. Individual is an integrated whole.

ii. Animal research is irrelevant to human behaviour.

iii. Human nature is essentially good.

iv. Man has creative potential.

v. Psychological health of man is more important.

The Shaping of Personality

How personality develops from its infant to grown up stage is an interesting and useful study. Psychologists have come out with different stages in the development of personality. The most important are discussed below.

Freudian Stages

Sigmund Freud was a pioneering stage theorist. Although the analysis of stages of development can be traced as far back as the ancient Greeks, it was Freud who first formulated a meaningful stage theory. He was the first psychologist to believe that childhood events might have a bearing on adult behaviour and consciousness. Freud theorized that there are 4 universal stages of psychological development which are decisive for the formation of personality: oral, anal, phallic and genital. A period of latency, normally occurring between the ages of 6 or 7 and the onset of puberty was included by Freud in the overall scheme of development, but strictly speaking it is not a stage. The first 3 stages of development extend from birth to five years and are called pregenital stages; since the genital zones of the body have not attained a dominant role in personality formation. The fourth stage coincides with the attainment of puberty. The names of these stages are based on the regions of the body whose stimulation allows for the discharge of sexual energy.

i. The Oral Stage: This stage extends throughout the first year of life. Infants are totally reliant upon others for survival, dependence is their only way of obtaining instinctual gratification. The mouth is the body zone through which biological drives are sought to be reduced. Freud believed that the mouth remains an important erogenous zone.

ii. The Anal Stage: During the second and third years of life, the focus shifts from mouth to the anal region.

iii. The Phallic Stage: Age about 4 years. —This is a stage of psychosexual development. Adults males fixate at the phallic stage are usually brash vain, boastful and ambitious while women are found to express traits of flirtatiousness.

iv. The Latency Period: Between the ages of 6 or 7 and the onset of adolescence, occurs the latency period (the elementary school age) which is very important for the social development of the child, for acquiring the knowledge and skills needed to get along in the workday world.

v. The Genital stage: The genital stage occurs during adolescence to adulthood.

Freud believed that in order for people to attain the ideal genital character, they must relinquish the passivity of early childhood days when love, security, physical comfort indeed all gratification's were freely given and nothing was expected in return. They have to work, postpone gratification, become responsible and above all assume a more active role in dealing with life's problems.

Assessment of Freud's Stages

Credit should be given to Freud, for he was the pioneering stage theorist. He provides some valuable insights which provoked further study on personality development. There exists hardly a sphere of modem life which has not been influenced more or less by Freudian thought - sociology, social welfare, politics, law, the family, education, the treatment of delinquency and mental illness, medicine, propaganda, advertising, entertainment and even religion. Freud has made our understanding of human personality both deeper and wider than we chose to dream.

Although the human mind is invisible and intangible, Freud has shown that it's study can be carried out with something like scientific precision. Human behaviour indeed seems unpredictable, swayed by unknown motives, but Freud showed that it is possible to discern law which governs people's words, thoughts and feelings and that they do not behave irrationally as it might seem, but in tune with their own inner dynamics. His works are considered to be a revolution in our knowledge of human personality for two reasons: firstly. Because he evolved a new scientific method of studying the human mind and secondly, because of the application of that method yielded results which compels us to revise our ideas about the human personality. However, Freud's high reliance on sex to explain stages in personality development has been criticized. The major disagreement centres on Freud's choice of words.

Neo-Freud Stages

Among Neo-Freudians, Erik Erikson gave a new dimension to the development of personality, which he claimed was nothing more than a systematic extension of Freud's psychosexual development. Erikson felt that, relatively more attention should be given to the social rather than the sexual adaptations of individual. He postulated that, the social problems encountered in the course of development were more important stages in which the child faces a wider range of human relationships as he grows up. Erikson asserted that, a psychosocial crisis occurs within each of the stages and that in order for the person to have a normal, fulfilling personality, each crisis should be optimally resolved. For Erikson, a crisis is not a catastrophe but a turning point in an individual's development. Erikson's eight stages of psychological development can be enlisted as:

1. Infancy: Birth to one year.
2. Early Childhood: One to three years.
3. Play age: Four to five years.
4. School age: Six to eleven years.
5. Puberty and adolescence: Twelve to twenty years.
6. Young adulthood: Twenty to twenty four years.
7. Middle adulthood: Twenty five to sixty five years.
8. Late adulthood: Old age.

Assessment of Psychosocial Stages

Eight stages of man, as postulated by Erikson, offer new perspectives about personality. First, Erikson has formulated a theory in which the roles of society and of persons themselves are accorded equal emphasis with respect to the development and organization of personality. Second, Erikson has been sensitive to the age of adolescence, a period largely ignored in the formation of the person's psychological and social well-being. Finally, Erikson has stimulated a sense of optimum by demonstrating that each stage of psychosocial growth has the potential for both strength and weakness, so that failure at one stage of development does not necessarily indicate doom at a later stage.

Although Erikson's theory has gained prominence in both clinical and academic setting, research efforts towards testing it have been sparse. Erikson himself admits that his own conceptions of personality may not be directly applicable to experimental verification.

Cognitive Stages

Jean Piaget, a Swiss psychologists is credited with 'cognitive' or 'conscious' stages of personality development. For Piaget it is 'conscious' instincts which are important variables in the development of personality. Being a lover of children, Piaget spent most of his life observing children in order to understand when and how they developed their reasoning abilities.

He identified four stages of personality development which are:

i. Sensorimotor: Age 0-2 years: By sensorimotor, Piaget means that the infant responds to stimuli quite directly with little in the way of complex information processing.

ii. Pre-operational Stage: During the pre-operational stage, the child learns to separate himself from the environment and initially classifies objects through the use of symbols and words.

iii. Concrete Operational Stage: The concrete operational stage is characterized by an intellectual understanding of the concept of conversation of a mass, irrespective of its shape.

iv. Formal Operation Stage: In this final stage, reasoning can take place on abstract as well as concrete levels.

Piaget's views on personality are valid as much as the cognitive stages do have influence on organizational behaviour, particularly the formal operational stage in which most people are active organization members. At this stage, concrete things need not be manipulated to cause behaviour, as employees are capable of analyzing reasoning, imagining and evaluating objects. But the problem with the cognitive theory is that it fails to unravel all dimensions of personality development.

Immaturity to Maturity

Professor Chris Argyris of Harvard has identified specific dimensions of the human personality as it develops. He proposes that the human, rather than going through distinct stages, progresses along a continuum from an infant to maturity as an adult. However, at any stage, people can have their degree of development plotted according to the seven dimensions as shown below:

Immaturity Characteristics	Maturity Characteristic
Passivity	Activity
Dependence	Independence
Few Ways of Behaving	Diverse Behaviour
Shallow interests	Deep interests

Short-time perspective	Long-time Perspective
Subordinate position	Super ordinate position
Lack of self-awareness	Self-Awareness Control

In contrast to the stage theories of Freud and Erikson, the Argyris's immaturity maturity model of personality is specifically directed to the study and analysis of organizational behaviour. Argyris assumes that the personalities of organizational employees can be generally described by the mature end of the continuum. In order to obtain full expression of employee's personalities, the formal organization should allow for activity rather than passivity, independence rather than dependence, long-time rather than short-time perspective, occupation of a position higher than that of peers and expression of deep, important abilities. Argyris argues that, too often the exact opposite occurs. The mature organizational participant becomes frustrated and anxious and is in conflict with the modern formal organization. Argyris sees a basic incongruity between the needs of the mature personality and the nature of the formal organization.

Determinants of Personality

What determinants go into the development of personality? Of all the complexities and unanswered questions in the study of human behaviour, this question may be the most difficult. For the convenience of study, the determinants of personality can be grouped into five broad categories:

Heredity

The role of heredity in the development of personality is an old argument in personality theory. Heredity refers to those factors that were determined at conception. Physical stature, facial attractiveness, energy level, muscle composition and reflexes and biological rhythms are characteristics that are generally considered to be imported either completely or substantially by one's parents. The heredity approach argues that the ultimate explanation of an individual's personality is the molecular structure of the genes, located in the chromosomes which contain thousands of genes, which seem to be transmitters of traits. The role of heredity on personality development is still an unsettled area of understanding. The problem is that geneticists face a major obstacle in gathering information scientifically on the human being. Nevertheless, the role of heredity on personality development cannot be totally minimized. Physical attributes, for instance, may be largely attributed to heredity.

The following classification of characteristics is said to be inherited by all humans:

a. Physical Structure (how tall or short one is, whether one has a long or short nose, large or small feet — briefly, how one is put together).

b. Reflexes (direct response to stimuli, such as withdrawing from a pin prick, blinking when something approaches the eye).

c. Innate drives (impulses to act based on physiological tensions; but these must be linked through learning with activities which will reduce the tensions).

d. Intelligence (the capacity to learn, to modify responses).

e. Temperament (patterned and recurrent responses associated with basic emotional makeup for e.g.- phlegmatic, excitable and or lethargic).

Environment

If all personality characteristics were by heredity, they would be fixed at birth and no amount of experience could alter them. Personality development owes as much to environment as it does to heredity. Environment is a broad term and includes such factors as culture. Culture establishes norms, attitudes and values that are passed along from one generation to the next and create consistencies overtime. Anthropologists, to whom culture as a subject belongs, have clearly demonstrated the important role culture plays in the development of the human personality.

While growing, the child learns to behave in ways expected by the culture of the family into which the baby was born. Most cultures expect different behaviour from males than from females.

Every culture has its own subcultures, each with its own views about such qualities as moral values, standards of cleanliness, style of dress and definitions of success. The cultural subgroup exerts its influence on personality. All boys are expected to show certain personality characteristics (as compared with girls), but a poor boy raised in an urban slum is expected to behave differently in some respects than a well-to-do raised in a middle class suburb.

Although culture has significant influence on personality development, linear relationship cannot be established between personality and the given culture, for 2 reasons:

a. The culture impacts upon an individual are not uniform, because they are transmitted by certain people-parents and others who are not all alike in their values and practices.

b. The individual has some experiences that are unique. Each individual reacts in his own way to social pressures, differences in behaviour being caused by biological factors.

Contribution from the Family

The family has considerable influence on personality development, particularly in the early stages. The parents play an important part in the identification process which is important to an individual's early development. The process can be examined from three different perspectives:

a. First, identification can be viewed as the similarity of behaviour (including feelings and attitudes between child and model).

b. Second, identification can be looked upon as the child's motives or desires to be like the model.

c. Third, identification can be viewed as the process through which the child actually takes on the attributes of the model.

The overall home environment created by the parents, in addition to their direct influence, is critical to personality development. Siblings (brothers and sisters) also contribute to personality. It has been argued that, sibling position is an important psychological variable because it represents a microcosm of the significant social experience of adolescence and adulthood. It is argued that those first born are more prone to be schizophrenic, more susceptible to social pressures and more dependent than those later-born. The first born are also more likely to experience the world as more orderly, predictable and rational than later-born children.

Socialization Process

There is greater realization that other relevant persons, groups and organizations exercise their due role in personality development. This is commonly called the socialization process. It is especially relevant to organizational behaviour, because the process is not confined to early childhood, rather taking place throughout one's life. In particular, evidence is accumulating that, socialization may be one of the best explanations of why employees behave the way they do in today's organizations.

Socializations involves the process by which a person acquires, from the enormously wide range of behavioural potentialities that are open to him or her, starting at birth, those behaviour patterns that are customary and acceptable to the standards of, initial', the family, and later the social group and the employing organization. Thus, socialization starts with the initial contact between mother and her new infant. After infancy, other members of immediate family (father, brothers, sisters and close relatives or friends) followed by the social group (peers, school friends and members of the working group) play influential roles.

Situational Considerations

Above determinants discussed are no doubt important to personality, but it must be recognized that, it is the immediate situation which may predominate finally.

While it seems logical to suppose that, situations will influence an individual's personality, a neat classification scheme that would tell us the impact of various types of situations has so far eluded us. However. we do know that certain situations are more relevant than others in influencing personality. What is of taxonomically, wrote Lee Sechrest, is that situations seem to differ substantially in the constraints they impose on behaviour with some situations, e.g. church. constraining many behaviours and others, e.g., a picnic in a public park — constraining relative few. From the above discussion, it is clear that personality is a complex concept that reflects many influences both within and outside the individual. Personality progresses through identifiable stages and never really stops developing. One can, however, examine personality at any point in time within its developmental sequence in order to compare and contrast individual personalities.

Personality Traits

A trait is understood as a predisposition to respond in an equivalent manner to various kinds of stimuli. Traits, in effect, are psychological entities that render many stimuli as well as many responses equivalent. Many stimuli may evoke the same response, or many responses (perceptions, interpretations, feelings, actions) have the same functional meaning in terms of the traits. Various attempts have been made to isolate traits, but the efforts have been hindered because there are so many of them. However, it is virtually impossible to predict behaviour when such a large number of traits requires to be considered. As a result, attention has been directed towards reducing these thousands to a manageable number to ascertain the source of primary traits.

One researcher identified 171 surface traits but concluded that they were superficial and lacking descriptive power. What he sought was a reduced set of traits that would identify underlying patterns. The result was the identification of sixteen personality factors, which he called source or primary traits that are basic underlying causes of surface traits.

1.	Reserved	Vs	Outgoing
2.	Less intelligent	Vs	More intelligent
3.	Affected by feelings	Vs	Emotionally more stable
4.	Submissive	Vs	Dominant
5.	Serious	Vs	Happy-go-lucky
6.	Expedient	Vs	Conscientious
7.	Timid	Vs	Venturesome
8.	Tough-minded	Vs	Sensitive
9.	Trusting	Vs	Suspicious
10.	Practical	Vs	Imaginative
11.	Fortright	Vs	Shrewd
12.	Self-assumed	Vs	Apprehensive
13.	Conservative	Vs	Experimenting
14.	Group dependent	Vs	Self-dependent
15.	Uncontrolled	Vs	Controlled
16.	Relaxed	Vs	Tense

These sixteen traits have been found to be generally steady and constant sources of behaviour, subject, of course, to the influence of particular situations.

The Myers - Briggs Framework

This is a popular questionnaire with 100 items and is widely used to understand personalities in organizations. Based on the classical work of Carl Jung, the Myers – Briggs Type Indicator (MBTI) asks people how they usually feel or act in particular situations. Based on the answers received, people are differentiated in terms of four general dimensions: sensing. intuiting, judging and perceiving. Highest and lower positions in each of the dimensions are used to classify people into sixteen different categories.

The MBTI is a popular instrument used to assess personality types. It is widely used in selection process. As many as two million people are reported to be taking it each year in the U.S. Research suggest that the MBTI is a very useful method for determining communication styles and interaction preferences. In terms of personality attributes, however, doubts exist about the validity and the stability of the instrument.

The Big Five Model

Stability and validity of the MBTI may be in doubt, but the same cannot be said for the five-factor model of personality – popularly called the "Big Five".

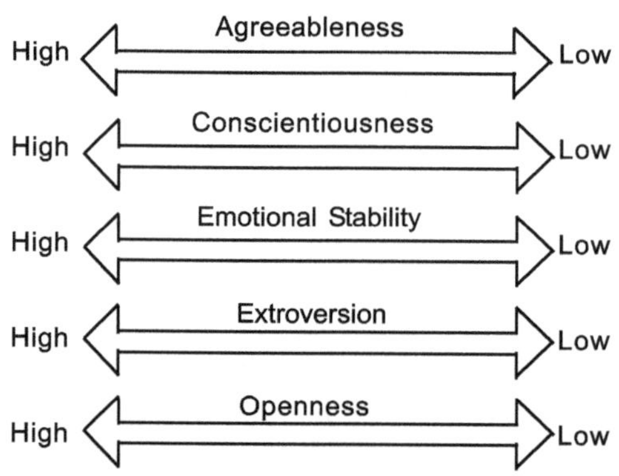

Agreeableness refers to a person's ability to get along with others. High agreeable people value harmony more than they value having their say or their way. They are cooperative and trusting others. People who low on agreeableness focus more on their own needs than the needs of are others.

Conscientiousness refers to the number of goals on which a person focuses. A high conscientiousness person focuses on relatively few goals at one time. He or she is likely to be organised; Systematic, careful, thorough, responsible, self-disciplined, and achievement-oriented. A person with low conscientious tends to focus on a more number of goals at one time. Consequently, the individual is more disorganized, careless and irresponsible, as well as less thorough and self-disciplined. Emotional stability focuses on an individual's ability to cope up the stress. The individual with positive emotional stability tends to be calm, enthusiastic and secure. He or she with negative score tends to be nervous, depressed and insecure. Extroversion reflects a person's comfort level with relationships. Extroverts are sociable, talkative, assertive and open to establishing new relationships. Introverts are less sociable, less talkative, less assertive and more reluctant to begin new relationships. Openness addresses one's range of interests. Extremely open people are fascinated by novelty and innovation. They are willing to listen to new ideas and to change their own ideas, beliefs and attitudes in response to new information. On the other hand, people with low levels of openness tend to be less respective to new ideas and less willing to change their minds. They also tend to have fewer and narrow interests and to be less curious and creative.

The "Big Five" framework continues to attract the attention of both researchers and managers. The potential value of this framework lies in the fact that it encompasses an integrated set of traits that appear to be valid predictions of certain behaviour in certain situations. However, the "Big Five" model is primarily based on research conducted in the U.S. Its generalibility to other cultures, therefore, presents unanswered questions.

Major Traits Influencing Organizational Behaviour

There are many different personality traits, but some of the more important ones for organizational behaviour are authoritarianism, locus of control, machiavellianism, introversion-extroversion, achievement orientation, self- esteem, risk taking, self-monitoring and type A personality.

Authoritarianism

It is a concept developed by the psychologist Adorn during World War II to measure susceptibility to autocratic, fascistic or antidemocratic appeals. Since that time, the concept has been extended to the authoritarianism personality, a generic term used to describe an individual who has a strong belief in the legitimacy of established mechanisms of formal authority, views obedience to authority as necessary, exhibits a negative philosophy of people, adheres to conventional and traditional value systems, is intellectually rigid and opposes the use of subjective feelings. Authoritarians also tend to be rigid in their positions, place high moral value on their beliefs and are strongly oriented towards conformity to rules and regulations. They naturally prefer stable and structured work environments which are governed by clean rules and procedures. Similarly, authoritarians are likely to prefer autocratic or directive leadership and would exhibit high respect for individuals in positions of authority

Locus of Control

It refers to an individual's belief that events are either within one's control (internal locus of control) or are determined by forces beyond one's control (external locus of control). These personality traits are manifested in different behaviour which are significant to manager. It has been proved that externals (those who believe that events are determined by external forces) are less satisfied with their jobs, have higher absenteeism rates, more alienated from work setting and are less involved on their jobs than internals (those who believe that events are within one's control). Internals typically have more control over their own behaviour, are more active in seeking information to make decisions, and are more active socially than externals.

Machiavellianism

It refers to an individual propensity to manipulate people. Machiavellians would be prone to participate in organizational politics. They are also adept at interpersonal game playing, power tactics and identifying influence system in organizations. Do the Machiavellians make good employees? The answer depends on the type of job and whether one considers ethical considerations in evaluating performance. In jobs that require bargaining skills (such as labour negotiation) or where there are substantial rewards for winning (commissioned sales), Machiavellians perform better.

Introversion and Extroversion

These are the most common descriptions of personality traits. These terms are normally associated with an individual's sociability and interpersonal orientation. Extroverts are gregarious and sociable individuals while introverts are shy, quiet and retiring. It is generally established that, introverts and extroverts have significantly different career orientations and require different organizational environments to maximize performance. Extroverts are more suitable for positions that require considerable interaction with others, whereas introverts are more inclined to excel at tasks that require thought and analytical skills. Not surprisingly, managerial positions are dominated by extroverts, thus suggesting that, this managerial trait is a factor in managerial success.

Achievement Orientation

It is yet another personality character which varies among people and which can be used to predict certain behaviours. Employees with a high need to achieve, continually strive to do things better. They want to overcome obstacles, but they want to feel that their success or failure is due to their own actions (read internals). This means that they like tasks of moderate difficulty. An easy task shall not evoke challenges and is, therefore, not liked by high achievers. Similarly, a task with high risk is not linked by these people as the failure rates are more. Given the high achievers propensity for tasks where the outcome can be directly attributed to his or her efforts, the high achiever looks for challenges having approximately a 50-50 chance of success on the job, high achievers will perform better where there is moderate difficulty, rapid performance feedback and direct relationship between effort and reward. This means that the high achievers tend to do better in sales, sports or in management.

Self-esteem

It refers to feeling of like or dislike of one-self. This trait, naturally, varies from person to person. Self- esteem is directly related to desire for success. People with high self-esteem believe that they have abilities to undertake challenging jobs. They tend to choose unconventional jobs than those with lower self-esteem. People with low self-esteem are more susceptible to external influence than are those with high esteem. Low esteems are dependent on the receipt of positive evaluation from others. As a result, they are more likely to seek approval from others and more prone to conform to the beliefs and behaviours of those they respect than high esteems. In managerial positions, low esteems will tend to be concerned with pleasing others, and therefore less likely to take unpopular stands than high esteems. Self-esteem is also related to job satisfaction. High esteems are more satisfied with their jobs than the low esteems.

Risk-taking

People differ in their willingness to take chances. Their propensity to assume or avoid risk has been shown to have an impact on how long it takes managers to make a decision and how much information they require before making their choice. For instance, 79 managers worked on simulated personnel exercise that required them to make decisions. High-risk-taking managers made more rapid decisions and used less information in making their choices than did low-risk- taking managers. Interestingly, the decision accuracy was the same for both groups.

While it is generally correct to conclude that managers in organizations are risk aversive, there are still individual differences on this dimension. As a result, it makes sense to recognise these differences and even to consider aligning risktaking propensity with specific job demands. For instance, a high-risk-taking propensity may lead to more effective performance for a stock trader in a brokerage firm. This type of job, demands rapid decision-making. On the other hand, this personality characteristics might prove a major obstacle to accountants performing auditing activities. This Iatter job might be better filled by someone with a low-risk taking propensity.

Self-monitoring

It refers to an individual's ability to adjust his or her behaviour to external factors. Individuals high in self-monitoring can show considerable adaptability in adjusting their behaviour to external, situational factors. They are highly sensitive to external cues and can behave differently in different situations. High self-monitors are capable of presenting striking contradictions between their public, personal and their private selves. Low self- monitors cannot deviate their behaviour. They tend to display their true dispositions and attitude in every situation, hence there is high behavioural consistency between who they are and what they do. The high self-monitors tend to pay closer attention to the behaviour of others and are more capable of conforming than are low self-monitors. We might also hypotheses that high self-monitors will be more successful in managerial positions where individuals are required to play multiple and even contradicting roles. The high self-monitor is capable of putting on different "faces" for different audiences.

Type of Personality

Finally, there is type 'A' personality and type 'B' personality. Type A personality typifies a person who is always in a hurry, is extremely competitive and is often hostile and irritable. Opposite is Type B personality who is relaxed, incompetent and easy going. How do the two perform in organizations? Type A's are no doubt highly competitive and hardworking. But it is the Type 'B' who climbs up to the top of organization. Type A's will make most successful sales people and senior executive yes are usually Type B's. Why this paradoxes? Answer lies in the tendency of Type A's to trade off quality of effort for quantity. Executive positions usually go to those who are patient rather than to those who are merely hasty, to those who are tactful rather than to those who are hostile and to those who are creative rather than to who are merely agile in competitive strife.

Personality and Organizational Behaviour

Personality is an important determinant of employee behaviour. If an employee likes monotonous or boring work; if he steadfastly refuses additional responsibilities in the form of promotion; if a supervisor fails to reprimand an unruly subordinate; or if a middle level manager tries to climb over you the ladder to reach the top of an organization callously ignoring ethical considerations; the explanation for such behaviour in each case depends on the individual personality, which predisposes an individual to certain behavioural patterns. Thoughtful application of personality concepts, through subjective, helps us understand unique beings and groups with similar personality characteristics.

Personality is the focal point determining motivation. It is impossible to give a full and comprehensive account of executive behaviour without raising questions of why they behave as they do. For e.g., why do effective executives spend so much time on personnel matters? Why don't they concentrate their efforts on production? When we ask such questions regarding executive behaviour, we are trying to explore questions of motivation. Motivation is concerned with the study of the direction and persistence of action. Personality is the organism centre around which people's motives form a unified and integrated system.

Personality characteristics into centrifugation of individuals to occupy various positions in an organization. The traits required for a successful sales manager are different from those required for an executive in charge of production.

The concept of personality is not be understood in an organizational context only. The need for understanding human characteristics, in general is more significant than comprehending personality in the context of organizations.

Despite serious attempts, experts have not been able to comprehend the real nature of personality. Of all the problems that have confronted human beings since the beginning of recorded history, perhaps the most significant has been the riddle of their own nature. Attempts to answer 'what is man?' are countless, a great many avenues have been explored with an enormous variety of concepts being employed along the way. Astrology, philosophy and the life sciences are but a few of the many directions that the quest to understand human nature has taken. At this point in history, some of these avenues have been proved to dead ends, while other are just beginning to flourish. And today the problem is more pressing than ever, since most of the world's ills, for example: overpopulation, war, pollution, prejudice are brought about by the behaviour of people. So it may not be overstating the case to say that the quality of human life in the future, indeed our own survival, may well depend upon an increased understanding of human nature.

Attitudes

Attitude is important variable in human behaviour.

Nature

The salient features which contribute to the meaning of attitudes are:

- Attitudes refer to feelings and beliefs of individuals or groups of individuals.
- The feelings and beliefs are directed towards other people, objects or ideas.
- Attitudes tend to result in behaviour or action.
- Attitude can fall anywhere along a continuum from very favourable to very unfavourable.
- Attitudes endure.
- All people, irrespective of their status or intelligence, hold attitudes. Some of the definitions of attitude are as below:
    - "The word attitude describes a persistent tendency to feel and behave in a particular way towards some object".

- "Attitudes are evaluative statements either favourable or unfavourable concerning objects, people or events. They reflect how one feels about something".
- "Attitudes are learned predispositions towards aspects of our environment. They may be positively or negatively directed towards certain people, service or institutions".

Individuals acquire attitudes from several sources, but the point to be stressed is that the attitudes are acquired, but not inherited.

The most important sources of acquiring attitudes are:

Direct Experience with the Object

Attitudes can develop from a personally rewarding or punishing experience with an object. Employees form attitudes about jobs on their previous experiences. For e.g. if everyone who has held a job has been promoted within six months, current job holders are likely to believe that they will also be promoted within six months. Attitude formed on experience are difficult to change.

Classical Conditioning and Attitude

One of the basic processes underlying attitude formation can be explained on the basis of learning principles. People develop associations between various objects and the emotional reactions that accompany them. For e.g., many soldiers who were stationed in the Persian Gulf during the war with Iraq reported that, they never wanted to sit on a sandy beach again. This is the soldiers formed negative attitudes towards sand. Similarly, positive associations can develop through classical conditioning. Advertisers make use of the principles of classical conditioning of attitudes by attempting to link a product they want consumers to buy with a positive feeling or event.

Operant Conditioning and Attitude Acquisition

Another learning process, operant conditioning, also underlies attitude acquisition. Attitudes that are reinforced, either verbally or non-verbally, tend to be maintained. Conversely, a person who states an attitude that elicits ridicule from others may modify or abandon the attitude. But it is not only direct reinforcement or punishment that can influence attitudes.

Vicarious Learning

In which a person learns something through the observance of others, can also account for attitude development — particularly when the individual has no direct experience with the object about which the attitude is held. It is through vicariously learning processes that children pick up the prejudice of their parents.

We also learn attitudes vicariously through television, films and other media.

Family and Peer Groups

A person may learn attitudes through imitation of parents. If parents have positive attitude towards an object and the child admires his parents, he is likely to adopt a similar attitude, even without being told about the object and even without having direct experience. Attitudes towards the opposite sex, religion, tolerance or prejudice, education, occupations and almost all other areas where attitudes are capable of expression are the result of our accepting or rejecting the attitudes held by members of our family. Similarly, attitudes are acquired from peer groups in colleges and organizations.

Neighbourhood

The neighborhoods we live has a certain structure in terms of its having cultural facilities, religious groupings and possibly ethnic differences. Further, it has people who are neighbours. Neighbouring — adults or children- tolerate, condone, or deny certain attitudes and behaviour and as a result we are either Northerners or Southerners. Further, we accept these moves and conform, or we deny them and possibly rebel. The conformity or rebellion in some respects is the evidence of the attitudes we hold.

Economic Status and Occupations

Our economic and occupational positions also contribute to attitude formation. They determine, in part, our attitudes towards unions and management and our belief that certain laws are "good" or "bad". Our socio-economic background influences our present and future attitudes.

Mass Communication

All varieties of mass communications — televisions, radio, newspaper and magazines feed their audiences large quantities of information. The presentation of news or information is constructed so as to cater to the attitude of the audience. In turn, the audience selects the specific form of mass communication that best reflects its attitudes on various subjects. The material we select helps us either to substantiate our opinions or to establish new ones.

Types of Attitudes

Individuals possess hundreds of attitudes. But in organizational behaviour, we are concerned with work related attitudes which are mainly three:

1. Job Satisfaction: Job satisfaction refers to one's feeling towards one's job. An individual having satisfaction is said to posses positive attitude towards the job. Conversely, a dissatisfied person will have negative attitude towards his orher job. When people speak of employee attitudes they invariably refer to job satisfaction.

In fact, the two terms are used interchangeably, though subtle difference does exist between the two.

2. Job Involvement: Job involvement refers to the degree with which an individual identifies psychologically with his or her job and perceives his or her perceived performance level important to self-worth. High degree of job involvement results in fewer absence and lower resignation rates.

3. Organizational Commitment: The last job attitude refers to organizational commitment. It is understood as one's identification with his or her organization and feels proud of being its employee. Job involvement refers to one's attachment to a job whereas organizational commitment implies an employee's identification with a particular organization and its goals. Needless to say, it is to state that, an individual may be attached to his or her job but may be indifferent to the organization and its objectives. Turnover and absenteeism are low when employees have organizational commitment.

Functions of Attitude

Why do we hold on to certain attitudes towards individuals or objects? It is because these attitudes help us respond to the individuals or objects in a meaningful way. Attitudes serve four important functions:

1. Utilitarian: An attitude may develop because either the attitude or the object of the attitude is instrumental in helping one to obtain rewards or avoid punishments. In some cases the attitude is a means to an end. A worker finds that when he expresses a negative attitude towards his boss, his co-workers pay attention to and sympathies with him, but when he expresses a positive attitude, he is ignored or chastened. The negative attitude is instrumental in obtaining rewards (acceptance) and avoiding punishment (reflection). In another case, the object is a means to an end, and the attitude develops from association of the object and its outcome.

   For Example: A car salesman may develop favourable attitudes towards blue-collar workers, to whom he can easily sell, and a negative attitude towards doctors, who he finds always searching for a bargain and difficult to sell to. He associates success and profit with blue collar workers and failure and difficulty with doctors and thus he develops appropriate attitudes towards those objects through association.

2. Ego-defence: People often form and maintain certain attitudes to protect their own self-images. For e.g., workers may feel threatened by the employment or advancement of minority or female workers in their organization. These threatened workers may develop prejudices against the new workers. They may develop an attitude that such newcomers are less qualified, and they might mistreat

these workers. Such an ego defensive attitude is formed and used to cope with a feeling of guilt or threat. Unless this feeling is removed, this kind of attitude will remain unchanged.

3. Value Expressive: Our attitude reflects our value systems. And our value expressive attitudes are closely related to our self- concept. One whose central value is freedom, the individual may express very positive attitudes towards decentralization of authority in the organization, flexible work schedules and relaxation of dress standards.

4. Knowledge: Attitude is often substituted for knowledge. In the absence of knowledge, we use our attitude to organise and make sense out of the perceived object or person. For e.g., people who are not familiar with nuclear energy may develop an attitude that it is dangerous and should not be used as an energy source. Stereotyping is another example. In the absence of knowledge about a person, we may use a stereotyped attitude for judging the person.

Why should managers know about these attitude functions? Such knowledge can serve two purposes. First, it helps us understand and predict how a certain person is likely to behave. For e.g., if a person is "prejudiced" against another, he is less likely to be fair in judging the other person. Moreover, this knowledge helps the manager see why the person has developed such an attitude. Second, it can help the manager change the attitude of another person. He can do this by changing the conditions that sustain the attitude. For e.g. he can change people with low self-images by helping them increase their ability to solve their problems, or by providing them with positive feedback on what they accomplish.

Changing Attitude

Attitudes of employees can be changed and it is in the best interest of the organization to try for the change. But change is difficult as there are barriers to it.

Barriers to Change

One obstacle to the change of attitude is the attitude theory of balance and consistency. That is, human beings prefer their attitudes about people ad things to be in line (i.e. balanced, consistent) with their behaviours towards each other and objects. When attitudes or behaviours are not consistent, people usually seek to reduce the inconsistency rewarding internally. Leon Festinger has developed a theory in support of attitude consistency called cognitive dissonance. Festinger's theory states that dissonance makes an individual feel uncomfortable. This feeling makes the individual try to reduce dissonance.

Cognitive dissonance also occurs when a person behaves in a fashion that is inconsistent with his or her attitudes. For e.g., a person may realize that smoking and overeating are dangerous, yet continue to do both. Because the attitudes and behaviour are not consistent with each other, the person probably will experience a certain amount of tension and discomfort and may engage in dissonance reduction, seeking ways to reduce the dissonance and tension it causes. The dissonance associated with smoking might be resolved by rationalizing. In general, the person attempts to change the attitude, alter the behaviour or perceptually distort the circumstances to reduce tension and discomfort. In the organizational setting, cognitive dissonance occurs when an employee desires to leave the present job as there is no use in continuing and working hard. The individual may rationalize his or her stay with such explanations as, "organization is not bad after all" or "what is the alternative?"

The Second Barrier

The second barrier to change of attitude is prior commitments. This occurs when people feel a commitment to a particular course of action and are unwilling to change.

The Third Barrier

The third barrier results from insufficient information. Sometimes people see no reason why they should change their attitudes. The boss may not like a subordinate's negative attitude, but the latter may be quite pleased with his behaviour. Unless the boss can show the individual why a negative attitude is detrimental to career progress or salary increases or some other personal objective, the subordinate may continue to have negative attitude.

Ways of Changing

A few important ways of changing attitudes have been described below:

1. Providing new information: New information will help change attitudes. Negative attitudes are mainly formed owing to lack of or insufficient information. Workers generally become pro-union because of the ignorance about the good intentions of the management. Once they come to know how the management cares for the welfare of the workers, they change their attitude and might turn pro-management.

2. Use of Fear: Fear can change attitude. However, the change depends on the degree of fear. For e.g., if low levels of fear arouses are used, people often ignore them. The warnings are not strong enough to warrant attention. If moderate levels of fear arousals are used, people often become aware of situation and will change their attitudes. However, if high degrees of fear arousal are used, people often reject the message, because it is too threatening and thus not believable. On the contrary, high degrees of fear may prove counter productive. On being

threatened too far, people tend to become stubborn in their attitudes and may refuse to change.

3. Influence of friends or peers: Change of attitude can come about through persuasion of friends or peers. Credibility of the others, specially peers, is important to effect change. Peers with high creditability shall exercise significant influence on change. The same is not true with peers who have low creditabilities.

4. The co-opting approach: Co-opting is another way of changing attitude. This means taking people who are dissatisfied with a situation and getting them involved in improving things.

5. Others: Research has shown that an individual is more likely to change a privately held attitude than one he has stated publicly. It is, therefore, necessary that a situation is avoided where the individual makes his attitude public prior to the change attempt.

The individual from a culturally deprived environment who holds an array of hostile attitudes, may change when he is given opportunities for education. A person from privileged subculture, who has always held to a democratic attitude, may become negative towards some group because of one unfortunate experience. Again, through continued association with others holding similar attitudes, one can be influenced in a positive or negative direction. Here the attitudes of both the reference group and the social climate are important.

Types of Change

Attitude change may be classified into congruent and incongruent change. Congruent change in attitude involves a movement in the same direction but with reduced intensity of feeling. For e.g., a negative or positive attitude of a boss towards his subordinate will persist, but the degree of like or dislike is reduced. Incongruent change involves change of direction itself from positive (or negative) attitude towards a person to negative (or positive) attitude towards the same person. This change is observable in behavioural terms such as change in retail store purchases, resigning from an organization or joining one.

Attitude and OB

Employee attitudes are important to management because of their influence on behaviour, attitudinal influences or perception, job-satisfaction, job-involvement, and organizational commitment.

Attitudinal Influences on Behaviour

Attitudes affect employee behaviour. However, a direct relationship between attitudes and actions is not agreeable to some, since attitude does not lead to any specific action.

For e.g., a manager may dislike certain people in minority groups, but he may nevertheless treat them fairly and pleasantly in his office. This inconsistency occurs because the manager does not allow his attitude to interfere with his professional judgement. However, these attitudes may manifest themselves in other behaviour. For e.g., the manager may treat the minority workers fairly on the job but not invite them to his son's or daughter's marriage.

Although the influence of attitudes on behaviour is not clearly discernible, two theories, i.e. cognitive dissonance and self-fulfilling prophecy, helps us understand the direction of attitudinal influences.

Cognitive dissonance will be more intense when any of the following conditions exist:

- The decision is an important one psychologically or financially.
- There are a number of foregone alternatives.
- The foregone alternatives have many positive features. Typically an individual will try to minimize the dissonance by using any of the four methods.

The methods are:

- The individual seeks information that confirms the wisdom of the decision.
- The individual selectively perceives (distorts) information in a way that supports the decision.
- The person adopts a less favourable attitude towards the foregone alternatives.
- The person down plays the importance of any negative aspects of the choice and magnifies the positive elements.

The self-fulfilling prophecy is the process by which we try to convert our attitudes, beliefs and expectations into reality. If we predict that something is going to happen, we will try very hard to make it happen. For e.g., if we feel that we are competent, we will undertake challenging tasks.

Consequently, we gain experience and skills that make us more competent, so that we accomplish even more. However, if we have a negative attitude towards ourselves, we will not provide ourselves with the chance to become competent.

Attitudinal Influence on Perception

Perceptual outcomes are derived from past experiences and perceptions, but they also influence the way we perceive stimuli such sayings as "Beauty is altogether in the eye of the beholder" and "one person's trash is another person's treasure" emphasise the importance of attitudes in perceiving the world around us. If our attitudes are positive, things will look brighter to us than if they are negative.

Job Satisfaction

Employee attitudes are important to monitor, understand and manage. They develop as a consequences of the feelings of equality or inequality in the reward system as well as from supervisory treatment. Managers are particularly concerned with three types of attitudes, namely job satisfaction, job involvement and organizational commitment.

Although many of the factors contributing to job satisfaction are under the control of managers, it is also true that people do differ in their personal dispositions as they enter organizations. Some people are optimistic, upbeat, cheerful and courteous. They are said to have positive affectivity. Others are generally pessimistic, downbeat, irritable and even abrasive. They are said to have negative affectivity. Appears that people are predisposed to be satisfied or dissatisfied. But it is important to explore the nature and effect of job satisfaction.

Elements of Job Satisfaction

Job satisfaction is a set of favourable or non-favourable feelings and emotions with which employees view their work. Job satisfaction is an affective attitude. Job satisfaction refers to the attitude of an individual single employee. The general term used to describe overall group satisfaction is MORALE. Group morale is important to monitor since individuals often take their social cues from their work associates and adapt their attitudes to conform to those of the group.

Job satisfaction studies focus on various parts that are believed to be important, since job-related attitudes predispose an employee to behave in certain ways. Important elements of job satisfaction include pay, one's supervisor, the nature of tasks performed, a employers co-worker's or team and the immediate working conditions. Managers should not allow an employee's high satisfaction on one element to offset high dissatisfaction on another by arithmetically bonding both feelings into an average rating. The attention should be divided between elements that are related to job content (i.e. nature of job) and those which are part of the job-context. (supervisor, co-workers and organization).

Like attitudes, job satisfaction or dissatisfaction emerges over a long period of time, but job satisfaction is dynamic. Manager must pay attention to employee attitudes week after week, month after month, year after year since the stability in job satisfaction varies in level.

Job satisfaction is one part of life satisfaction. So, it is said that there is a spill-over effect that occurs in both directions between job and life satisfaction. Therefore, managers need to monitor not only job and immediate work environment but also their employee's attitudes towards other parts of life.

The level of job satisfaction across groups is not constant, but is related to number of variables. The key variables revolve around age, occupational level and organizational size. The level of job satisfaction are higher in smaller organization units. Larger organizations tend to overwhelm with people, disrupt supportive processes and limit the amounts of personal closeness, friendship, and small group team work that are important aspects of job satisfaction for many.

Job Involvement

Two other distinct but related, employee attitudes are important to many employers in addition to job satisfaction. Job involvement is the degree to which employees immerse themselves in their job, invest time and energy in them and view work as a central part of their overall lives. Job-involved employees are likely to believe in the work, to exhibit high growth needs, and to enjoy participation in decision making. As a result, they are willing to work long hours and they will attempt to be high performers.

Organizational Commitment

Organizational commitment or employee loyalty, is the degree to which an employee identifies with the organization and wants to continue actively participating in it. It is a measure of the employee's willingness to remain with a firm in the future. It reflects the employee's belief in the mission and goals of the firm, willingness to expend effort in their accomplishment and intentions to continue working here. Commitment is usually stronger among longer term employees. Organizationally committed employees will usually have good attendance records, demonstrate a willing abstinance to company policies, lower turnover rates. A comprehensive approach to OB suggests that a manager should consider ways in which the work environment can help produce all three key employee attitudes — job satisfaction, job involvement and organizational commitment. Higher job involvement tends to higher levels of dedication and productivity in workers. High performance and equitable rewards encourage high satisfaction through a performance-satisfaction-effort loop. Higher job satisfaction usually is associated with lower turnover and fewer absence. Committed employees are also more likely to embrace company values and its culture.

Values

Value is generally used in two different ways: as a characteristic of an object or as an attribute possessed by an individual and thought desirable. The focus here is on the latter.

A value is defined as a "concept of the desirable, an internalizes criterion of standard of evaluation a person possesses. Such concepts and standards are relatively few and determined or guide an individual's evaluation of the many objects encountered in everyday life".

Values are tinged with moral flavor, involving an individual's judgement of what is right, good or desirable. Thus, values provide standards of competence and morality.

- Are fewer in number than attitudes.
- Transcend specific objects, situations or persons.
- Are relatively permanent and resistant to change.
- Are most central to the core of a person.

Values and Attitudes

There are differences between values and attitudes. Attitudes essentially represent predisposition's to respond. Values focus on the judgement of what ought to be. This judgement can represent the specific manifestation of a determining tendency below the surface of the behaviour. Attitudes represent several beliefs focussed on a specific object or situation. Value, on the other hand, represents a single belief that transcendently guides actions and judgements across objects and situations. Finally, a value stands in relation to some social or cultural standards or norms while attitudes are mostly personal experiences.

There are similarity between values and attitudes. Both are powerful instruments influencing cognitive process and behaviour of people both are learned and acquired from the same sources — experience with people and objects. Values and attitudes are relatively permanent and are resistant to change. Finally, values and attitudes influence each other and are, more often than not, used interchangeably.

Types of Values

In extensive research conducted during the last 2 decades, Milton Rokeach has identified 2 basic types of values- terminal and instrumental. A terminal value is an ultimate goal in a desired status or outcome. An instrumental value, on the other hand, is a tool or means for acquiring a terminal value. For e.g., a person may desire and strive to achieve happiness, a terminal value by being ambitious, independent and responsible (instrumental values).

Some of the terminal values are - Equality, Freedom, Family Security, Happiness, National security. Some of the Instrumental values are — Ambitious, Broad-minded, Capable, Cheerful, Honest.

The different values an individual has, both terminal and instrumental, combine to create an enduring cluster of values, a value system. Our values and value system then are primary determinants of who and what we are as individual.

Another way of categorizing values is given below:

Theoretical — Interest in the discovery of truth through reasoning and systematic thinking.

- Economics - Interest useful and practicality, including the accumulation of wealth.
- Aesthetic - Interest in beauty, form and artistic harmony.
- Social - Interest in people and love as a relationship.
- Political - Interest in gaining power and influencing people.
- Religious - Interest in unity and understanding the cosmos as a whole.

Formation of Values

Values are learned and acquired primarily through experience with people, institution. Parents, for e.g., will have substantial influence on the values of their children values. Parents relation to everyday events demonstrates what is good and bad, acceptable and unacceptable, and important and unimportant values are also taught and reinforced interest in schools, religious organization, and social groups. As we grow and develop, each source of influence contributes to our definition of what is important in life.

Cultural moves have influence on the formation of values. Basic conviction of what is good or bad are derived from one's satisfaction about own culture.

Values and OB

An understanding of values is useful to a manager interest following ways:

- Values are important to the study of OB because they lay the foundation for the understanding of attitudes and motivation as well as influencing our perception. Individual enter an organization with preconceived notion of what "ought" and what "ought not" to be. Of course, these notions are not value free. On the contrary they contain interpretation of right and wrong. Further, they imply that certain behaviours or outcomes are preferred over others. As a result, it clouds objectivity and rationality.
- Values generally influence attitudes and behaviour. Suppose an individual enters an organization with the view that allocating pay on the basis of performance is right, whereas allocating pay on the basis of seniority is wrong or inferior. He is likely to get disappointed if the organization rewards seniority and merit, disappointment is likely to lead to dissatisfaction and decline interest performance. His attitude and behaviour would be different if his values are aligned with the organization's pay policies.
- The challenge and relationship-examination of established work values constitute of the cornerstones of the current management revolution all over the world. Hence, an understanding of values becomes a necessity.

- Values differ across culture What is permissible in the U.S may be simple considreation. Strangely, majority of the principles and concepts of OB have been developed by American, using American subjects within domestic context. A study of more than 11000 articles published in 24 management and OB journals over a ten-year period reveals that, approximately 80% of studies have been done in the U.S and have been conducted by Americans. This implies that OB specialists should remember that, no theories and principles are universally applicable to managing people around the world. They should take into consideration cultural values when trying to understand the behaviours of people's interest different in countries.

Job Satisfaction

It is useful to highlight the important aspects of job satisfaction. The important dimensions to Job satisfaction are:

- Job satisfaction refers to one's feeling towards one's job. It can only be inferred but not seen.
- Job satisfaction is often determined by how well outcomes meet or exceed expectations. Satisfaction with one's job means increased commitment in the full-fillment of formal requirements. There is greater willingness to invest personal energy and time into job performance.
- The terms job satisfaction and job attitudes are typically used interchangeably. Both refer to effective orientation on the part of individuals towards their work and roles which they are presently occupying. Positive attitudes towards the job are conceptually equivalent to job satisfaction and negative attitudes towards the job dissatisfaction.

Though the terms job satisfaction and attitudes are used interchangeably, there are differences between the two. Job satisfaction, on the other hand, relates to performance factor. Attitudes reflect ones feeling towards individuals, organizations and objects. But satisfaction refers to one's attitude to a job. Job satisfaction is therefore, a specific subset of attitudes. Attitudes endue generally, but job satisfaction is dynamic, it can decline ever more quickly than developed. Managers, therefore, cannot establish the conditions leading to high satisfaction as now and then employee needs may change. Managers need to pay attention to job satisfaction constantly.

Some of the few definitions of job satisfaction:

- Job satisfaction is defined as a "pleasurable or positive emotional state resulting from the appraisal of one's job or job experience".
- Job satisfaction is a set of favourable or unfavourable feeling with which employees view their work.

- Job satisfaction will be defined as the amount of overall positive affect (or feeling) that individual have towards their jobs.

Consequences of Satisfaction

High job satisfaction may lead to improved productivity, increased turnover, improved attendance, less job stress and lower unionization.

Productivity

The relationship between satisfaction and productivity is not definitely established. The result, however, is that in the long run job satisfaction leads to increased productivity. But, 4 decades of research into this issue, unfortunately, does not lend support to this belief.

First, the relationship between job satisfaction and job performance is weak. Interestingly, the latest finding is that the median correlation between satisfaction and performance is only 0.14.

Second, there is more evidence to suggest that job performance leads to job satisfaction and the other way round. An employee who performs well in his job gets both intrinsic and extrinsic rewards which will lead to his satisfaction. A poor performance will make him feel worse about his incompetence and will receive fewer rewards. He will be less satisfied with his work experience.

Third, there are some conditions under which high productivity, more clearly leads to high job satisfaction. One condition is that the employee perceives that, intrinsic and extrinsic rewards are contingent upon his productivity. The second condition is that, the extrinsic rewards (pay for example) be distributed equitably. Inequitable distribution fails to convince the employees that there is close correlation between hard work and rewards.

However, the adage "a happy worker is a productive worker" is not always wrong. True, there may not be a relationship between job satisfaction and productivity. Performance may be affected indirectly by absenteeism or turnover which is related (negatively) to satisfaction.

Job satisfaction and Employee Turnover

High employee turnover is of considerable concern for employee because it disrupts normal operations, causes morale problems for those who stick on and increases the cost involved in selecting and training replacements. The employer does whatever possible to minimize turnover, making the employee feel satisfied on their jobs, being one such.

Unlike the relationship between satisfaction and productivity, the connection with turnover is established beyond doubt.

However, the withdrawal behaviour of employee is modified by certain factors. Loyalty to the organization is one such. Some employees cannot imagine themselves working elsewhere, however dissatisfied they are in their present jobs. Availability of other places of employment also influence turnover. If greener pastures are available, an employee does not mind going in search of them, not with-standing the present level of job satisfaction he enjoys.

Satisfaction and Absences

Correlation of satisfaction to absenteeism is also proved conclusively. Workers who are dissatisfied are more likely to take "mental health" days i.e. days off due to illness or personal business. Simply stated, absenteeism is high when satisfaction is low. As in turnover, absenteeism is subject to modification by certain factors. The degree to which people feel that their jobs are important has a moderating influence on their absences. Employees who feel that their work is important tend to clock in regular attendance. Besides, it is important to remember that while high job satisfaction will not necessarily result in low absenteeism, low satisfaction is likely to bring about high absenteeism.

Satisfaction and Safety

Poor safety practices are a negative consequence of low satisfaction level. When people are discouraged about their jobs, company and superiors, they are more liable to experience accidents. An underlying reason for such accidents is that, discouragement may take one's attention away from the task at hand. Inattention leads to accidents. For e.g., many hand injuries from poorer tools can be attributed to the operator not paying careful attention.

Satisfaction and Job Stress

Job stress is the body's response to any job- related factor that threatens to disturb the person's equilibrium. In the process of experiencing stress, the employee's inner state changes. Prolonged stress can cause the employee serious ailment such as heart disease, ulcer, lower back pain and muscles aches. Chronic job dissatisfaction is a powerful source of job stress. The employee may see no satisfactory short- term solution to escaping this type of stress. An employee trapped in a dissatisfying job may withdraw by such means as high absenteeism and tardiness or the employee may quit.

Employee under prolonged stress stemming from job dissatisfaction often consume too much alcohol, tobacco and drugs. These employees are costly to the management in terms of time lost due to frequent absences and increased payment towards medical reimbursement.

Unionization

It is proved that job dissatisfaction is a major cause for unionization. Dissatisfaction with wages, job security, fringe benefits, chances for promotion and treatment by superiors are reasons which make employees join unions. Another dimension is that job dissatisfaction can have an impact on the tendency to take action within the union, such as filing grievances or striking.

Other Effects of Job-Satisfaction

In addition to above, it has been claimed that a satisfied employee tend to have better mental and physical health and learn new job- related tasks more quickly. Practicing manager and OB researcher would agree that, job satisfaction is important to an organization. Critics however, point out that, this is pure conjecture because there is so much we do not know about the positive effects of satisfaction. On the other hand, when job satisfaction is low, there seems to be negative effects on the organization that have been documented. So, if only from the stand point of viewing job satisfaction as a minimum requirement or point of departure, it is of value to the organization's overall health and effectiveness and is deserving of study and application in the field of OB.

Sources of Job Satisfaction

Several job element contribute to job satisfaction .The most important amongst them are wage structure, nature of work, promotion chances, quality of superior, work group and working conditions.

1. Wages: Wages play a significant role in influencing job satisfaction. This is because of 2 reason. First, money is an instrument in fulfilling one's needs, and two, employees often see pay as a reflection of management's concern for them. Employee want a pay system which is simple, fair and in line with their expectations. When pay is seen as fair, based on job demands, individual skill level, and community pay standards, satisfaction is likely to result. What needs emphasis is that, it is not the absolute pay that matters, rather it is one's perception of fairness.

2. Nature of works: Most employees crave intellectual challenges on jobs. They tend to prefer being given opportunities to use their skills and abilities and being offered a variety of tasks, freedom and feedback on how well they are doing. These characteristics make jobs mentally challenging. Jobs that have too little challenge create boredom. But too much challenge creates frustration and a feeling of failure. Under conditions of moderate challenge, employees experience pleasure and job satisfaction.

3. Promotions: Promotional opportunities affect job satisfaction considerably. The desire for promotion is generally strong among employees as it involves change in job content, pay, responsibility, independence, status and the like. An average employee in a typical government organization can hope to get two or three promotions in his entire

service, though chances of promotion are better in the private sector. It is no surprise that the employee takes promotion as the ultimate achievement in his career and when it is realized, he feels extremely satisfied.

4. Supervisions: There is a positive relationship between the quality of supervisor and job satisfaction. Supervisor who establish a supportive personal relationship with subordinates and takes a personal interest in them, contributes to their employee satisfaction. On realizing the role of supervision in creating satisfaction, a number or supervisory roles have been suggested for the purpose. Some of the supervisory roles are:

a. Maintain open lines of communication

b. Create a good physical environment

c. Remedy sub-standard conditions

d. Transfer discontent employees

e. Change the perception of dissatisfied employees

f. Display concern for employees

g. Give ample recognition

h. Allow for participative in management

i. Practice good management

j. Conduct morale building programs.

5. Work Group: Work Group does serve as a source of satisfaction to individual employees. It does so, primarily by providing the group member, with opportunities for interaction, with each other. It is well known that, for many employees, work fills the need for social interaction. The work group is a even stronger source of satisfaction when members have similar attitudes and values. Having people around with similar attitudes causes less friction on day to day basis. Co-worker's with similar attitudes and values can provide some confirmation of people's self-concept.

6. Working condition: Working condition that are compatible with an employee's physical comfort and that facilitate doing a good job, contribute to job satisfaction. Temperature, humidity, ventilation, lighting and noise, hours of work, cleanliness of work place and adequate tools and equipment are the features which affect job satisfaction.

The assumption that working condition and satisfaction are interrelated contradicts the two-factor theory of motivation. According to this theory, working conditions are a part of maintenance factor which, when provided, help remove dissatisfaction. And the opposite of dissatisfaction is no dissatisfaction, but not satisfaction. Thus, while working condition constitute a source of job satisfaction they are a relatively minor source. Generally, unless working conditions are either extremely good or bad, they are taken for granted by most employees. Only when employees themselves change jobs or when working conditions change dramatically over time. (e.g.; moving into new facilities) do working conditions assume more relevance. In other words, all workers are not satisfying dissatisfaction by favourable or unfavourable work environment.

Motivation

Motivation is a process that starts with a physiological or psychological need that activates a behavior or a drive that is aimed at a goal.

Every employee is expected to show increased and qualitative productivity by the manager. To achieve this is the behavior of the employee is very important. The behavior of the employees is influenced by the environment in which they find themselves. Finally, an employee's behavior will be a function of that employee's innate drives or felt needs and the opportunities he or she has to satisfy those drives or needs in the workplace. Behaviors on the job determined by:

- Needs the individual brings to the job: unique to each person
- The situation" outside the person"
- Opportunities for satisfying needs

If employees are never given opportunities to utilize all of their skills, then the employer may never have the benefit of their total performance. Work performance is also contingent upon employee abilities. If employees lack the learned skills or innate talents to do a particular job, then performance will be less than optimal. A third dimension of performance is motivation.

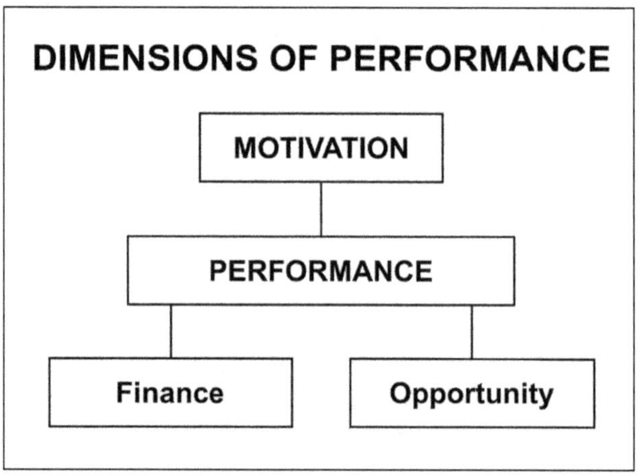

"Motivation is the act of stimulating someone or oneself to get desired course of action, to push right button to get desired reactions."

The following are the features of motivation:

- Motivation is an act of managers
- Motivation is a continuous process
- Motivation can be positive or negative
- Motivation is goal oriented
- Motivation is complex in nature
- Motivation is an art
- Motivation is system-oriented
- Motivation is different from job satisfaction.

Motivational Factors

There are several factors that motivate a person to work. The motivational factors can be broadly divided into two groups:

Monetary Factors

- Salaries or wages: Salaries or wages is one of the most important motivational factors. Reasonable salaries must be paid on time. While fixing salaries the organization must consider such as:
    - Cost of living
    - Company ability to pay
    - Capability of company to pay etc.
- Bonus: It refers to extra payment to employee over and above salary given as an incentive. The employees must be given adequate rate of bonus.
- Incentives: The organization may also provide additional incentives such as medical allowance, educational allowance, hra, allowance, etc.
- Special individual incentives: The company may provide special individual incentives. Such incentives are to be given to deserving employees for giving valuable suggestions.

Non Monetary Factors

- Status or job title: By providing a higher status or designations the employee must be motivated. Employees prefer and proud of higher designations.
- Appreciation and recognition: Employees must be appreciated for their services. The praise should not come from immediate superior but also from higher authorities.
- Delegation of authority: Delegation of authority motivates a subordinate to perform the tasks with dedication and commitment. When authority is delegated, the subordinate knows that his superior has placed faith and trust in him.
- Working conditions: Provision for better working conditions such as air-conditioned rooms, proper plant layout, proper sanitation, equipment, machines etc. motivates the employees.
- Job security: Guarantee of job security or lack of fear dismissal, etc. can also be a good way to motivate the employees. Employees who are kept temporarily for a long time may be frustrated and may leave the organization.
- Job enrichment: Job enrichment involves more challenging tasks and responsibilities. For instance an executive who is involved in preparing and presenting reports of performance, may also asked to frame plans.
- Workers participation: Inviting the employee to be a member of quality circle, or a committee, or some other form of employee participation can also motivate the workforce.
- Cordial relations: Good and healthy relations must exist throughout the organization. This would definitely motivates the employees.
- Good superiors: Subordinates want their superiors to be intelligent, experienced, matured, and having a good personality. In fact, the superior needs to have superior knowledge and skills than that of his subordinates. The very presence of superiors can motivate the subordinates.
- Other factors: There are several other factors of motivating the employees:
    - Providing training to the employees
    - Proper job placements
    - Proper promotions and transfers
    - Proper performance feedback

- Proper welfare facilities
- Flexible working hours.

Need and Importance of Motivation

Motivation offers several importance of the organization and to the employees:

- Higher efficiency.
- Reduce absenteeism.
- Reduces employee turnover.
- Improves a corporate image.
- Good relations.
- Improved morale.
- Reduced wastages and breakages.
- Reduced accidents.
- Facilitates initiative and innovation.

Money as a motivator

It is normally believed that money acts as a motivator. In general the role of money as a motivator depends upon certain factors:

- Money fails to motivate people, when there is no direct relationship between reward and effort.
- Economic conditions of people influence the Importance of money. For poor person, the value of certain amount of money is quite high as compared to rich.
- Money is a significant motivator at lower level of employee's level however money may not be a significant factor for senior executives who have already fulfilled their lower level needs.
- Employees are concerned not only with the amount of money paid to them, but it should be fair and equitable as paid to that of other employees of same level or status.
- Social attitudes towards money and wealth also decides the motivation to earn more and more.

Motivational Theories

Maslow's-Hierarchy of Needs Theory: This theory was proposed by Abraham Maslow and is based on the assumption that people are motivated by a series of five universal needs. These needs are ranked, according to the order in which they influence human behavior, in hierarchical fashion.

- Physiological needs are deemed to be the lowest- level needs. These needs include the needs such as food and water:
    - So long as physiological needs are unsatisfied, they exist as a driving or motivating force in a person's life. A hungry person has a felt need. This felt need sets up both psychological and physical tensions that manifest themselves in overt behaviors directed at reducing those tensions (getting something to eat). Once the hunger is sated, the tension is reduced, and the need for food ceases to motivate. At this point (assuming that other physiological requirements are also satisfied) the next higher order need becomes the motivating need.
- Thus, safety needs - the needs for shelter and security - become the motivators of human behaviour:
    - Safety needs include a desire for security, stability, dependency, protection, freedom from fear and anxiety, and a need for structure, order, and law.. In the workplace this needs translates into a need for at least a minimal degree of employment security; the knowledge that we cannot be fired on a whim and that appropriate levels of effort and productivity will ensure continued employment.
- Social needs include the need for belongingness and love:
    - Generally, as gregarious creatures, human have a need to belong. In the workplace, this need may be satisfied by an ability to interact with one's co-workers and perhaps to be able to work collaboratively with these colleagues.
- After social needs have been satisfied, ego and esteem needs become the motivating needs:
    - Esteem needs include the desire for self-respect, self-esteem, and the esteem of others. When focused externally, these needs also include the desire for reputation, prestige, status, fame, glory, dominance, recognition, attention, importance, and appreciation.
- The highest need in Maslow's hierarchy is that of self-actualization; the need for self-realization, continuous self-development, and the process of becoming all that a person is capable of becoming.

Alderfer's Hierarchy of Motivational Needs: Clayton Alderfer reworked Maslow's Need Hierarchy to align it more closely with empirical research. Alderfer's theory is called the ERG theory Existence, Relatedness, and Growth.

- Existence refers to our concern with basic material existence requirements; what Maslow called physiological and safety needs.
- Relatedness refers to the desire we have for maintaining interpersonal relationships; similar to Maslow's social/love need, and the external component of his esteem need.
- Growth refers to an intrinsic desire for personal development; the intrinsic component of Maslow's esteem need, and self-actualization.

Alderfer's ERG theory differs from Maslow's Need Hierarchy insofar as ERG theory demonstrates that more than one need may be operative at the same time. ERG theory does not assume a rigid hierarchy where a lower need must be substantially satisfied before one can move on.

Alderfer also deals with frustration-regression. That is, if a higher-order need is frustrated, an individual then seeks to increase the satisfaction of a lower-order need.

According to Maslow an individual would stay at a certain need level until that need was satisfied. ERG theory counters by noting that when a higher- order need level is frustrated the individual's desire to increase a lower- level need takes place. Inability to satisfy a need for social interaction, for instance, might increase the desire for more money or better working conditions. So frustration can lead to a regression to a lower need.

In summary, ERG theory argues, like Maslow, that satisfied lower- order needs lead to the desire to satisfy higher-order needs; but multiple needs can be operating as motivators at the same time, and frustration in attempting to satisfy a higher- level need can result in regression to a lower- level need.

Table: Alderfer's hierarchy of motivational needs.

Level of Need	Definition	Properties
Growth	Impel a person to make creative or productive effects on himself and his environment	Satisfied through using capabilities in engaging problems; creates a greater sense of wholeness and fullness as a human being
Relatedness	Involve relationships with significant others	Satisfied by mutually sharing thoughts and feelings; acceptance, confirmation, understanding, and influence are elements
Existence	Includes all of the various forms of material and psychological desires	When divided among people one person's gain is another's loss if resources are limited

A Reorganization of Maslow's and Alderfer's Hierarchies

Level	**Introversion**	**Extroversion**
Growth	Self-Actualization (development of competencies [knowledge, attitudes, and skills] and character)	Transcendence (assisting in the development of others' competencies and character; relationships to the unknown, unknowable)
Other (Relatedness)	Personal identification with group, significant others (Belongingness)	Value of person by group (Esteem)
Self (Existence)	Physiological, biological (including basic emotional needs)	Connectedness, security

Two-factor Theory

Herzberg's Two Factor Theory, also known as the Motivation Hygiene Theory, was derived from a study designed to test the concept that people have two sets of needs:

1. Their needs as animals to avoid pain.
2. Their needs as humans to grow psychologically.

Herzberg' Study

Herzberg's study consisted of a series of interviews that sought to elicit responses to the questions:

1. Recall a time when you felt exceptionally good about your job. Why did you feel that way about the job? Did this feeling affect your job performance in any way? Did this feeling have an impact on your personal relationships or your well- being?
2. Recall a time on the job that resulted in negative feelings? Describe the sequence of events that resulted in these negative feelings.

Research Results: It appeared from the research, that the things making people happy on the job and those making them unhappy had two separate themes.

1. Satisfaction (Motivation): Five factors stood out as strong determiners of job satisfaction:
    - Achievement
    - Recognition
    - Work itself
    - Responsibility
    - Advancement.

The last three factors were found to be most important for bringing about lasting changes of attitude. It should be noted, that recognition refers to recognition for achievement as opposed to recognition in the human relations sense.

2. Dissatisfaction (Hygiene): The determinants of job dissatisfaction were found to be:
    - Company policy
    - Administrative policies
    - Supervision
    - Salary
    - Interpersonal relations
    - Working conditions.

From the results Herzberg concluded that the replies people gave when they felt good about their jobs were significantly different from the replies given when they felt bad. Certain characteristics tend to be consistently related to job satisfaction and others to job dissatisfaction. Intrinsic factors, such as work itself, responsibility and achievement seem to be related to job satisfaction. Respondents who felt good about their work tended to attribute these factors to themselves. On the other dissatisfied respondents tended to cite extrinsic factors such as supervision, pay, company policies and working condition. Herzberg proposed that his findings indicated the existence of a dual continuum: the opposite of "satisfaction" is "No satisfaction" and the opposite of "Dissatisfaction" is "No Dissatisfaction.

According to Herzberg, the factors leading to Job satisfaction are separate and distinct form those that lead to job dissatisfaction. Therefore, managers who seek to eliminate factors that can create job dissatisfaction may bring about peace but not necessarily motivation. They will be placating their workforce rather than motivating them. As a result, conditions surrounding the job such as quality of supervision, pay , company policies, physical working conditions relations with others and job security were characterized by Herzberg as hygiene factors, when they're adequate, people will not be dissatisfied; neither will they be satisfied. If we want to motivate people on their jobs, Herzberg suggested emphasizing factors associated with the work itself or to outcomes directly derived form it, such as promotional opportunities, opportunities for personal growth, recognition, responsibility and achievement. These are the characteristics that people find intrinsically rewarding.

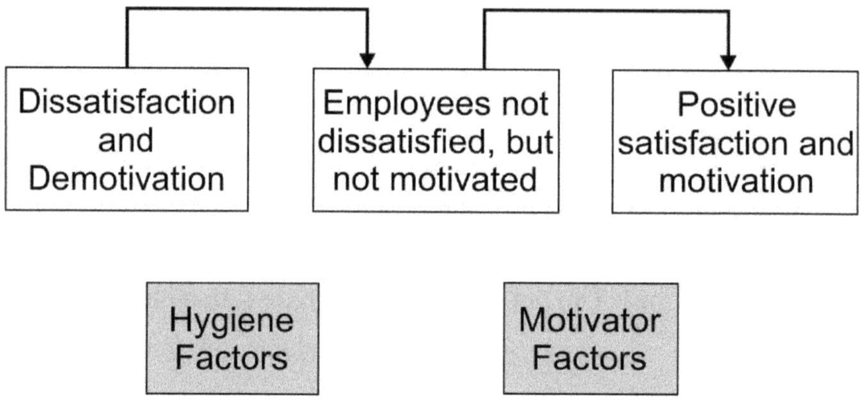

Expectancy Theory

In recent years, probably the most popular motivational theory has been the Expectancy Theory (also known as the Valence-Instrumentality- Expectancy Theory). Although there are a number of theories found with this general title, they all have their roots in Victor Vroom's 1964 work on motivation.

Alternatives and Choices

Vroom's theory assumes that behavior results from conscious choices among alternatives whose purpose it is to maximize pleasure and minimize pain. The key elements to this theory are referred to as Expectancy (E), Instrumentality (I), and Valence (V). Critical to the understanding of the theory is the understanding that each of these factors represents a belief.

Vroom's theory suggests that the individual will consider the outcomes associated with various levels of performance (from an entire spectrum of performance possibilities), and elect to pursue the level that generates the greatest reward for him or her.

Expectancy: "What's the probability that, if we work very hard, we'll be able to do a good job?"

Expectancy refers to the strength of a person's belief about whether or not a particular job performance is attainable. Assuming all other things are equal, an employee will be motivated to try a task, if person believes that it can be done. This expectancy of performance may be thought of in terms of probabilities ranging from zero (a case of "we can't do it!") to 1.0 ("we have no doubt whatsoever that we can do this job").

A number of factors can contribute to an employee's expectancy perceptions:

- The level of confidence in the skills required for the task.
- The amount of support that may be expected from superiors and subordinates.
- The quality of the materials and equipment.
- The availability of pertinent information.

Previous success at the task has also been shown to strengthen expectancy beliefs.

Instrumentality: "What's the probability that, if I do a good job, that there will be some kind of outcome in it for me?"

If an employee believes that a high level of performance will be instrumental for the acquisition of outcomes which may be gratifying, then the employee will place a high value on performing well. Vroom defines Instrumentality as a probability belief linking one outcome (a high level of performance, for example) to another outcome (a reward).

Instrumentality may range from a probability of 1.0 (meaning that the attainment of the second outcome - the reward - is certain if the first outcome - excellent job performance - is attained) through zero (meaning there is no likely relationship between the first outcome and the second). An example of zero instrumentality would be exam grades that were distributed randomly (as opposed to be awarded on the basis of excellent exam performance). Commission pay schemes are designed to make employees perceive that performance is positively instrumental for the acquisition of money.

For management to ensure high levels of performance, it must tie desired outcomes (positive valence) to high performance, and ensure that the connection is communicated to employees.

The VIE theory holds that people have preferences among various outcomes. These preferences tend to reflect a person's underlying need state.

Valence: "Is the outcome we get of any value to us?"

The term Valence refers to the emotional orientations people hold with respect to outcomes (rewards). An outcome is positively valent if an employee would prefer having it to not having it. An outcome that the employee would rather avoid (fatigue, stress, noise, layoffs) is negatively valent. Outcomes towards which the employee appears indifferent are said to have zero valence.

Valences refer to the level of satisfaction people expect to get from the outcome (as opposed to the actual satisfaction they get once they have attained the reward).

Vroom suggests that an employee's beliefs about Expectancy, Instrumentality, and Valence interact psychologically to create a motivational force such that the employee acts in ways that bring pleasure and avoid pain.

People elect to pursue levels of job performance that they believe will maximize their overall best interests (their subjective expected utility).

There will be no motivational forces acting on an employee if any of these three conditions hold:

1) The person does not believe that he/she can successfully perform the required task.
2) The person believes that successful task performance will not be associated with positively valent outcomes.
3) The person believes that outcomes associated with successful task completion will be negatively valent (have no value for that person).

MF= Expectancy x Instrumentality x Valance

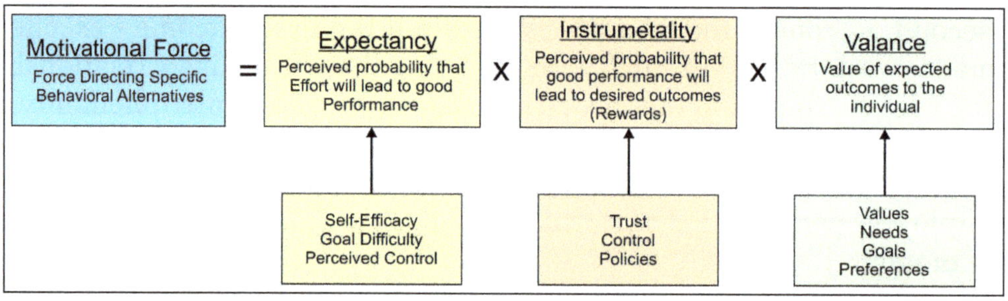

McClelland's Theory of Needs

According to David McClelland, regardless of culture or gender, people are driven by three motives:

- Achievement
- Affiliation and
- Influence.

Since McClelland's first experiments, over 1,000 studies relevant to achievement motivation have been conducted. These studies strongly support the theory.

- Achievement: The need for achievement is characterized by the wish to take responsibility for finding solutions to problems, master complex tasks, set goals, get feedback on level of success.
- Affiliation: The need for affiliation is characterized by a desire to belong, an enjoyment of teamwork, a concern about interpersonal relationships, and a need to reduce uncertainty.
- Power: The need for power is characterized by a drive to control and influence others, a need to win arguments, a need to persuade and prevail.

According to McClelland, the presence of these motives or drives in an individual indicates a predisposition to behave in certain ways. Therefore, from a manager's perspective, recognizing which need is dominant in any particular individual affects the way in which that person can be motivated.

People with achievement motives are motivated by standards of excellence, delineated roles and responsibilities and concrete, timely feedback. Those with affiliation motives are motivated when they can accomplish things with people they know and trust. And the power motive is activated when people are allowed to have an impact, impress those in power, or beat competitors.

Theory of "X" and Theory of "Y": Douglas McGregor observed two diametrically opposing view points of managers about their employees, one is negative called "Theory of X" and one is positive called "Theory of Y".

a) Theory of X: Following are the assumptions of managers who believe in the "Theory of X" in regard to their employees.

   - Employees dislike work; if possible avoid the same.
   - Employees must be coerced, controlled or threatened to do the work.
   - Employees avoid responsibilities and seek formal direction.
   - Most employees consider security of job, most important of all other factors in the job and have very little ambition.

b) Theory of Y: Following are the assumptions of managers who believe in the "Theory of Y" in regard to their employees.

   - Employees love work as play or rest.
   - Employees are self-directed and self-controlled and committed to the organizational objectives.
   - Employees accept and seek responsibilities.

  - Innovative spirit is not confined to managers alone, some employees also possess it.

Theory of X assumes Maslow's lower level needs dominate in employees. Whereas Theory of Y, assumes Maslow's higher level needs dominate in employees.

Goal Setting Theory

Edwin Locke proposed that setting specific goals will improve motivation. Salient features of this theory are the following:

- Specific goal fixes the needs of resources and efforts.
- It increases performance.
- Difficult goals result higher performance than easy job.
- Better feedback of results leads to better to better performance than lack of feedback.
- Participation of employees in goal has mixed result.
- Participation of setting goal, however, increases acceptance of goal and involvements.
- Goal setting theory has identified two factors which influences the performance. These are given below:
  - Goal commitment
  - Self-efficiency.
- Goal commitment: Goal setting theory presupposes that the individual is committed to the goal. This commitment depends on the following:
  - Goals are made public
  - Individual has an internal locus of control
  - Goals are self-set.
- Self –Efficiency: Self Efficiency is the belief or self-confidence, that he/she is capable of performing task. Persons with high self-efficiency put up extra-efforts when they face challenges. In the case of low self-efficiency level they will lessen or even abandon when meeting challenges.

Reinforcement Theory

This theory focus its attention as to what controls behaviour. In contrast to goal setting theory, which is cognitive approach focus attention on what initiates behaviour.

Behaviour, as per cognitive approach is initiated by internal events. Reinforcement theory argues that behaviour is reinforced and controlled by external events. The classical conditioning proposed by Pavlov which we have already studied in our earlier lessons explains this in a better way.

Equity Theory

This theory of motivation centres around the principle of balance or equity. According to this theory level of motivation in an individual is related to his or her perception of equity and farness practiced by management. Greater the fairness perceived higher the motivation and vice versa. In this assessment of fairness, employee makes comparison of input in the job (in terms of contribution) with that of outcome (in terms of compensation) and compares the same with that of another colleague of equivalent cadre.

Perception

Perception is how people look at and understand the things. It is a unique interpretation of the situation rather than recoding of it. Perception is a complex cognitive process of understanding the world, sometimes not in its real form. Perception is a learning process and hence it differs from person to person. As a result, the same stimuli may produce different behaviours and responses. In managing the organizations, particularly in dealing with the people, managers should be able to understand the perceptions of the people. It is in this context, an attempt is made here to explain the perceptual process, factors influencing perceptions and managing the perceptions to the advantage of the organization.

Perceptual Process

Perception is the process by which people select, organize, interpret and respond to information from the world around them. This information is obtained through the senses namely, seeing, hearing, touch, taste and smell.

Perception may be defined as the process of receiving, selecting, organizing, interpreting, checking, and reacting to sensations. It is also defined as 'a process by which individuals organize and interpret their sensory impressions in order to give meaning to their environments.' The perceptional processes show that their functioning is affected by three variables – the objects perceived, the environment in which perception occurs, and the individual perceiving the objects.

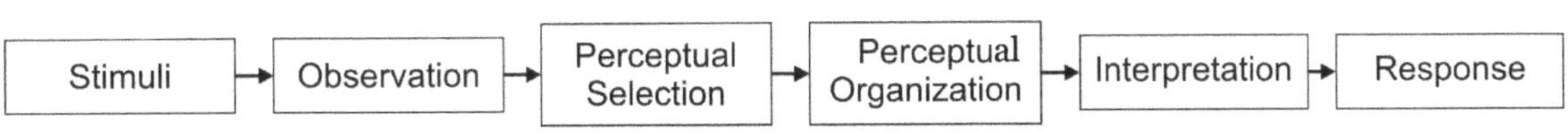

The Perceptual Process.

In the above diagram, you may find that the important aspects of perception are selection and organization. Different people perceive an object differently both in terms of what they selectively perceive and how they organize and interpret the things perceived. A person's selection process involves factors internal to the person as well as external to him. It is, in fact, a complex set of factors that determine the perception of an individual.

Similarly, an individual organizes the selected stimuli into meaningful patterns. The interpretation of what is perceived may vary widely. For example, a wave of hand may be interpreted as a friendly gesture or it may be interpreted as a sign of threatening depending on the circumstances and the state of mind of the two people. Therefore, quite often the people perceive things differently and behave on the basis of those perceptions. Managers in organizations should understand that people's perceptions differ and at times they also go wrong.

External Factors Influencing Selection

The external factors influencing selection are nature, intensity, size, contrast, repetition, motion, and novelty and familiarity.

Nature

By this we try to understand the nature of the object. Is it a visual object? Does it have words, pictures, people or animals? Pictures attract attention more than words and a picture with human beings attracts attention more than a picture with inanimate objects. That is why cartoons and caricatures draw more attraction.

Intensity

The intensity principle conveys that if the external stimulus is more intense in nature, the more it is likely to be perceived by the individual. That is why people pay more attention to loud noise, strong odour or bright light. At work places, superiors speak loudly to subordinates for this reason only.

Size

Like intensity, size also matters very much. Larger objects are likely to be perceived more by the individuals than the smaller ones. A maintenance engineer gives greater attention to a bigger machine than a smaller one.

Contrast

The contrast principle suggests that the external stimulus that stands out distinctly against the background or the one that is quite unusual will receive greater attention of the people.

Repetition

The principle of repetition suggests that a repeated external stimulus draws more attention than a single one. The several advertisements of various products shown daily on TVs are based on the principle of repetition only. This principle also explains why supervisors have to give directions to workers repeatedly for even simple tasks.

Motion

According to this principle, people pay greater attention to moving objects rather than stationary objects. That is why advertisers create signs that incorporate moving parts.

Novelty and Familiarity

This principle states that either a novel or a familiar external situation can better serve to draw attention. New objects in familiar settings or familiar objects in new settings are likely to draw the attention of the perceiver. Job rotation is followed in organizations for this reason. For instance, workers will pay greater attention to the tasks assigned to them in the new jobs in order to prove themselves and gain acceptance in the new job.

Internal Factors Influencing Selection

Internal factors influencing selection of stimuli are personality, learning, and motivation. They are explained below:

1. Personality: It cannot be disputed that personality has a significant impact on what and how people perceive. The various personality dimensions influence the perceptual process. A conscientious person is likely to pay greater attention to external environmental stimuli than a less conscientious person who is likely to be careless, impulsive and irresponsible. On the other hand, conscientious people tend to organize their perceptions into clear categories, receive information quickly and in an organized manner. They are careful and methodical in their perceptual selection and organization.

2. Learning: Perceptual selection is also affected by learning. Learning determines the development of perceptual sets. Perceptual set means the expectation of particular interpretation based on past experience with the same object. This is also known as cognitive awareness by which the minds organizes information and form images and compare them with previous exposures to similar stimuli. In organizations employees' experiences are influenced by their perception very much. In making decisions, managers are also influenced by their functional background. However, it is necessary for managers to rise above their own experiences and be able to solve the problems in an appropriate way. Individual differences lead to perceptual bias. This bias can be overcome through education and experience.

3. Motivation: Motivation also plays an important role in influencing the process of

perception. For example, a hungry person is likely to be sensitive to the sight or smell of food than a non-hungry person. Likewise if the person is deprived of sleep, he looks for a situation in which he can have a comfortable sleep. Generally, people perceive things that help in satisfying needs and those that were found rewarding in the past. The relationship between motivation and perception is explained through Collenyannia Principle which states that people process pleasant events more efficiently and accurately than the unpleasant events.

Factors Influencing Perception

A number of factors operate to shape and sometimes to distort perception. These factors emanate from three sources – the perceiver, the perceived and the situation.

The Perceiver

When a person looks at a target, his interpretation of it is influenced by his personal characteristics like his needs, past experience, habits, personality, values, and attitudes. A person with a strong need for ego satisfaction may select out from a situation and emphasize signals that tend to satisfy the desire for self-esteem. Similarly, negative attitudes toward unions may cause a manager to look for antagonisms in even routine visits by local union officials to the organization. These and other personal factors will determine what a person gives attention to in a situation and how these cues are interpreted as a basis for decision-making and action responses.

The Perceived

Characteristics in the target/object that are being observed may influence what is perceived. The physical attributes, appearance, and behaviour of other persons in the situation also influence how the object is perceived. Physical attributes of a person are related to age, sex, height, and weight. A young person exercising authority in a situation is viewed differently from an older person doing the same thing. Personal attire and appearance are also relevant factors in the formation of perceptions.

The Situation

The context in which we see the objects or events is important. The physical, social and organizational elements of the situation or event may also influence perceptions. A subordinate calling his boss by the first name may be perceived quite differently when observed in a typical Indian office as opposed to in a social reception. Though the perceiver and the perceived are the same, it is the situation that makes a difference. Such background characteristics of the situation or context are additional factors that can affect how the situation is perceived by the different persons. The following Diagram shows the summary of the factors influencing perception.

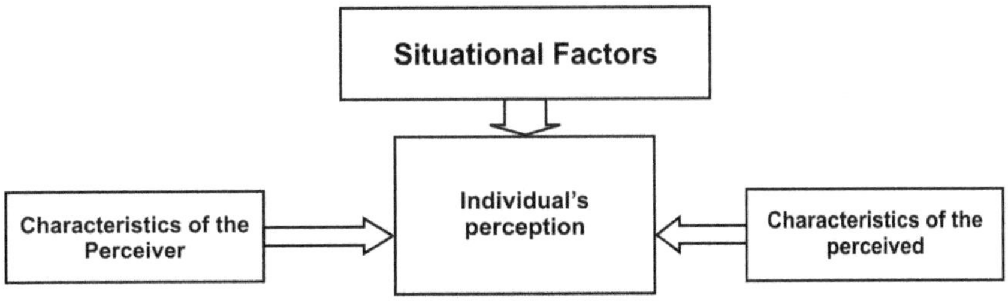

Factors Influencing Perception.

Managing the Perception Process

Successful managers understand the importance of perceptions as influences on behaviour, and handle them accordingly. They are aware of perceptual distortions and accept that perceptual differences are likely to exist in any situation. With this knowledge, they make appropriate decisions that are acceptable to all persons concerned. The perceptual skills of a manager will help him in the following ways.

High level of Self-awareness

As already made clear, individual needs, experience, and expectations will all affect perceptions. The successful manager understands this and is able to identify when he is inappropriately distorting a situation because of such perceptual tendencies.

Seek Information from Various Sources for Decisions

The successful manager minimizes the bias of personal perceptions by seeking out the viewpoints of others. These insights are used to gain additional perspective on situations and the problems or opportunities they represent.

Empathy

As is understood, different people look at the same situation differently. The successful manager rises above the personal impressions and tries to understand problems as felt by other people.

Influence of Perceptions on Other People

People act according to their own perceptions. If felt necessary, the successful manager influences the perceptions of others in such a way that the work events are interpreted as accurately as possible and to the advantage of all concerned.

Avoid Common Perceptual Distortions

Perceptual distortions include the use of stereotypes and halo effects, as well as selective perception and projection. Successful managers are self-disciplined and sufficiently aware that the adverse impact of these distortions is minimized.

Avoid Inappropriate Attributions

A person has a tendency to explain why events happened the way they did or why people behaved as they did. The successful manager is wise enough to establish the real reasons for the things that happen and avoid the tendency of making quick or inappropriate attributions.

Learning

Now, let us understand the term 'learning' and the various processes of learning. Learning is any relatively permanent change in behaviour that occurs as a result of experience.

There are two important elements in learning:

a. Change must be relatively permanent. It means after 'learning' the behaviour of a person must be different from the previous behaviour. If a person learns car driving, it will last for a long time indicating the changed behaviour. Temporary changes may be only reflexive and fail to represent any learning. Therefore, this requirement rules out behavioural changes caused by fatigue or other temporary adaptations.

b. The second element is that the change of behaviour should take place as a result of some kind of experience. Learning must be because of some interaction with the environment and some feedback from such environment that affects behaviour. The experience may be direct or indirect. Sometimes we learn to change our behaviour when our colleagues are punished for that kind of behaviour.

You may note that learning itself cannot be observed. The behavioural changes consequent upon learning only can be seen. This kind of change in behaviour should be differentiated from change in behaviour caused by other factors. For example, aging may cause behavioural changes. A change in the individual's thought process or attitudes, if accompanied by no change in behaviour, would not be learning.

Learning certainly has its own impact on training activities in an organization. It can give insights into how to best develop the skills and talents of employees for performing the jobs effectively. But it is the desire to change individuals that is of the greatest importance. The manager who undertakes to produce such changes acts like a teacher. He guides the employees to engage in behaviours that will help the organization achieve its objectives. When the employees are late for work, lazy, disobey the rules or engage in any type of dysfunctional behaviour, the manager attempts to teach behaviours of functional nature. Further, if the employee is performing well, he gives the employee feedback and also rewards to strengthen such desirable behaviour.

You may understand that individuals enter an organization with a host of learned attitudes and behaviours. Their job performance is a function of their learned experiences. Learning is a continuous experience for employees. It is because of learning, employers recruit people with college degrees or those with job experience. The employer presumes that not only education or experience provides learning, but that learning will lead to higher job performance.

Learning Theories

In an organization, employees have to learn and practice productive work behaviours. The manager's task is to provide sufficient learning experiences to employees in an environment that will facilitate learning process and promote desired behaviours. Training prepares employees to meet the challenges of the job, for which incentives are to be provided to learn and practice right behaviours. The following are the important theories of learning.

Classical Conditioning

Classical conditioning is the process by which individuals learn to link the information from a neutral stimulus to a stimulus that causes a response. This response may not be under an individual's conscious control. Pavlov, in his experiments, hanged some meat in front of dogs. This meat is unconditioned stimulus or unlearned stimulus. The dogs responded to this stimulus by salivating. This kind of response was instinctive or unconditioned. Afterwards Pavlov started to ring a bell at the same time when meat was offered. Ringing the bell without offer of meat was not connected to any responses. However, by ringing the bell every time when meat was offered, Pavlov established a relationship between the two stimuli that is the bell and the meat. With the continuation of the process, the ringing of the bell alone acted like a stimulus to evoke the response of salivating even without presentation of meat. As a result, the bell became a conditioned stimulus leading to conditioned response.

Operant Conditioning

B.F. Skinner coined the term operant conditioning to refer to a process by which individuals learn voluntary behaviour. Voluntary behaviours are called operant because they operate or have some influence on the environment. Learning occurs from the consequences of behaviour, and many employee work behaviours are operant behaviours. As a matter of fact, most behaviours in everyday life are forms of operant behaviour. Managers are interested in operant behaviours because they can influence the results of such behaviours. On the basis of the direct relationship between the consequences and behaviour, the management can identify the relationship and try to modify the behaviour. That is how the behaviour can be controlled by manipulating its consequences. Two principles guide this relationship.

- The behaviour that results in positive rewards is likely to be repeated and behaviour with negative consequences is likely to be extinguished.
- Based on such consequences, the behaviour can be predicted and controlled.

Therefore, some consequences can be used to increase the recurrence of desired behaviour and some other consequences can be used to decrease the recurrence of undesired behaviour.

Principle of Reinforcement

We understand that some behaviors are strengthened by the process of reinforcement. Reinforcer may be any stimulus that prompts a behavior to be repeated or stopped. Managements expect that the employee should behave in a desirable manner in the organization and avoid undesirable behaviour. By the appropriate use of reinforcers, the organizations are able to maintain or increase the probability of behaviours like quality oriented performance, wise decision making, regular attendance and punctuality and so on. Some reinforcers work by their application to a situation whereas other reinforcers work by their removal from this situation.

Positive Reinforcement

Positive reinforcement is provided by offering rewards for desired behaviours. Such rewards should be powerful and durable so as to increase the probability of occurrence of desirable behaviour. Money, as you understand, is the most powerful reinforcement for positive behaviour since money can be used for a number of other purposes. Some other positive reinforcers are recognition for good performance, challenging task, participation in decision making and so on. As individuals have different motivations of performance, positive reinforcers should be individually tailored with a view to facilitate the repetition of desired behaviour. That means reinforcer must be valued by the employee. For example, money would be a less reinforcer who values praise for his performance more. The reward must be directly linked with behaviour so that the higher the performance of an employee, the grater would be the reward.

Negative Reinforcement

In negative reinforcement, an unpleasant event that precedes the employee behaviour is removed when the desired behaviour occurs. This procedure increases the likelihood of the desired behaviour to follow. Negative reinforcement is sometimes confused with punishment because both use unpleasant events to influence behaviour. However, negative reinforcement is used to increase the frequency of a desired behaviour, whereas punishment is used to decrease the frequency of an undesired behaviour. Managers frequently use negative reinforcement when an employee hasn't done something that is desired.

Omission

Omission is the removal of all reinforcing events. While reinforcement increases the frequency of a desirable behaviour, omission decreases the frequency and eventually extinguishes an undesirable behaviour. Managers use omission to reduce undesirable employee behaviours that obstruct achievement of organizational goals. The omission procedure consists of three steps.

1. Identifying the behaviour to be reduced or eliminated,
2. Identifying the reinforcer that maintains the behaviour, and
3. Stopping the reinforcer.

Omission is a useful technique for reducing and eventually eliminating behaviours that disrupt normal workflow.

Punishment

Punishment is an unpleasant event that follows a behaviour and decreases its frequency. As in positive reinforcement, a punishment may include a specific antecedent that cues the employee that a consequence will follow a specific behaviour. While a positive consequence of reinforcement encourages the frequency of a desired behaviour, a consequence of punishment decreases the frequency of an undesired behaviour.

Organizations typically use several types of unpleasant events to punish individuals. They may be a wage cut, a suspension without pay, a demotion, or a transfer. The severe punishment is the dismissing an employee for failure to perform. In general, organizations use punishments of unpleasant nature sparingly for cases of serious behavioural problems.

It may be kept in mind that punishment should be used as a lost resort. The use of punishment should be limited to those undesirable behaviours that cause a significant damage to the organizational operations. It may also be remembered that punishment should not lead to hostility to such an extent of making solution more harmful than the problem itself. Punishment may cause undesirable emotional reactions. An employee who has been reprimanded for a mistake may react with anger toward the manager and the organization. Such reactions may lead to retaliatory behaviour harmful to the organization. Sabotage, you remember, typically is a result of a punishment-oriented management system. It is clear that punishment leads to short-term suppression of the undesirable behaviour, rather than to its elimination. Further, the punished individual may develop a tendency of avoiding the situation. High absenteeism is a form of avoidance and quitting is the final form of escape.

You should also note that punishment suppresses employee initiative and flexibility. Overusing punishment produces apathetic employees, who are not assets to an organization. Sustained punishment can also lead to low self-esteem. Low self-esteem, in turn, undermines the employee's self-confidence, which is necessary for performing most of the jobs.

Diversity

Diversity is any dimension that can be used to differentiate groups and people from one another, in which the dimensions can be visible or invisible. The existence of workplace diversity, within a workplace, indicates that the workplace is heterogeneous in terms of gender, race, and ethnicity, in which employees possess distinct elements and qualities, differing from one another. Also Hazard defines workplace diversity as a broad range of differences that influence how people interact and achieve business results. Workplace (also called workforce) diversity can be characterized as an organization, in which employees possess distinct elements and qualities, differing from one another. These different elements include employees' beliefs, values, and actions that vary by gender, ethnicity, age, lifestyle and physical abilities. Managing these elements can create an old way of staffing related problems that are the main focus for human resource departments. There are several important components associated with workplace diversity, problems concerning workplace diversity, and the management of workplace diversity. The intent of this study was to precisely define workplace diversity, examine the policies and procedures associated with workplace diversity management, and explore how managing workplace diversity can effect diversity awareness and employees job satisfaction. In the past, companies were driven towards creating a homogenous workplace in which employees acted and thought in identical way. "Nowadays managers and supervisors are looking at a workplace that is somehow different from those managed by their ancestors".

Managing diversity is focused on the assumption that diverse segments will create new methods of working together and that morale, profit, and productivity will increase. These authors stated that managing diversity includes building specific skills and creating policies that increases the best work behaviors and attitudes from each employee. Implementing workplace diversity has become a major focus in many Human Resource departments. In order to meet the demands of modern technologically advanced society, corporations must rethink what diversity means and how the concepts of developing, valuing, and managing a truly diverse corporation must go beyond traditional strategies. Human resource management allows Human Resource departments to strategically utilize personnel, in a fashion that will meet the demands of society, through improvements in the corporation's productivity and performance. Human resources in their role of managing diversity must be aware of problems and elements that may impact this role. Several elements are included in managing workplace diversity. One of the main elements is equal employment opportunity. Equal employment opportunity warrants the treatment of employees in a fair and impartial way, in all aspects of employment. Equal Employment Opportunity (EEO) regulation includes legislation and policies that enforce fair and impartial treatment of employees. The Equal Employment Opportunity Commission and Office of Federal Contract Compliance Programs are agencies that are responsible for enforcing legislation and policies. In addition to Equal Employment Opportunity, affirmative action, and discrimination law are also elements that corporations use to manage and regulate workplace diversity.

Almost everyone is now able to communicate and work with other people from different parts of the world due to the advancements in technology. One great proof of the technology advancement is the outsourcing of many administrative jobs. U.S companies can now hire their Human Resource personnel from India or Philippines and have them do the HR work in less than half the price they will pay workers in US. Because of this, many question the importance of diversity in the workforce, but studies have shown that having a diverse workforce proves to be a beneficial asset in a company. Workplace diversity despite having numerous benefits does have its flaws. Workplace diversity should be one of the top things businesses today should address. Businesses should prioritize hiring diverse employees because of the many great things associated with it. The main goal of workplace diversity management is the prohibition of discrimination against individuals, which would cause them to be unfairly differentiated from co-workers. In addition to globalization, diversity has also increased as a result of an increase in women and people with disabilities entering the work force. One of the tasks of managing workplace diversity is to recognize the differences among individuals and provide opportunities and means for individuals to contribute their talents to the organization.

Three Theories about Workplace Diversity

The fundamental to social justice within business is to make certain that the workplace remains a place of diversity. Not only does this ensure recognition of basic rights and liberties, but it also creates an atmosphere of trust that is often lacking between corporation and consumer.

- The meaning of diversity has changed from what it used to be in the past. One theory states that, before businesses can implement a strategy to get diversity, they should gain a clear understanding of what it means. According to this theory, many people are still focused on old models of diversity, which focus on social justice issues such as concerning gender or race. Conversely, diversity now should focus on creating an atmosphere that fosters connection.

- A second theory requires leveraging diversity in order to attract new clients. By building a diverse team of employees, a business will be better able to reach specific audiences. Staffing a company with one demographic would make it very hard to connect with anyone outside of that demographic.

- A third theory requires that businesses focus more on understanding the client, rather than focusing on workplace diversity. Making a product marketable is more about clear advertising, rather than anything that goes on behind closed doors.

When it comes down to it, there are many different definitions of diversity and many different ways to achieve it. It has now been a long time since anti-discrimination laws were entered into the books, but that does not mean that we should stop focusing on them. Implementing a diverse working class is fundamental to maintaining social justice on multiple levels. Its importance should never be forgotten and should always be a tool for positive change whenever possible.

Benefits of a Diverse Workplace

There are several benefits of a diverse workplace. Some economic benefits include increase in the pool of qualified personnel from different backgrounds, and it widens the scope of eligible candidates for hire. Another benefit of a diverse workplace is it improves communication with an organization's clients. Additionally, a sense of harmony is recreated when a company recognizes and accommodates the differences within its diverse workforce. A diverse workplace increases productivity, increases creativity, and improves problem solving.

A diverse workplace helps build work practices that create harmony. If a company is able to recognize the differences between its employees, it will be able to formulate work practices that will not exclude a certain culture. Also, if a company is able to develop desirable work practices that strives to unite all the employees together despite their differences, no one individual will feel left out or unsure about their position within the company. This in turn increases productivity among the employees.

A diverse workplace also allows an organization to effectively execute its plans. As previously stated, if a company recognizes the differences among its diverse employees, it will be able to create a work plan that optimizes productivity. The increase in productivity allows employees and managers to reach their goals within the organization.

The impact of diversity in the workplace is surprisingly greater than one would think. Studies show that putting together a team composed of people with the same ethnic background and personality may cause conflicts and decrease productivity. As opposed to a team that is composed of people with different ethnic backgrounds and personalities which allows for a higher rate of productivity and a lower rate of conflict. A study that was conducted, people with the same backgrounds tend to have many internal issues dealing with pride and competitiveness amongst one another that may reduce productivity process due to unmade decisions by the group. Teams assembled together that consist of different ethnicities and backgrounds tend to have less conflict because people have more understanding for one another, tend to be more creative and have skills that accent each other. These teams also seem to have a higher rate of productivity simply because each brings a set of different tools to the table, from different kinds of experiences and trainings.

Because people all have a unique way of learning, thinking and processing, it is more likely to be that a group composed of different minds may have several solutions to a problem. Teams like this have a tendency to see things in different angles and are able to catch any errors that may be presented. Businesses that have these types of groups, have a lower turnover rate, have less chances of having flaws in their product(s) and tend to be able to come up with many creative techniques as opposed to their competitors. An unhealthy work atmosphere is often the cause of high conflict levels in a company. People require a feeling of belongingness and security. When they feel supported in their ideas and beliefs they become more productive. At the foundation, all of today's skilled workers expect to be treated fairly and with respect. If not, they will soon find other jobs elsewhere, where they will receive their reward. Turnover is expensive and unproductive yet some employers ignore it. Moreover, stakeholders are now demanding that any organization they invest in must conform to practices that encourages low employee turnover, provides a healthy workplace, rewarding team performance, and empowers workers to express themselves with an open mind.

Workplace Diversity Challenges

As with any positive aspects to diversity in a work place environment, there are also negative ones that can cause problems for a division and more importantly, a company. There can be numerous issues that can be identified that can undoubtedly affect the performance of a company. The first challenge is communication problems in a work environment and how it hinders performance of workers when left unresolved. Employers should ensure that communication barriers are fixed at once due to the huge effect that it will have when workers are left unable to communicate with each other due to differences in languages. It will greatly affect not only the workplace environment, but also the whole business as well. Another type of challenge that a business may face is when they have workers that show resistance to change. Some workers sometimes are stubborn and do not adhere to new rules that are being set up by the company. These type of workers rebel and retaliate to the company by sabotaging their employers in different ways just to show their discontent. The final challenge is ethnocentrism and discrimination in the workplace. It is unfortunate, sometimes, that some business establishments show favoritism among their employees. Some managers or bosses favour one person or group of people over another. This is unhealthy for a business because fairness and equality is what makes up a great team. Without a great team and teamwork among the workers, no business will thrive long enough. Bosses who climb the ladder through favoritism will put employees who know the job down because they feel threatened and cause most of those employees to leave for other employers who are looking for better performance. Also bosses who for some reason will hate or envy a particular employee tend to gang up with other subordinates against that individual, making the environment unhealthy to work in for that individual. Diversity in some corporations is fake because it is almost always because the company is influenced by fear of lawsuits rather than by a genuine desire for greater diversity. They are just using a process of putting on a public relations show that has very little or no true commitment to the underlying principles entailed in diversity training or implementation.

Workplace Diversity Solutions

Addressing the main problem is the first step in finding a solution. Workplace diversity will be a permanent fixture in the workforce, and companies will need to create better diversity management action plans in order to better accommodate the changing business environment. In addition to effectively managing a diverse workforce, companies will need to create and or learn how to create a diverse workplace. In the following paragraphs below author will address both issues and provide useful tips for companies to use in order to manage diversity in the workplace and solutions to common issues that arise in a diverse workplace.

Workplace diversity is much more prominent nowadays than ever before. This growing change calls for immediate action from organizations in order to better accommodate the changing business environment. Organizations will need to rethink and remove any preconceived notions about previously thought knowledge of diversity management, because it has since evolved into a greater force in today's business environment. Overall, management will need to invest wisely and spend a considerable amount of resources in diversity management in order to better equip their companies to handle the issues that accompany a diverse workplace. "A strategy must be created and implemented to create a culture of diversity that permeates every department and function of the organization".

Greenberg lists two recommended steps that an organization must address in order for a company to successfully manage diversity in the workplace, as Assessment and implementation of diversity in the workplace.

Assessment of Diversity in the Workplace

a. Assessing and evaluating the diversity process should be an integral part of your organizations management system. This can help your management team determine challenges and obstacles to diversity which are present in your workplace and which policies need to be added or eliminated.

b. Pass out flash cards to employees to write down their most valued co-workers on a quarterly basis. The employee's name that does not show up in most cards should be monitored. A conversation should be held with this worker to find out what is going on. This way, you will know whether there is discrimination or conflict going on.

Implementation of Diversity in the Workplace Plan

a. Personal commitment of executive and managerial teams is a must. It is imperative that leaders and managers within organizations must incorporate diversity policies into every aspect of the organization's functions and purpose. Overall, the diversity workplace plan must flow through all levels of the organization in order for the diversity management and workplace plan to be successful.

b. Some of the tools as suggested by McLaren, are as follows:

- Organize diversity training for employees at all levels.
- Allow affinity networking among employees with similar backgrounds.
- Conduct learning sessions among groups, during which employees share with each other how their varying beliefs, cultures, and traditions shape their professional and personal lives.
- Set-long term goals and develop diversity practices during recruitment, appraisal and lay-off.
- Encourage employees to confide in their superiors about problems of discrimination.
- Carefully analyze the diversity at each employment rank and level.
- Reward the attainment of diversity goals from time to time.
- Develop training for diversity leadership.
- Actively promote successes of diversity.

It is also essential that businesses incorporate training in cultural diversity in the workplace, not only to top management but to every member of the workforce. Education and training in cultural diversity can better prepare employees to better understand and respect cultural differences amongst each other. Training and education in cultural diversity also helps employees learn to collaborate and work together to achieve the company's goals. It is also important to include employment laws regarding discrimination in the workplace as part of the education and awareness training in cultural diversity.

The key to create a successful diverse work place lies within your organization. When a business addresses the issues and problems that are unique to their organization, diversity is sure to have a positive impact on their business. In addition, when an organization understands the importance of investing in diversity management and how it will benefit the company overall, they sure will reap the sweet fruits of their investment. Diversity should be a voluntary and strong exercise instead of a mandatory training just because you fear lawsuits. It should not be a safety measure to keep corporations from getting into trouble.

Workplace diversity is very important in every business. It is essential that management in any business focus and prioritize diverse hiring due to the many benefits that diversity brings. Although there are some minor setbacks, the impact of diversity in every organization is more beneficial. Diversity will soon be a fixture in the future work environment, the globalization of business is fast approaching and the need to create a work environment that will foster a diverse workforce is pressing on the heels of businesses everywhere. It will be futile to fight it and remain stuck in the traditional form of management, because there is no such thing as a one size fits all management plan for all businesses. Each of the different companies will have to create a diversity management plan that will fit them and their unique needs. The advantages of having a diverse workplace are great and are very beneficial to any company. Although it will be more of a challenge at first, businesses will soon learn that they have done the right thing in choosing a diverse work force. Creating a strong diversity plan should be the first thing any business should do prior to embarking on anything related with a diverse workforce and workplace. A diversity management plan need not sound tedious to make and enforce, there are many studies that show what usually works for companies and also includes common problems that often occur from diverse workplaces. Diversity training or management should not be created for the lone purpose of legal requirements. Workplace diversity is not a trend, businesses need to take note of its importance and do something now because, in the future, they will surely reap the benefits of having a diverse workplace and you will see that it is a good idea and if it is done correctly and with an open mind to it.

3

Team Behavior and Group Dynamics

People forms groups in order to interact and achieve particular objectives. The different types of communication which take place within organizations and groups are downward communication, upward communication, horizontal communication and diagonal communication. This chapter discusses in detail these theories related to group dynamics and team behavior.

Team

The people working in a factory form a group because, in the context of their occupation, they interact with one another more than they interact with other people, so far as their occupation goes. Group is basically a collection of two or more persons. The society or the organisations are themselves huge groups of people.

Group can be defined as two or more individuals interacting and interdependent, who have come together to achieve particular objectives. According to Edgar H. Schien, "a group may be defined as a social phenomenon in which two or more persons decide to interact with one another, share common ideology and perceive themselves as a group." A group is defined as two or more individuals who are connected to one another by social relationships.

Features of a Group

1. Two or more people in social interaction.
2. Rewards to members.
3. Stable structure.
4. Members share common interests or goals.
5. Individuals must perceive themselves as a group.

Classification of Groups or Teams

All persons who are working in an organisation belong to different groups within the organisation. Groups may be classified on the basis of purpose, extend of structuring, process of formation and size of group membership. On analytical point of view groups may be classified into.

Formal Groups: A designated work group defined by the organization's structure. A formal group is set up by the organization to carry out work in support of the organization's goals. In formal groups, the behaviours that one should engage in are stipulated by - and directed toward - organizational goals. Examples include a book-keeping department, an executive committee, and a product development team. Formal groups may be command groups or task groups.

- Command Group: A command group consists of a manager and the employees who report to him or her. Thus, it is defined in terms of the organization's hierarchy. Membership in the group arises from each employee's position on the organizational chart.
- Task Group: A task group is made up of employees who work together to complete a particular task or project. A task group's boundaries are not limited to its immediate hierarchical superior. It can cross command relationships. An employee's membership in the group arises from the responsibilities delegated to the employee -that is, the employee's responsibility to carry out particular activities. Task group may be temporary with an established life span, or they may be open ended.
- Committee: A group of people officially delegated to perform a function, such as investigating, considering, reporting, or acting on a matter. Committee, one or more persons appointed or elected to consider report on, or take action on a particular matter. It investigates analyses and debates the problem and makes recommendation. Committee usually has their own committee member comprising of advisory authority, secretary and others. Recommendation is sent to the authority that is responsible for implementing them.

Characteristics of Formal groups

- Created to carry out some specific task or to meet a required goal.
- Explicitly stated defined structure, procedural rules and membership.
- Relatively permanent of temporary (e.g. steering group or problem solving group).
- Defined roles and designated work assignments.
- Well Defined norms.
- Specified goals and deadlines.

Informal Groups: An organization's informal groups are the groups that evolve to meet social or affiliation needs by bringing people together based on shared interests or friendship. Thus, informal groups are alliances that are neither formally structured nor organizationally determined. These groups are natural formations in the work environment that appear in response to the need for social contact. Many factors explain why people are attracted to one another. One explanation is simply proximity; when people work near one another every day, they are likely to form friendships. That likelihood is even greater when people also share similar attitudes, personalities, or economic status.

- Friendship Groups: Groups often develop because the individual members have one or more common characteristics. We call these formations 'friendship groups'. Social alliances, which frequently extend outside the work situation, can be based on similar age, same political view, attended the same college, etc.
- Interest Groups: People who may or may not be aligned into common command or task groups may affiliate to attain a specific objective with which each is concerned. This is an interest group.
- Reference Groups: Sometimes, people use a group as a basis for comparison in making decisions or forming opinions. When a group is used in this way, it is a reference group. Employees have reference groups inside or outside the organization where they work. For most people, the family is the most important reference groups. Other important reference groups typically include co-workers, friends, and members of the person's religious organization. The employee need not admire a group for it to serve as a reference group. Some reference groups serve as a negative reference; the employee tries to be unlike members of these groups.
- Membership Groups: When a person does belong to a group (formal and informal groups to which employees actually belong) the group is called a membership group (or affiliation group) for that person. Members of a group have some collection of benefits and responsibilities that go beyond the group serving as a reference point. In a membership group, each member would be expected to contribute to the group's well being and would enjoy the benefits arising from the group members' friendship.
- Cliques: A relatively permanent informal groups that involves friendship. Most of the relationships came down to two cliques, each with a hanger-on, and some isolates. The groups included several different professions. They developed ideas about each other. Clique membership acted as a form of social control, forcing people to conform to group desires. The groups established norms regarding output, treatment of supervisor, reciprocity and other interpersonal relations. The cliques served as a system for sense making about organizational events. They developed their own set of beliefs, explaining things to each other.

Table: difference between formal and informal groups.

Basis	Formal group	Informal groups
Formation	Legally consitituted, rationally designed, and consciously planned	Emerges naturally and spontaneously
Existence	Normally formal group does not arise because of informal group	Informal group emerges while working in formal group
Purpose	Well-defined and centres around survival, growth, profit, service to society	Ill-defined and centres around friendship, goodwill, unity and so on
Relationship	Superior-subordinate relationship	Personal, and social relationship
Influenced by	Rationality and leaves no scope for personal, social and emotional factors	Personal, social and emotional factors
Communication	Unity of command and line of authority followed	Pattern is grapevine, which is natural, haphazard and intricate
Leadership	Based on formal authority and position	Based on individual competence and group acceptance
Boundaries	Operates within set boundaries	No bounds, operates in different directions
Nature & Emphasis	Normative and idealistic, emphasis on efficiency and control bring in rigidity and bureaucracy in processes and practices	Reflects actual functioning, characterised by relative freedom, spontaneity, homeliness and warmth

Work Groups

Work groups are a part of task groups in employment settings and goal focussed groups in a variety of non-employment situations. A work group is a group that interacts primarily to share information and to make decisions to help one another perform within each member's area of responsibility with a given work or organisation.

Features of Work groups

1. Work groups are composed of two or more individuals.
2. It is formed to perform organisationally designed tasks.
3. The members of the group are attracted to it and are loyal to its members, including the leader.
4. The superior of each work group exerts a major influence in establishing the tone and atmosphere of that work group by his or her leadership principles and practices.
5. There is high motivation in the group to use the communication process so that it best serves the interests and goals of the group.
6. It exhibit task interdependencies.

7. The group is eager to help each member develop to his or her full potential.
8. These work groups have a developmental life span. They form, mature and evolve over time.

Types of Work Groups

1. Production Groups - consists of core employees who involved in producing of tangible products. e.g., automobile assembly. It includes bottom line employees, supervisors and foreman.
2. Service Groups - they engage in repeated transactions with customers e.g., airline attendants.
3. Management groups - include all medium level and top level managers. The primary responsibility of these managers is directing and coordinating lower level units under their authority.
4. Project Groups - are formed to accomplish certain tasks or projects which are completed within a period of stipulated time. These are temporary groups that execute specialised time constrained tasks and eventually dissolve after the completion of the project. E.g., new product development.
5. Action and performing groups - are composed of interdependent exerts who engage in complex time-constrained performance events,. Examples include aircrews, surgical teams and military units.

The Reasons of People joining Groups

People join in groups for a variety of reasons like

1. Security
2. Status
3. Self-esteem
4. Affiliation
5. power
6. Goal achievement.

They join functional groups simply by virtue of joining organizations. People you accept employment to earn money or to practice their profession. People in existing functional groups are told, are asked, task forces and teams. People join informal or interest groups for a variety of reasons, most of them quit complex. Indeed, the need to be team players has grown so strong today that many organizations will actively resist hiring someone who does not want to work with others.

- Interpersonal Attraction: One reason why people choose to form informal or interest groups is that they are attracted to one another. Many different factors contribute to interpersonal attraction. Attraction is increased when people have similar attitude, personalities, or economic standings.
- Group Activities: Individuals may also be motivated to join a group because the activities of the group appeal to them. Jogging, playing war games and flying model airplanes are all activities that some people enjoy. Many of them are more enjoyable to participate in as a member of a group and most require more than one person. Of course, if the groups level of interpersonal attraction is very low, a person may choose to forget the activity rather than join the groups.
- Group Goals: The goal of a group may also motivate people to join. The Sierra Club, which is dedicated to environmental conservation, is an example of this kind of interest group. Member may or may not be personally attracted to the other fund raisers, and they probably do not enjoy the activity of knocking on doors asking for money but they join the group because they subscribe to its goal. Workers join unions like the United Auto Workers because they support its goal.
- Need Satisfaction: Still another reason for joining a group is satisfy the need for affiliation. New residents in a community may join the New Comers Club partially just to be around other people. Likewise, newly divorced people often join support groups as away to have companionship.
- Stages of group development: Groups tend to develop in stages. As you work with a support group, or with almost any group of people who are working together toward a common cause, you'll be able to see the progression. As a facilitator, knowing what to look for and how to manage the challenges can have a big impact on how your group progresses.

As with many things, the progress of a group isn't always neat and tidy. Sometimes groups will regress to an earlier stage if there's a major change, if a group member leaves or another is added, or for various other reasons. Having said that, here's an overview of how groups typically develop and progress.

Stage 1- Orientation (Forming)

Group members are learning what to do, how the group will operate, what's expected, and what's acceptable. Students watch the facilitator and each other for cues and clues, and seek guidelines and stated expectations. They want to feel safe and comfortable, and many will do only limited sharing until that comfort zone is established.

Some students will be comfortable sharing openly even on the first day, either because they enjoy this type of interaction, or because they already feel comfortable with the facilitator and the other students in the group. As a facilitator, you can call on these students to give examples, be the first to answer questions, and model positive interactions for the other group members.

- In this stage, most team members are positive and polite. Some are anxious, as they haven't fully understood what work the team will do. Others are simply excited about the task ahead.
- As leader, you play a dominant role at this stage, because team members' roles and responsibilities aren't clear.
- This stage can last for some time, as people start to work together, and as they make an effort to get to know their new colleagues.

Stage 2- Power Struggle (Storming)

A things progress, it's normal for some power struggles to emerge. As students become more comfortable, they may challenge each other or the facilitators, attempt to form cliques and exclude or ignore certain students, and push limits. This can be frustrating for everyone involved, but it helps to know it's just a stage, and things tend to get much better once it's past.

- Next, the team moves into the storming phase, where people start to push against the boundaries established in the forming stage. This is the stage where many teams fail.
- Storming often starts where there is a conflict between team members' natural working styles. People may work in different ways for all sorts of reasons but, if differing working styles cause unforeseen problems, they may become frustrated.
- Storming can also happen in other situations. For example, team members may challenge your authority, or jockey for position as their roles are clarified. Or, if you haven't defined clearly how the team will work, people may feel overwhelmed by their workload, or they could be uncomfortable with the approach you're using.
- Some may question the worth of the team's goal, and they may resist taking on tasks.
- Team members who stick with the task at hand may experience stress, particularly as they don't have the support of established processes, or strong relationships with their colleagues.

Stage 3- Cooperation and Integration (Norming)

This is where being in group becomes fun and enjoyable most of the time. Group interaction becomes easier, more cooperative, and productive, with balanced give and take, open communication, bonding, and mutual respect. If there is a conflict or disruption, it's relatively easily resolved and the group gets back on track. Group leadership is still important, but the facilitator can step back a little and let group members initiate more and move forward together.

- Gradually, the team moves into the norming stage. This is when people start to resolve their differences, appreciate colleagues' strengths, and respect your authority as a leader.
- Now that your team members know one another better, they may socialize together, and they are able to ask one another for help and provide constructive feedback. People develop a stronger commitment to the team goal, and you start to see good progress towards it.
- There is often a prolonged overlap between storming and norming, because, as new tasks come up, the team may lapse back into behaviour from the storming stage.

Stage 4 – Synergy (Performing)

Not every group reaches this level, and if you spend most of a school year in Stage 3, it will still be a productive and enjoyable group. Synergy emerges when the group shifts or evolves into another level, often without realizing what's happening. Here, there's a sense of group unity, group members looking out for each other even outside of the group setting, deepening friendships or bonds, and a dynamic energy no matter what the task. This is the epitome of "The whole is greater than the sum of its parts."

- The team reaches the performing stage, when hard work leads, without friction, to the achievement of the team's goal. The structures and processes that you have set up support this well.
- As leader, you can delegate much of your work, and you can concentrate on developing team members.
- It feels easy to be part of the team at this stage, and people who join or leave won't disrupt performance.

Stage 5 – Closure (Adjourning)

The closure stage of a group can be confusing and disconcerting if you don't know it's coming. After weeks or months of a smoothly running group, as the end of group or the school year approaches, things may start to fall apart for no apparent reason. Students may bicker with and criticize each other, and anger may surface in unexpected ways.

This is a normal part of group process. Many students (and adults, for that matter) have no idea how to deal with endings, goodbyes, or losses, and they don't know how to find closure. Being angry with each other, or in conflict, is easier for many students than feeling or addressing the sadness of saying goodbye. It's easier for most to be angry than to be vulnerable. Students who have abandonment issues may become especially argumentative or unruly.

- Many teams will reach this stage eventually. For example, project teams exist for only a fixed period, and even permanent teams may be disbanded through organizational restructuring.
- Team members who like routine, or who have developed close working relationships with colleagues, may find this stage difficult, particularly if their future now looks uncertain.

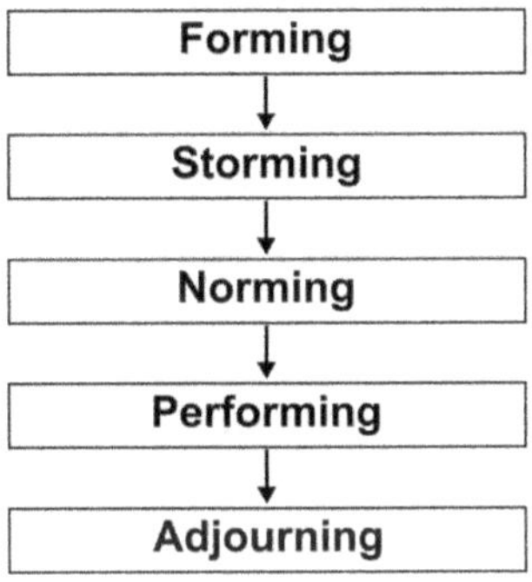

process of group deveopment.

Group Behaviour

Group behaviour" refers to the ways people behave in large- or small-group situations. People join groups for a multitude of reasons, most frequently because membership satisfies a need of the individual. Group membership can provide companionship, survival and security, affiliation status, power and control, and achievement. There is currently no universal description of what constitutes a group, though research has identified a few common requirements that contribute to recognition of a group:

- Interdependence — Individual members must depend, to some degree, on the output of the collective members.
- Social interaction — Accomplishing a goal requires some form of verbal or nonverbal communication among members.
- Perception of a group — All members of the collective must agree they are part of the group.
- Commonality of purpose — All members of the collective come together to attain a common goal.
- Favouritism—Members of the same group tend to be positively prejudiced toward other members and discriminate in their favour.

How Groups Influence Individual Behaviour

Individual behaviour and decision making can be influenced by the presence of others. There are both positive and negative implications of group influence on individual behaviour. For example, group influence can often be useful in the context of work settings, team sports, and political activism. However, the influence of groups on the individual can also generate negative behaviours.

While there are many ways a group can influence behaviour, we will focus on three key phenomena: groupthink, group shift, and individuation.

Groupthink happens when group members, faced with an important choice, become so focused on making a smooth, quick decision that they overlook other, possibly more fruitful options. Group shift is a phenomenon in which the initial positions of individual members of a group are exaggerated toward a more extreme position. Deindividuation happens when a person lets go of self-consciousness and control and does what the group is doing, usually with negative goals or outcomes. Besides these, the important forces of group behaviour are:

1. Member resources - members' knowledge, abilities, skills and personality characteristics such as sociability, self-reliance and independence are the resources which decides the success of a group.
2. Group size - it may vary from a small size of two to a large number of people. Small groups are effective than large groups.
3. Group roles - in formal groups, roles are always predetermined and assigned to members. Group roles may be:
    - Work roles - like initiator, informer, clarifier, summariser and reality master.
    - Maintenance roles-social - emotional activities including harmonizer, gatekeeper, consensus tester, encourager and compromiser.
    - Blocking roles - are activities that disrupt the working of a group. They often resist ideas, disagree with group members for personal reasons and will have hidden agendas. This behaviour may be positive or negative. Their roles includes aggressor, blocker, dominator, comedian and avoidance behaviour.
4. Group Norms – define the acceptable standard or boundaries of acceptable and unacceptable behaviour, shared by group members. Each group will create its own norms to follow by group members. Group apply pressure on members and force them to conform to the group's standards. The norms often reflect the level of commitment, motivation and performance of the group.

5. Group cohesiveness - refers to bonding of group members or unity, feelings of attraction for each other and desire to remain part of the group. Many factors are responsible for group cohesiveness such as agreement to group goals, frequency of interaction, personal attractiveness, inter group competition, favourable evaluation, etc. It also depends on the degree of difficulties to obtain group membership. If it is difficult to obtain an entry into a group, the cohesiveness of the group will be more and vice versa. Groups also show more cohesive when there are strong competitions with other groups or face a serious external threat to survival. Smaller groups and those who spend considerable time together also tend to e more cohesive. Cohesiveness has many positive effects like worker satisfaction, low turnover and absenteeism and higher productivity. But highly cohesive group may be detrimental to organisational performance if their goals are contradictory to organisational goals.

6. Group Processes - decision making by a group is superior, because group generates more information and knowledge, generates diverse alternatives, increases acceptance of a solution, and increases legitimacy. The demerits are decisions take longer time, minority is dominated, pressure is applied to conform to group decisions, and none is responsible for the decisions.

Group Dynamics

The term "group dynamics" refers to the interactions between people who are talking together in a group setting. Group dynamics can be studied in business settings, in volunteer settings, in classroom settings, and in social settings. Any time there are three or more individuals interacting or talking together, there are group dynamics.

Group dynamics involve the study and analysis of how people interact and communicate with each other in face-to face small groups. The study of group dynamics provides a vehicle to analyse group communications with the intent of rendering the groups more effective.

In its most basic sense, Group dynamics is used to describe something that is happening in all groups at all times, whether anyone is aware of it or not. "Group dynamics" used in this way refers to the complex forces that are acting upon every group throughout its existence which cause it to behave the way it does.

We can think of every group as having certain relatively static aspects – its name, constitutional structure, ultimate purpose, and other fixed characteristics. But it also has dynamic aspects -- it is always moving, doing something, changing, becoming, interacting, and reacting. And the nature and direction of its movement is determined by forces being exerted on it from within itself and from outside. The interaction of these forces and their resultant effects on a given group constitute its dynamics. In this sense, "group dynamics" is to groups what "personality dynamics" is to individuals. It is a phenomenon that occurs naturally; nobody invents it.

Dynamics of Group Formation

There is no single reason why individuals join groups. Different groups offer different benefits to their members. The most popular reason for joining a group are:

1. Proximity, Interaction and Influence: One of the most common reasons why people join groups is because they work near each other. Informal groups seem to form among those who are in close proximity. When people have frequent interaction or contact with one another, there is likelihood that they will form a group. Finally, if the behaviour of one individual influences that of others, they are likely to form a group.

2. Security: Probably the strongest reason to join the group is the need for security. By joining a group we can reduce our insecurity – we feel stronger. New or experienced, no employee likes to stay alone. We derive reassurance from interacting with others and being part of a group. This often explains the appeal of unions – if management creates an environment in which employees feel insecure, they are likely to turn to unionization in order to reduce their feelings of insecurity.

3. Affiliation: people join the groups because it provides them an opportunity to have regular company with those with whom they share something common. Individuals may seek out others at work who shares common hobbies or common back grounds.

4. Power: Membership of groups offers power to members in at least two ways. First, there are sayings such as "United we stand, divided we fall" and "there is strength in number." Secondly, leadership of an informal group enables an individual to use power over group members, even if he does not enjoy a formal position of authority in the organization.

5. Esteem: An individual can increase his self-esteem through group membership. One may gain esteem by becoming a member of a high status group. Associating with high status people is reinforcing.

6. Task functions:

    - Generating new ideas or creative solution requires inputs from a large number of individuals.
    - Co-ordination of several groups.
    - Teaching methods to new comers.
    - Facilitate the implementation of complex decisions.
    - A complex task which cannot be performed individually.

Group Norms

Norms are acceptable standards of behaviour within a group that are shared by the members of the group. Norms define the boundaries of acceptable and unacceptable behaviour. They are typically created in order to facilitate group survival, make behaviour more predictable, avoid embarrassing situations, and express the values of the group. Each group will establish its own set of norms that might determine anything from the appropriate dress to how many comments to make in a meeting. Groups exert pressure on members to force them to conform to the group's standards. The norms often reflect the level of commitment, motivation, and performance of the group.

Group norms are the informal guidelines of behaviour and a code of conduct that provides some order and conformity to group activities and operations. These rules are expected to be followed by all the group members. These norms and rules usually develop gradually and informally as group members learn as to what behaviours are necessary for the group to function effectively.

Performance norms determine how quickly members should work and how much they should produce. They are created in an effort to determine levels of individual effort.

Reward-allocation norms determine how rewards are bestowed upon group members. For example, the norm of equality dictates equal treatment of all members. Every member shares equally so rewards are distributed equally to everyone. Equity norms suggest that rewards are distributed according to the member's contribution.

The majority of the group must agree that the norms are appropriate in order for the behaviour to be accepted. There must also be a shared understanding that the group supports the norms.

It should be noted, however, that members might violate group norms from time to time. If the majority of members do not adhere to the norms, then they will eventually change and will no longer serve as a standard for evaluating behaviour. Group members who do not conform to the norms will be punished by being excluded, ignored, or asked to leave the group.

Types of Group Norms

Behaviour Norms

These are rules and guidelines defining the day-to-day behaviour of people at work. This behaviour pattern may include punctuality as a habit, completing any given assignments within the required time framework, not losing temper, showing respect for other member's opinions, not monopolizing the conversation and so on. Certain professionalism is expected from all members and this professionalism is predictable form of behaviour.

Work Norms

Work norms regulate the performance and productivity of individual members. An overly ambitious worker who produces more is considered as much a deviate from the norms as a worker who is an under producer. Work norms usually put an acceptable level of productivity, within reasonable tolerances so that comparatively poor performers can also be accommodated and that they do not become a burden on their peers.

Workers performing below the lower acceptable level are generally informally reprimanded and encouraged to produce more. On the other hand, rate-busters who perform above the upper acceptable limit set by the group are also ostracized for encouraging the management to raise its expectations.

Reasons for Strong Enforcement of Norms

Group norms are generally reinforced if all members agree to abide by them and the members will agree if they firmly believe that adherence to such norms will facilitate group goals achievement or ensure group survival and additionally, such norms do not conflict with individual values and principles. Also, the norms are reinforced if the members value their membership in the group and do not like the outcomes of violating them. The outcome of violating the group norms must be sufficiently consequential in order to discourage members to deviate from them.

The groups enforce compliance with norms in many ways. They can reward people who comply with group norms by appreciating them, by listening to them in a respectful manner and by making them leaders of the group. Also, they can take negative actions against those persons who deviate from group norms in the form of ridicule or 'silent treatment' or by withdrawing privileges or by ultimate action of expelling them from the membership of the group.

Conditions where group norms will be strongly enforced are as follows:

- If the norms facilitate group success or ensure group survival,
- If the norms simplify or predict regarding the behaviour which is expected from group members,
- If the norms emphasize the roles of specific members within a group, and
- If the norms help the group to solve the inter-personal problems themselves.

Group Cohesiveness

Cohesiveness refers to the bonding of group members and their desire to remain part of the group. Many factors influence the amount of group cohesiveness. Generally speaking, the more difficult it is to obtain group membership the more cohesive the group. Groups also tend to become cohesive when they are in intense competition with other groups or face a serious external threat to survival. Smaller groups and those who spend considerable time together also tend to be more cohesive.

Cohesiveness in work groups has many positive effects, including worker satisfaction, low turnover and absenteeism, and higher productivity. However, highly cohesive groups may be detrimental to organizational performance if their goals are misaligned with organizational goals. Highly cohesive groups may also be more vulnerable to groupthink. Groupthink occurs when members of a group exert pressure on each other to come to a consensus in decision making. Groupthink results in careless judgments, unrealistic appraisals of alternative courses of action, and a lack of reality testing. It can lead to a number of decision-making issues such as the following:

1. Incomplete assessments of the problem,
2. Incomplete information search,
3. Bias in processing information,
4. Inadequate development of alternatives, and
5. Failure to examine the risks of the preferred choice.

Evidence suggests that groups typically outperform individuals when the tasks involved require a variety of skills, experience, and decision making. Groups are often more flexible and can quickly assemble, achieve goals, and disband or move on to another set of objectives.

Many organizations have found that groups have many motivational aspects as well. Group members are more likely to participate in decision-making and problem-solving activities leading to empowerment and increased productivity. Groups complete most of the work in an organization; thus, the effectiveness of the organization is limited by the effectiveness of its group.

Consequences of Group Cohesiveness

More participation, more conformity, high productivity, more success, more influence, more communication and more personal satisfaction are some of the consequences of group cohesiveness. These positive outcomes of group cohesiveness are as follows:

1. More Participation: Because group cohesiveness involves close interpersonal relationship, the members consider the group as their own, just like a family and they are motivated to participate actively in group affairs and activities. Members also try to assist and support other members of the group in times of need and this strengthens the bonds of friendship.

The turnover rate of members is very low and they look forward to group meetings and group activities as it gives them an opportunity of social interaction in addition to devising strategies for achieving individual and group goals.

2. More Conformity: While all individuals who are in the group are unique in many ways with their own norms, values, beliefs and attitudes and sometimes these characteristics may be in conflict with the group norms, the members usually make sacrifices in order to conform to group norms. The cohesive group is generally able to put subtle pressure on the individual member who 'deviated' from the group norms in order to bring him back to the mainstream.

3. More Success: Success and cohesiveness are interdependent factors. Cohesiveness makes the goal achievement easier and goal achievement adds to cohesiveness. Cohesive groups are more successful in achieving their goals. The reason for this relationship is that a high degree of cohesiveness involves a high degree of communication, participation and conformity to group norms and this result in successes in achieving them. Thus such coordinated efforts tend to result in successes in achieving such goals.

4. More Influence: Individual members will respond favourably to the demands of the cohesive groups in comparison to less cohesive groups. An informally accepted and respected leader of the group can have quite an autocratic authority and influence over the group members specially when confronting an external threat.

   Thus the leader will have considerable influence over the members in shaping their opinions and operations.

5. More Communication: Communication reduces conflict. The better the communication, the less likely is any misunderstanding among members. Because the members of the cohesive groups share common values and goals, they are inclined greater communicativeness. Since communication is key to understanding, respect and closeness, it tends to foster and cement positive social relations as well as deep personal relationships.

6. More Personal Satisfaction: Satisfaction, though a state of mind, is primarily influenced by positive external factors. These factors include friendliness, respect from other members and self-respect, support, opportunity to interact, achievement, protection against threats and a feeling of security. Members of cohesive groups report that they are more satisfied than members of less cohesive groups. This is expected since the members of a cohesive group will not stay as members if they were dissatisfied.

7. High Productivity: It is quite easy to understand that unity has synergetic effect. The group effort is expected to bring better results than the sum efforts of individual members. However, the outcome of the efforts is a function of not only group cohesiveness but also group compliance with the organizational goals.

According to Richard M. Steers, 'specifically, when cohesiveness is high and acceptance of organizational goals is high; performance will probably be high. Similar results would be expected for low cohesiveness and high goal acceptance, although the results may not be as strong. On the other hand, performance would not be expected to be high when cohesiveness is high and goal acceptance is low.' In that case, group effort will probably be directed away from organizational goals and towards goals valued by the group.

Factors Influencing Group Cohesiveness

Group size, degree of dependency, physical distances, time spent together, severity of initiation, cooperation, threat history of past successes are the major factors. These factors are influencing the group cohesiveness in an organization. We shall discuss about the above factors below:

1. Group size: Small group size is a greater probability of being cohesive than large groups in an organization When team size increases, in this circumstance, possibility of agreement towards the common goal and mutual interaction decreases. When team increases it restricts inter group and intra group communication and encourages for the formation of sub groups.

2. Degree of Dependency: It is a positive between the degree of cohesiveness and dependency in an organization. It requires greater attractiveness towards goals in an organization. The greater the degree of dependency which will be greater attraction and consequently the higher group cohesiveness in an organization.

3. Physical Distance: It is very important when people working together at a very close distance are likely to have greater opportunity for interaction in an organization.

   It enhances the free exchange of ideas, sharing the problems and prospects in an organization. Therefore, it develops closeness among the team members who leading to greater cohesiveness.

4. Time spent Together: Time spent together and cohesiveness is positively related people who met frequently and spend time together for developing mutual attraction and interpersonal interaction. Team members are developing friendship and communication among members in an organization.

5. Severity of Initiation: It is positively correlated towards with cohesiveness when strict admission procedures are prescribed for entry into group that is creating severity of initiation.

   In this case, the group becomes unique and elite in the eyes of other teams in an organization.

   It arises out of the natural human tendency which share among the team members and get benefits for their efforts in an organization.

6. Cooperation: It is the team spirit that is developed by all team members in the team. It helps to share their personal opinion, suggestion, and recommendation relating to group tasks, reward system in a team and teamwork. Well-designed organization structure promotes greater cooperation in this way cohesiveness is enhanced.

7. Status: Status and cohesiveness are positively related in an organization. Status is identity of team and team members and their tasks in an organization Status will come to heard dedication, achievement, growth and development of the organization.

8. Threat: It is also considered for determining factors of cohesiveness. External threat are unpredictable and uncontrollable. Internal threat can be predictable and controllable, Its impact on the group, its identity, and process in an organization. Strong and united team can easily face threat in an organization.

9. History of Past Successes: It is very important factors influencing the group cohesiveness in an organization Past result, performance, growth and development is the step stone towards the future goals and mission and vision of an organization Team will be evaluated the past results and analysis and interpret future result for survival and growth and development of an organization.

Group Decision Making

Group decision-making (also known as collaborative decision-making) is a situation faced when individuals collectively make a choice from the alternatives before them. The decision is then no longer attributable to any single individual who is a member of the group. This is because all the individuals and social group processes such as social influence contribute to the outcome. The decisions made by groups are often different from those made by individuals. Group polarization is one clear example: groups tend to make decisions that are more extreme than those of its individual members, in the direction of the individual inclinations.

There is much debate as to whether this difference results in decisions that are better or worse. According to the idea of synergy, decisions made collectively tend to be more effective than decisions made by a single individual.

1. Brainstorming: It is a combination of group problem solving and discussions. It works on the belief that the more the number of ideas, greater the possibility of having a solution to the problem that is acceptable to all. It starts with the group generating ideas which are then analysed, with action points based on the discussions.

2. Nominal group technique: In a nominal group technique, the team divides itself into smaller groups and generates ideas quietly. Possible options are noted

down in writing and the team members further discuss these to narrow down the possible choices they would like to accept. Team members then discuss and vote on the best possible choice. The choice that receives the maximum vote is accepted as the group decision.

3. Multi-voting: It starts with a number of rounds of voting where an individual casts his/ her vote for the options that are shortlisted. Each individual can cast one vote at a time. In this way the options favouring the maximum number of votes is carried to the next round. This process is repeated until a clear winning option is obtained.

4. Delphi method: In this method of decision making, the facilitator allows team members to individually brainstorm their ideas and submit their ideas "anonymously". The other team members do not know the owner of the ideas. The facilitator then collects all the inputs and circulates them among others for modifying or improving them. This process continues until a final decision is made.

5. Electronic meeting: Here, the decision making process takes place virtually with the help of technology. Participants type any message they want to convey and this flashes on the screen of other participating members. In this process, the identity of the participants can be kept a secret and they can voice their opinions without any inhibitions.

Turning Groups into Effective Teams

All teams are groups but not all groups are teams. Teams often are difficult to form because it takes time for members to learn how to work together. People in every workplace talk about building the team, working as a team, and my team, but few understand how to create the experience of team work or how to develop an effective team. Belonging to a team, in the broadest sense, is a result of feeling part of something larger than oneself. It has a lot to do with your understanding of the mission or objectives of your organization.

In a team-oriented environment, one contributes to the overall success of the organization. One works with fellow members of the organization to produce these results. Even though you have a specific job function and you belong to a specific department, you are unified with other organization members to accomplish the overall objectives. The bigger picture drives your actions; your function exists to serve the bigger picture.

It is on record that teams are better than groups, because they are more flexible and responsive to dynamic environment. A work group has no opportunity to involve in collective works.

It is the work team whose members 'work intensely on a specific, common goal using their positive synergy, individual and mutual accountability, and complementary skills'.

Table: Difference between a Group and a Team.

Group	Team
No opportunity to engage in collective work, which requires joint effort.	Members work intensely with individual and mutual accountability and complementary skills.
No positive synergy to create.	Generates positive synergy due to capability of group members to bounce ideas off one another to correct one another's mistakes, to bring a diverse knowledge base to bear on a problem, and to accomplish work that is too vast for any one individual to achieve.
Performance not greater than the sum of inputs	Generates greater outputs with no increase in inputs.
Less responsive to dynamic environment	More flexible and more responsive to dynamic environment.

Team Management - Meaning and Concept

There are some tasks which can't be done alone. Individuals need to come together, discuss things among themselves and work together towards the realization of a common goal. The individuals forming a team should ideally think more or less on the same lines and should have similar interests and objective. People with absolutely different tastes can't form a team. Their goals have to be the same. Every team is formed to achieve a predefined goal and it is the responsibility of each and every member to contribute his level best and accomplish the assigned task within the stipulated time frame. The team members must complement each other and come to each other's help whenever required. Individual performances do not matter much in a team and every individual should strive hard and work in unison.

Understanding Team Management

Team management refers to the various activities which bind a team together by bringing the team members closer to achieve the set targets. For the team members, their team must be their priority and everything else should take a back seat. They should be very focused on their goals.

Let us understand Team Management with the help of a real life situation.

Maria was representing the training and development vertical of a leading firm. Joe, Kathy, Sandra and Tim were reporting to Maria and helped her in designing the various training programs. Maria left no stone unturned to ensure that all her team members were satisfied with their job responsibilities. The workload was shared equally among four of them. Ideas were discussed on an open forum and each of them contributed to his level best. They went out for movies and stayed in touch even after work.

Maria being the team leader was actually responsible for bringing her team members closer so that none of them feels left out and all are motivated to deliver their level best.

With the help of the team management activities, she managed to create a positive ambience at the workplace and promoted healthy competition in her team.

Types of Teams

1. Permanent teams - These teams perform on a permanent basis and are not dissolved once the task is accomplished. Let us understand the concept with an example.

   Mike, Peter, Joe and Ana had a strong inclination towards branding as well as promotions and hence were a part of the branding team with a leading organization. They were primarily responsible for promoting their brand and designing marketing strategies to generate maximum revenue for their organization. They worked extremely hard and always managed to achieve their targets well in advance, but their team was always in place and never dissolved. Their organization never asked them to leave or ever dissolved their team. Such teams are called permanent teams.

   Work or no work, the human resources team, operation team, administration team always function effectively throughout the year and hence are permanent teams.

2. Temporary teams - Unlike permanent teams, temporary teams lose their importance, once the task is accomplished. Such teams are usually formed for a shorter duration either to assist the permanent team or work when the members of the permanent team are busy in some other When organizations have excess of work, they generally form temporary teams which work in association with the members of the permanent team for the accomplishment of the task within the stipulated time.

3. Task Force - Such teams are formed for a special purpose of working on any specific project or finding a solution to a very critical problem.

   The government generally appoints special teams to investigate critical issues like bomb blasts, terrorist attacks and so on. The task force explores all the possible reasons which led to a severe problem and tries to resolve it within a given deadline.

4. Committee - Committees are generally formed to work on a particular assignment either permanently or on a temporary basis. Individuals with common interests, more or less from the same background, attitude comes together on a common platform to form a committee and work on any matter.

   To organize any cultural event, organizations generally make committees to raise funds, invite celebrities and all the major tasks involved to successfully organize any event. The committee members work together, design strategies to successfully accomplish the task.

In educational institutes, various committees are formed where students with a common interest join hands to organize cultural events and various other activities required for the all -round development of students.

5. Organization/Work Force - Such groups are formed in organizations where team members work together under the expert guidance of leader. A leader or a supervisor is generally appointed among the members itself and he along with his team works hard to achieve a common goal. The leader all through must stand by his team and extract the best out of each team member. He must not underestimate any of his team members and take his team along to avoid conflicts.

   Samuel was working with a leading advertising firm with two members reporting to him. Samuel always believed in his team members and worked together with his team and no doubts his team always did wonders and was way ahead of others.

6. Self-Managed Teams - Self Managed Teams consist of individuals who work together again for a common purpose but without the supervision of any leader. Here as the name suggests every individual is accountable for his individual performance. The team members of self-managed teams must respect each other and should never lose focus on their target. No leader is appointed and the team members have to take their own responsibility. Individuals take the initiative on their own and are their own guides and mentors.

7. Cross Functional Team - Let us understand this with the help of an example.

   Maria and Andy both were part of the branding team. They got an assignment from their superiors to be completed within two days. Unfortunately Andy met with an accident and was advised complete bed rest. To avoid delays, Peter from the operations team was shifted to the marketing team to assist Maria for the time being and form a team. Such teams are called cross functional teams. Ideally the employees should be more or less on the same level to avoid ego hassles. Individuals from different areas come and work together for a common objective to form a cross functional team. In such teams, people from different areas, interests and likings join hands to come out with a unique idea to successfully complete a task.

8. Virtual Teams - Virtual teams consist of individuals who are separated by distances and connected through computer. Here individuals communicate with each other online through internet. Sam at Los Angeles can form a team with Mandy at Mexico and Sara at Denver all working for a common objective but the communication is totally digital through internet. Such teams are helpful when employees need to connect with each other and are located at different places. Individuals supporting any community in social networking sites such

as facebook or orkut also form a virtual team as all the members are from different locations but support a common community. They all have a common objective - to support and promote their community.

Characteristics of Effective Teams

- There is a clear unity of purpose: There was free discussion of the objectives until members could commit themselves to them; the objectives are meaningful to each group member.
- The group is self-conscious about its own operations: The group has taken time to explicitly discuss group process how the group will function to achieve its objectives. The group has a clear, explicit, and mutually agreed-upon approach: mechanics, norms, expectations, rules, etc. Frequently, it will stop to examine how well it is doing or what may be interfering with its operation. Whatever the problem may be, it gets open discussion and a solution found.
- The group has set clear and demanding performance goals: The group has set performance goals into well-defined concrete milestones against which it measures itself. The group defines and achieves a continuous series of "small wins" along the way to larger goals.
- The atmosphere tends to be informal, comfortable, relaxed: There are no obvious tensions, a working atmosphere in which people are involved and interested.
- There is a lot of discussion in which virtually everyone participates: It remains pertinent to the purpose of the group. If discussion gets off track, someone will bring it back in short order. The members listen to each other. Every idea is given a hearing. People are not afraid of being foolish by putting forth a creative thought even if it seems extreme.
- People are free in expressing their feelings as well as their ideas: The people in a group are free to express their feelings, ideas and emotions in the group.
- There is disagreement and this is viewed as good: Disagreements are not suppressed or overridden by premature group action. The reasons are carefully examined, and the group seeks to resolve them rather than dominate the dissenter.

  Dissenters are not trying to dominate the group; they have a genuine difference of opinion. If there are basic disagreements that cannot be resolved, the group figures out a way to live with them without letting them block its efforts.
- Most decisions are made at a point where there is general agreement: However, those who disagree with the general agreement of the group do not keep their opposition private and let an apparent consensus mask their disagreement. The group does not accept a simple majority as a proper basis for action.

- Each individual carries his or her own weight: Meeting or exceeding the expectations of other group members. Each individual is respectful of the mechanics of the group: arriving on time, coming to meetings prepared, completing agreed upon tasks on time, etc. When action is taken, clears assignments are made (who-what-when) and willingly accepted and completed by each group member.
- Criticism is frequent, frank and relatively comfortable: The criticism has a constructive flavour - oriented toward removing an obstacle that faces the group.
- The leadership of the group shifts from time to time: The issue is not who controls, but how to get the job done.

Team building is the collective term for various types of activities used to enhance social relations and define roles within teams, often involving collaborative tasks. It is distinct from team training, which is designed to improve the efficiency of the process, rather than the interpersonal aspect of it.

Steps to Building an Effective Team

The first rule of team building is an obvious one: to lead a team effectively, you must first establish your leadership with each team member. Remember that the most effective team leaders build their relationships of trust and loyalty, rather than fear or the power of their positions.

- Consider each employee's ideas as valuable: Remember that there is no such thing as a stupid idea.
- Be aware of employees' unspoken feelings: Set an example to team members by being open with employees and sensitive to their moods and feelings.
- Act as a harmonizing influence: Look for chances to mediate and resolve minor disputes; point continually toward the team's higher goals.
- Be clear when communicating: Be careful to clarify directives.
- Encourage trust and cooperation among employees on your team: Remember that the relationships team members establish among themselves are every bit as important as those you establish with them. As the team begins to take shape, pay close attention to the ways in which team members work together and take steps to improve communication, cooperation, trust, and respect in those relationships.
- Encourage team members to share information: Emphasize the importance of each team member's contribution and demonstrate how all of their jobs operate together to move the entire team closer to its goal.

- Delegate problem-solving tasks to the team: Let the team work on creative solutions together.
- Facilitate communication: Remember that communication is the single most important factor in successful teamwork. Facilitating communication does not mean holding meetings all the time. Instead it means setting an example by remaining open to suggestions and concerns, by asking questions and offering help, and by doing everything you can to avoid confusion in your own communication.
- Establish team values and goals; evaluate team performance: Be sure to talk with members about the progress they are making toward established goals so that employees get a sense both of their success and of the challenges that lie ahead.
- Make sure that you have a clear idea of what you need to accomplish: That you know what your standards for success are going to be; that you have established clear time frames; and that team members understand their responsibilities.
- Use consensus: Set objectives, solve problems, and plan for action. While it takes much longer to establish consensus, this method ultimately provides better decisions and greater productivity because it secures every employee's commitment to all phases of the work.
- Set ground rules for the team: These are the norms that you and the team establish to ensure efficiency and success. They can be simple directives (Team members are to be punctual for meetings) or general guidelines (Every team member has the right to offer ideas and suggestions), but you should make sure that the team creates these ground rules by consensus and commits to them, both as a group and as individuals.
- Establish a method for arriving at a consensus: You may want to conduct open debate about the pros and cons of proposals, or establish research committees to investigate issues and deliver reports.
- Encourage listening and brainstorming: As supervisor, your first priority in creating consensus is to stimulate debate. Remember that employees are often afraid to disagree with one another and that this fear can lead your team to make mediocre decisions. When you encourage debate you inspire creativity and that's how you'll spur your team on to better results.
- Establish the parameters of consensus-building sessions: Be sensitive to the frustration that can mount when the team is not achieving consensus. At the outset of your meeting, establish time limits, and work with the team to achieve consensus within those parameters. Watch out for false consensus; if an agreement is struck too quickly, be careful to probe individual team members to discover their real feelings about the proposed solution.

Team Advantages and Disadvantages

The advantages and disadvantages of teams also need to be considered before deciding to transition to teams. The following table of team advantages and disadvantages is an adaptation of work by Medsker and Campion. This list can also be used by existing teams to self- evaluate their efficacy.

Team Advantages	Team Disadvantages
Team members have the opportunity to learn from each other.	Some individuals are not compatible with team work.
Potential exists for greater work force flexibility with cross-training.	Workers must be selected to fit the team as well as requisite job skills.
Opportunity provided for synergistic combinations of ideas and abilities.	Some members may experience less motivating jobs as part of a team.
New approaches to tasks may be discovered.	Organization may resist change.
Teams membership can provide social facilitation and support for difficult tasks and situations.	Conflict may develop between team members or other teams.
Communication and information exchange may be facilitated and increased.	Teams may be time-consuming due to need for coordination and consensus.
Interdependent work flow can be enhanced.	Evaluation and rewards may be perceived as less powerful.
Potential exists for greater acceptance and understanding of team-made decisions.	“Free-riding” within the team may occur.
Greater autonomy, variety, identity, significance, and feedback for workers can occur.	Less flexibility may be experienced in personnel replacement or transfer.

Directions of Communication

Four directions of business communication are: I. Downward Communication II. Upward Communication III. Lateral or Horizontal Communication IV. Diagonal or Crosswise Communication.

Every organisation has a multidimensional or multidirectional communication.

The directions in which communication are carried out are:

Downward Communication

Traditionally, the emphasis in business organizations has been on downward communication. This is because of the hierarchical nature of organizations where all communication basically and naturally flows from top to bottom. It is the communication that comes from superiors and flows down to the subordinates.

Methods of Downward Communication

Downward communication can be written as well as oral. The oral communication is mostly through information channels. The written downward communication takes the form of orders, circulars, policy statements, memos and procedural documents.

Example- A CEO (Chief Executive Officer) or a General Manager issuing instructions or sending letters to various departmental heads.

Objectives

1. To give specific directions about a job
2. To explain procedures
3. To apprise subordinates of their performance
4. To explain the significance of a job given to a subordinate with respect to the organization's goals.

Limitations

1. Distortion: Downward communication is often marred by distortion or contortion of the message. Any piece of information loses a bit of its accuracy whenever it passes from one person to another.

   In fact, some directions or instructions may not even be understood. This often affects the accuracy of the information. By the time it reaches the receiver, the very crux of the communication may be lost.

2. Loss of Information: There is every likely hood of information getting lost in the huge labyrinth that a business organisation often is. Information in a written form is considered safer, but even this is likely to get lost.
3. Delay: Downward communication may take a long time to reach the person concerned. The communication has to go through various levels before reaching the grassroots. This makes downward communication time-consuming. Often, this delay in downward communication frustrates the top managers who have issued the communication.
4. Under-Communication and Over-communication: Downward communication may also be hampered by under-communication or over-communication by the intervening superiors. The superiors may talk too much at times, and too little at others. They may, thus, dilute or modify the communication.
5. Built-in Resistance: Downward communication reflects an authoritarian setup. It prevents subordinates from participating in the decision-making process. It

gives them a feeling of being talked down to. Subordinates may, therefore, oppose the decision or not welcome it wholeheartedly.

Upward Communication

As the term suggests, this channel of communication pushes information upwards. It starts from the people at the lowest level of an organisation and reaches the top. An open-door policy, social gatherings, reports, direct correspondence, counseling, etc. are some common methods of upward communication.

Managers have now recognized the importance of this channel of organizational communication. Until now, it was felt that the right to communicate had been vested only in the top management.

Methods of Upward Communication

1. Periodical meetings: These are regular meetings with the staff and subordinates conducted to invite suggestions, opinions or other ideas.
2. Written Representations: An example of upward communication is a written representation given by employees to their superiors as regards what they feel about the work environment and suggestions regarding improvement.
3. Informal Gatherings: Parties and get-togethers provide opportunities for the employees to share their feelings and have an interaction with the superiors.
4. Suggestion Schemes: The employees are encouraged to give suggestions on the practices and the systems being followed in the organisation. For this purpose, a suggestion box may be kept.

Objectives

1. Feedback: This channel provides the management with the necessary feedback. On the basis of the feedback, the management can ascertain whether the subordinates have understood a given set of directions properly.
2. Outlet for held-up Emotions: The employees get an opportunity to vent their problems and grievances when they communicate with the management.
3. Positive Suggestions: Quite often, this channel brings forward some very useful suggestions from the employees, which can be implemented for the organization's benefit.
4. Harmony: Upward communication creates a congenial atmosphere and brings the management and the employees closer to each other. It creates a positive psychological factor as employees feel involved.

Limitations

1. Most problems in upward communication are psychological in nature. Most higher-ups still do not like to be 'told' anything about or against their own decisions or wishes.
2. The employees are also hesitant to walk up to managers and initiate upward communication.
3. A common belief among employees is that it may not really be in their interest to communicate their problems to superiors.
4. Sometimes managers may not accept certain unpleasant facts. This may lead to the distortion of this channel of communication.
5. Subordinates may become too bold and directly approach the top authority with their complaints. This proves harmful as the relations between the workers and their immediate superior get strained.
6. Upward communication may also be used by sycophants for personal gains. Such employees may try to endear themselves to the superiors by passing on selective information. Genuine information may, thus, get suppressed or distorted.

Lateral or Horizontal Communication

This kind of communication takes place between departments or people on the same level in an organizational structure. It is one of the most frequently used channels of communication.

Face-to-face discussions, telephonic talks, periodical meetings, memos, etc. are the ways of carrying out this type of communication. It is very important for the smooth functioning of every organisation as it promotes understanding and coordination between various departments. Embarrassing situations can arise when there is a lack of proper horizontal communication.

For example, the production and the marketing departments must interact with each other because marketing tactics and production planning go hand-in-hand.

Objectives

1. To create a friendly atmosphere in an organisation.
2. To cut across departmental barriers.
3. To ensure quick feedback.

Limitations

1. Lateral communication may give birth to gossip. It can be used for rumour on-going and spreading false information.
2. Good ideas may get suppressed because such communication often comes without authority or sanction for implementation.
3. Lateral communication can be effective only if there is proper coordination.

Diagonal or Crosswise Communication

Diagonal or crosswise communication envisages a horizontal flow of information as well as interaction across different levels of an organization's hierarchy. Communication flows across different levels in an organisation among people who may not have direct reporting relationships. Diagonal communication is used to speed up the flow of information.

It makes effective efforts for achieving organizational goals. A great deal of communication does not follow the organizational hierarchy, but cuts across well-drawn lines. Channels of such communication are general notices, informal meetings, formal conferences, lunch hour meetings, etc.

Objectives

1. To help in proper coordination.
2. To communicate effectively whether laterally, horizontally and diagonally.
3. To improve mutual understanding.
4. To boost the morale of lower level staff through interaction across all the levels in the organisation.

Limitations

1. There is a fear of encroachment in diagonal communication. The superiors may feel bad when their subordinates are given importance, and may even end up feeling bypassed.
2. The superiors may resist suggestions just because these have come from subordinates. This comes out of a subconscious feeling of not having been part of the consultation process.
3. Diagonal communication can lead to a network that is extremely complex. An absence of accepted procedures may lead to internal chaos. The fallout can then be external displeasure.

Comparison between Upward and Downward Communication:

Basis of comparison	Downward communication	Upward communication
Direction	Downward communication flows from higher to bottom level.	Upward communication flows from bottom to higher levels.
Speed	Its speed is fast, empowered by authority.	Its speed is slow.
Purpose	Its purpose may be to give orders for implementing plans.	Its purpose is to provide feedback and give suggestions.
Nature	Its nature is authoritative and directive.	Its nature is informative and that of an appeal.
Examples	Its examples include orders, circulars, notices, etc.	Its examples include reports, suggestions, grievances, etc.

Models of Communication

Oral Communication

Oral communication implies communication through mouth. It includes individuals conversing with each other, be it direct conversation or telephonic conversation. Speeches, presentations, discussions are all forms of oral communication. Oral communication is generally recommended when the communication matter is of temporary kind or where a direct interaction is required. Face to face communication (meetings, lectures, conferences, interviews, etc.) is significant so as to build a rapport and trust.

Advantages of Oral Communication

- There is high level of understanding and transparency in oral communication as it is interpersonal.
- There is no element of rigidity in oral communication. There is flexibility for allowing changes in the decisions previously taken.
- The feedback is spontaneous in case of oral communication. Thus, decisions can be made quickly without any delay.
- Oral communication is not only time saving, but it also saves upon money and efforts.
- Oral communication is best in case of problem resolution. The conflicts, disputes and many issues/differences can be put to an end by talking them over.
- Oral communication is an essential for teamwork and group energy.

- Oral communication promotes a receptive and encouraging morale among organizational employees.
- Oral communication can be best used to transfer private and confidential information/matter.

Disadvantages of Oral Communication

- Relying only on oral communication may not be sufficient as business communication is formal and very organized.
- Oral communication is less authentic than written communication as they are informal and not as organized as written communication.
- Oral communication is time-saving as far as daily interactions are concerned, but in case of meetings, long speeches consume lot of time and are unproductive at times.
- Oral communications are not easy to maintain and thus they are unsteady.
- There may be misunderstandings as the information is not complete and may lack essentials.
- It requires attentiveness and great receptivity on part of the receivers/audience.
- Oral communication (such as speeches) is not frequently used as legal records except in investigation work.

Written Communication

Written communication has great significance in today's business world. It is an innovative activity of the mind. Effective written communication is essential for preparing worthy promotional materials for business development. Speech came before writing. But writing is more unique and formal than speech. Effective writing involves careful choice of words, their organization in correct order in sentences formation as well as cohesive composition of sentences. Also, writing is more valid and reliable than speech. But while speech is spontaneous, writing causes delay and takes time as feedback is not immediate.

Advantages of Written Communication

- Written communication helps in laying down apparent principles, policies and rules for running of an organization.
- It is a permanent means of communication. Thus, it is useful where record maintenance is required.

- It assists in proper delegation of responsibilities. While in case of oral communication, it is impossible to fix and delegate responsibilities on the grounds of speech as it can be taken back by the speaker or he may refuse to acknowledge.
- Written communication is more precise and explicit.
- Effective written communication develops and enhances an organization's image.
- It provides ready records and references.

Legal defenses can depend upon written communication as it provides valid records.

Disadvantages of Written Communication

Written communication does not save upon the costs. It costs huge in terms of stationery and the manpower employed in writing/typing and delivering letters.

Also, if the receivers of the written message are separated by distance and if they need to clear their doubts, the response is not spontaneous.

Written communication is time-consuming as the feedback is not immediate. The encoding and sending of message takes time.

Effective written communication requires great skills and competencies in language and vocabulary use. Poor writing skills and quality have a negative impact on organization's reputation.

Too much paper work and e-mails burden is involved.

Nonverbal Communication

Scenario 1 – You are sitting in front of an interview panel with arms crossed. So far you have not been asked a single question, however, your crossed arms have spoken louder than the words.

Tip 1 – Never keep your arms crossed especially during formal one-on-one meetings. It suggests you are not open to feedback and could also suggest that you are trying to dominate the situation.

Scenario 2 – You are giving a presentation to a group of 20 people. You keep your gaze fixed at the centre of the class / room through the presentation – your gaze has spoken louder than your words.

Tip 2 – Your gaze at one person should not be more than 4 - 5 seconds while delivering a presentation / communicating with a large group unless you are addressing an individual.

Scenario 1 and 2 clearly demonstrate the importance of Non Verbal Communication.

Non Verbal Communication

It is communication of feelings, emotions, attitudes, and thoughts through body movements / gestures/eye contact, etc.

The components of Non Verbal Communication are:

- Kinesics: It is the study of facial expressions, postures & gestures. Did you know that while in Argentina to raise a fist in the air with knuckles pointing outwards expresses victory, in Lebanon, raising a closed fist is considered rude?
- Oculesics: It is the study of the role of eye contact in non verbal communication. Did you know that in the first 90 sec - 4 min you decide that you are interested in someone or not. Studies reveal that 50% of this first impression comes from non-verbal communication which includes oculesics. Only 7% of comes from words - that we actually say.
- Haptics: It is the study of touching. Did you know that acceptable level of touching vary from one culture to another? In Thailand, touching someone's head may be considered as rude.
- Proxemics: It is the study of measurable distance between people as they interact. Did you know that the amount of personal space when having an informal conversation should vary between 18 inches - 4 feet while, the personal distance needed when speaking to a crowd of people should be around 10-12 feet?
- Chronemics: It is the study of use of time in non-verbal communication. Have you ever observed that while AN employee will not worry about running a few minutes late to meet a colleague, a manager who has a meeting with the CEO, a late arrival will be considered as a nonverbal cue that he / she does not give adequate respect to his superior?
- Paralinguistics: It is the study of variations in pitch, speed, volume, and pauses to convey meaning. Interestingly, when the speaker is making a presentation and is looking for a response, he will pause. However, when no response is desired, he will talk faster with minimal pause.
- Physical Appearance: Your physical appearance always contributes towards how people perceive you. Neatly combed hair, ironed clothes and a lively smile will always carry more weight than words.

Group Communications and Behavior

Interpersonal communication refers to one-on-one or small group interactions. Research generally suggests that this type of communication is influential in changing opinions, dealing with resistance and apathy to issues, and generally maintaining harmony in social situations – more so than its opposite, mass communication. The main features of interpersonal media are:

1. They provide a two-way exchange of information. Individual participants can obtain clarification, explanation and negotiation. This characteristic of interpersonal networks often allows them to overcome problems of message distortion caused by excessive noise.

2. They generally have a significant effect in persuading an individual to form or to change a strongly held attitude.

3. In many situations, they can help to resolve conflict because they provide a means to air personal feelings and deal with misunderstandings or grudges.

Here we discuss interpersonal communication in business and management contexts, by focusing on cultural influence, team interaction, conflict, information management, and project management.

Culture

Individuals interact in networks or groups which carry expectations, rules, norms and ideals. These regulative practices are based on assumptions about the order of things, values, ethical beliefs, and attitudes towards status and authority - all characteristics of the misleadingly transparent concept 'culture'. Meanings about the world and its objects are constructed in social interactions within or between cultural groups and then serve to identify the group both socially and globally.

Culture can be defined as a system of activities and discourses, which have been codified and crystallized by usage, and which reflect the conventional practices of a group. All collectivities develop a culture over time – a nation has a culture, as do an organization, a fan club and a gang. Complex societies have a diversity of cultures, including those of minority groups, such as ethnic cultures, gay culture, etc. The more complicated a culture becomes, the greater the chance that groups will break apart to form sub-cultures, which may be alternative (different from the mainstream, but not challenging it), or oppositional (different from the mainstream and attempting to change it in their light).

As regards the culture of business or government organisations, this is manifest in such factors as the organisation's objectives and 'mission', hierarchy (allocation of roles in order of seniority), internal and external patterns of negotiation, and conflict management. The organisation's public image is also significant in making cultural values apparent and known to others. This is achieved through various community oriented projects and ecological initiatives, encompassed under the umbrella term Corporate Social Responsibility (CSR).

Researchers in business communication have offered several models and taxonomies of features that help to define the culture of an organisation.

Robbins and Barnwell, for example, distinguish the following as key elements in analysing business culture:

1. Individual initiative: how much and what kind of responsibility, freedom and independence do individuals have?
2. Risk tolerance: are employees encouraged to take initiatives and engage in risk taking behaviour?
3. Direction: are the organisation's objectives and performance expectations clearly communicated and implemented?
4. Integration: is it easy for groups within the organisation to operate in a coordinated manner and are they motivated to do so?
5. Management contact: are managers accessible, supportive and helpful to their subordinates?
6. Control: to what degree and what kind of rules and supervision regulations does the organisation employ to oversee employee performance?
7. Identity: does the organisation encourage employees to identify with the company and the company's public image?
8. Reward system: how and to what degree are employees rewarded for their performance (i.e. through promotion, salary increases, bonus schemes, etc.)
9. Conflict tolerance: is there a mechanism and/or procedure that allows employees to communicate conflicts and criticisms?
10. Communication patterns: are communication channels restricted to the formal hierarchy of command, or are they diverse (i.e. do junior employees have easy access to senior managers; can members of one section cooperate with members of another)?

Answers to these questions would come from surveys of company employees, an examination of formal company procedures, and case studies involving particular situations where action and decision making reflect the company's structure and value system, i.e. its culture.

Two influential models in the analysis of organisational culture are Geert Hofstede's practice dimensions, and House's GLOBE model.

Hofstede's work spans approximately a 20 year-period, and is based on two surveys, one conducted of 116,000 IBM employees scattered over 72 countries, and another conducted of 1150 male and 1150 female students from 23 countries.

From this research, Hofstede distinguished five practice dimensions which he used to classify cultures. These are:

1. Power distance: The different attitudes to inequality between people. High-power distance cultures tend to value the following elements: hierarchy, fixed roles, authoritarian decision-making styles, and conformity. In addition, in such cultures subordinates are not often consulted in decision-making, and, in situations that involve negotiation, individuals tend to prefer to work with high-status negotiators rather than lower-level representatives (exemplified by the 'I want to talk to your manager' symptom). Low-power distance cultures, on the other hand, tend to value these elements: low hierarchical structure, independence, individual initiative, freedom (which could manifest in anything from the ability to voice dissent to being allowed to dress eccentrically), and consultative decision-making styles. In such cultures, subordinates tend to be consulted, and there is more emphasis on rewards and negotiation.

2. Uncertainty avoidance: The level of acceptance of an unknown future. High uncertainty avoidance cultures tend to exhibit the following characteristics: a preference for engaging in risky behaviour (such as initiating legal action), rather than waiting to see how a situation will unfold; security through predictability and routine; adherence to rules, regulations and operating procedures; traditional gender roles; controlled presence of innovators; and belief in specialists and experts. Low uncertainty avoidance cultures tend to exhibit these characteristics: patience in taking action; belief in the importance of emotive or intuitive response to situations; freedom in gender roles; support for innovation and experimentation; and belief in generalists.

3. Individualism versus collectivism: The manner in which individuals are integrated in groups. Individualist cultures generally define identity according to personal and separate values. They tend to exhibit these characteristics: appreciation of an individual 'voice' or opinion; guiltless pursuit of self-interest and material gain; calculative relationships (exemplified by the 'what's in it for me?' symptom); and individual incentive. On the other hand, collectivist cultures generally define identity according to group positioning and communal values. They tend to exhibit these characteristics: decision-making in groups; focus on the pursuit of the public good; emotional commitment to group membership; collaborative incentive.

4. Masculine versus feminine: The manner in which roles and emotive responses are divided according to gender. This practice dimension reflects traditional gender roles that associate males with assertiveness and females with nurturance, and extends these into the organisational domain. Typical characteristics of masculine cultures include: importance of challenge and recognition; performance or results orientation; a division of individuals into 'losers' and

'winners'; more men in top management positions; competitive advantage in manufacturing industries and price competition. Typical characteristics of feminine cultures include: cooperative orientation; process orientation and reflexive practice; more sympathy for the disadvantaged; easier for women to reach top management positions; competitive advantage in service industries and consulting.

5. Long-term versus short-term orientation: The different values attached to future as opposed to immediate results. Long term oriented cultures tend to value savings and investments, while short-term oriented cultures may be more entrepreneurial and focus on immediate gains. Long-term oriented cultures tend to exhibit these traits: persistence; deferral of gratification; a strong market position and relationship marketing; equality; and provision for old age (which is not seen as a negative factor). Short-term oriented cultures tend to exhibit these characteristics: schemes that produce fast results; appreciation of leisure time; grasping opportunities in business affairs; and deferral of concerns regarding old age.

Hofstede's practice dimensions do not represent exclusive or rigid categories, but rather a continuum of degrees between the two extremes of each dimension. Thus, for example, some cultures would probably fall somewhere in between long-term and short-term oriented or between individualist and collectivist. Also, a temporal element would come into play, with some cultures changing their positioning over time and under different circumstances.

For all its success as a research tool, Hofstede's model carries certain dangers typical of attempts to construct an abstract modelling of human behaviour. First, as happens in research based on surveys, the findings tend to be influenced by the wording of the questions and the circumstances in which the surveys were administered. It cannot be certain that the results would have remained the same if different wording was used and the surveys were repeated in different contexts. Second, even if the populations chosen to be surveyed constituted a representative sample and a substantial number of respondents were interviewed, the results would still be abstracted from the general attitudes of a majority. Exceptions that would actually contest the findings or that would highlight the circumstantial nature of responses are overshadowed. Finally, even though the results can be used for taxonomies and classifications of cultures, the evaluative or interpretative dimension is absent. For example, what does being an individualist or a collectivist actually mean to particular members of an organisation, and how does it play out in the social arena?

Bearing these reservations in mind, as anyone who has worked in different organisations or who has lived in different countries knows, culture is indeed a very influential factor in behaviour and attitude, in what one can and cannot do, and even in what one can or cannot imagine doing. In fact, structures and mental frames that determine our patterns of thinking are deeply embedded in social institutions and in language. To take one example, the Japanese language has different forms reserved for men and women, and for degrees of respect based on levels of seniority. In this case, unless a speaker actually impersonates another, s/he cannot express an identity that his/her social role is not culturally associated with. Identity is already inscribed in the status system of the culture and reflected in linguistic form. As Harry Irwin points out with regard to gender equality in Japan, this begs the question of whether a Japanese female manager could ever succeed in giving a direct order to a male, and presents a long-term and deeply rooted difficulty for Japanese women seeking workplace equality'.

The second approach to organisational culture that we consider here is based on Robert House's Global Leadership and Organisational Behaviour Effectiveness (GLOBE) model. The GLOBE model is based on surveys that asked participants to describe cultural situations both as they experience them in their organisations, and as they think they should ideally be. The GLOBE survey draws on data from around 17,000 questionnaires completed by middle managers from approximately 825 companies in 62 countries. The GLOBE project broke the countries surveyed into ten clusters based on geography, common language, religion and historical factors. The ten GLOBE clusters are:

- Anglo
- Latin Europe
- Nordic Europe
- Germanic Europe
- Eastern Europe
- Latin America
- Sub-Saharan Africa
- Arab
- Southern Asia
- Confusian Asia.

Building on Hofstede and others' work on cultural influences on behaviour, the GLOBE study distinguishes nine cultural dimensions, as set out in the following table:

Table: The Globe Dimensions.

Globe Dimension	Description	Examples
Assertiveness	The degree to which a culture encourages individuals to be confrontational and competitive as opposed to modest and accommodating.	High-scoring cultures (e.g. USA, Austria) value competition and show sympathy for strong people. Low-scoring cultures (e.g. Sweden, New Zealand) value cooperation and solidarity. They show sympathy for the underprivileged.

Future orientation	The degree to which a culture encourages such future oriented practices as investing, planning and delaying gratification.	High-scoring cultures (e.g. Singapore, the Netherlands) have a higher tendency to save and plan for the future. Low-scoring cultures (e.g. Italy, Russia) tend to make shorter term plans and to value immediate gratification.
Gender differentiation	The degree to which a culture emphasizes gender roles.	High-scoring cultures (e.g. South Korea, China) favour traditional gender dichotomies. They tend to accord males higher social status than females. Low-scoring cultures (e.g. Poland, Denmark) do not favour strict gender dichotomies and tend to give females a stronger 'voice' in decision making.
Uncertainty avoidance	The degree to which a culture uses rules and procedures to counteract unpredictability.	High-scoring cultures (e.g. Sweden, Germany) favour predictability and consistency, and have clear specifications of social expectations. Low-scoring cultures (e.g. Russia, Greece) tolerate ambiguity and uncertainty more, and have less structured social expectations.
Power distance	The degree to which a culture distributes power unequally.	High-scoring cultures (e.g. Thailand, Spain) clearly distinguish between those with and those without power, and expect obedience towards superiors. Low-scoring cultures (e.g. Denmark, the Netherlands) favour stronger participation in decision making and expect a more equal distribution of power.
Collectivism versus individualism	The degree to which a culture expects individuals to be integrated in groups and categories.	High-individualism scoring cultures (e.g. Italy, Greece) value self-interest, and reward individual performance. Highcollectivism scoring cultures (e.g. Japan, South Korea) value similarity rather than difference, and are more likely to classify and group individuals, They tend to favour the collective good and cooperation more than individual autonomy.
In-group collectivism	The degree to which a culture expects individuals to belong to non-organisational groups, such as family units and circles of friends.	High-scoring cultures (e.g. India, China) favour belonging to an in-group of family or friends. Nepotism (favouring one's relatives and friends in work situations) is common in such cultures, as is foregoing work commitments for family or personal reasons. Low-scoring cultures (e.g. Denmark, New Zealand) do not favour in- groups and individuals are not pressured to ignore work commitments for family or personal reasons.

Performance orientation	The degree to which a culture rewards individuals for performance improvement and excellence.	High-scoring cultures (e.g. Singapore, USA) value initiative and a 'can-do' attitude. They favour a direct style of communication. Low-scoring cultures (e.g. Russia, Italy) tend to value loyalty and belonging, emphasising tradition and an individual's background rather than performance. These cultures tend to see feedback as negative, and associate competition with defeat.
Humane orientation	The degree to which a culture rewards altruism, generosity and a caring attitude.	High-scoring cultures (e.g. Malaysia, Ireland) value human relations, sympathy and support for the weak or underprivileged. Low-scoring cultures (e.g. France, Germany) value power and material possessions as motivators. They tend to prefer assertive styles of conflict resolution, and expect individuals to solve their own problems.

Probably the first impression one would get from this classification is that it is based largely on stereotype. In fact, in many ways it is reminiscent of such generalizations as 'Southern Europeans are emotional', 'Scandinavians are well-organised', etc. In addition, as we discussed earlier regarding survey-based research, answers to questionnaires carry the risk that respondents may not have been truthful or that what they understood by particular terms may not be what the researcher intended. Also, the clustering itself may be based on assumptions that are quite arbitrary or at least not self-evident. For example, the GLOBE model classifies Japan as Confucian Asia – but how Confucian is Japan actually? Latin Europe includes Israel – but does Israel really have enough similarities with France, Italy and Spain to justify its inclusion in this cluster?

On the other hand, there is little doubt that such research is useful in bringing to light possible group reactions to situations, and in indicating the similarities and differences among these reactions. Classifying individual attitudes also plays an instrumental role in being able to talk about and understand these attitudes. In fact, the process of categorizing is part of human mental and cognitive make-up and is vital in the ability to reflect upon the objective world. The popularity of cultural models in business consulting and executive professional development courses shows that they are perceived as relevant and useful by industry practitioners.

As cognitive scientists Glass and Holyoak point out:

If each experience were given a unique mental representation, we would be quickly overwhelmed. By encoding experiences into an organized system of categories, we are able to recognize significant commonalities in different experiences.

What do these considerations imply for cultural influence on professional communication? Allowing for the fact that cultural models are general and therefore approximate, and also that the dichotomies they distinguish are two ends of a continuum and not disconnected polar opposites, such models are useful in analyzing how different organizational structures and policies are often influenced by cultural values and expectations. Therefore, if they are used as analytical tools as opposed to as vehicles for negative stereotyping, they do have a role to play in helping to prevent cultural misunderstandings, acknowledge diversity, and enhance international collaboration.

Collaboration and misunderstandings, however, do not occur only between different cultures; they occur as part of any interpersonal act of communication. How these social phenomena play out among team members is the topic of the next section.

Groups and Teams

This section looks at the ways humans communicate in a group situation. Research in group interaction has shown that, when formed, a group attains its own identity that exists irrespective of the identities or personal characteristics of each individual member. A group has a 'personality' of its own, so to speak. At the same time, the group with which one identifies or is a member of has a great effect in the individual's identity and social potential. As Hogg and Abrams point out, 'the groups to which people belong will be massively significant in determining their life experience'.

Teams are also groups, but it is important to distinguish between a group and a team. As defined by Hogg and Abrams, a group comprises a number of individuals who 'perceive themselves to be members of the same social category'. So, groups include those who share the same ethnicity, those who share the same gender, those who share the same music tastes, those who share the same sexual orientation, and those who share the same hobby – to name just a few possibilities. Teams, on the other hand, are groups that have been formed for a specific purpose or task. The groups formed in work situations to carry out a project as well as the groups formed to play a game are examples of teams. A team may include members of different groups; people of different races, genders, sexual preferences and leisure tastes can come together to form a team for a purpose. Teams tend to have clear objectives, and more or less specified roles and duties, usually related to professional concerns. Since the aim of this chapter is to discuss interpersonal communication in business contexts, teams will be our main focus.

Team Dynamics

Those working in collaborative projects or in situations that require negotiation skills often use reasoning techniques to manage conflict and to sway others' opinions. The problem with this is that, in reality, issues of power play a major role in interpersonal communication, which means that many decisions are not made rationally. In fact, people are much more likely to respond positively to someone they believe is 'on their side', protects their interests, and shares their ideals than to someone who can produce a perfectly reasoned argument.

At their best, teams can produce excellent results by combining the specialised skills that individual team members bring. At their worst, teams produce delays, misunderstandings, At their best, teams can produce excellent results by combining the specialised skills that individual team members bring. At their worst, teams produce delays, misunderstandings, and conflicts. For this reason, the ability to deal productively with other people, peers, juniors and superiors is a highly valued skill that contributes greatly to the smooth and successful management of an organization.

Teams can be effective problem solvers for many reasons, including:

- More extensive information is available in a team than an individual may have alone.
- Individuals bring different approaches to a problem within the team. This allows for a wide range of options to be considered.
- Improved understanding of the problem and possible solutions is possible, because team members are aware of the reasoning used in problem analysis.
- It is more likely that consensus will be achieved if a decision was made in consultation with members of the team, so that no one feels 'left out', and therefore is not likely to oppose a decision.
- Risks can often be managed more effectively in teams. What can be a high-risk decision for an individual could actually be a moderate-risk decision for a team, because different team members bring new knowledge to the issue, and because risk is often a function of knowledge.
- Motivation and confidence are likely to increase in decisions made in team situations because individual team members feel supported by others.

Major disadvantages of reaching important decisions as part of a team include:

- Decisions can be made too soon: teams that feel uncomfortable with conflict may decide on the first option which meets with some support from the team members, regardless of whether this would be the best option.
- On the other hand, decisions can take too long, if the team cannot agree on a topic.
- If the team structure is too democratic, there may be a lack of initiative and responsibility.
- Teams may be influenced by one person, whose charismatic or persuasive strengths may induce members to overlook pertinent factors in the problem involved.

- If there is too much conflict in a team, the team may become inoperable or ineffective.
- Teams may displace responsibility so that it may be difficult to hold a team or an individual member accountable for a negative outcome.

Good team dynamics are generally achieved in three main ways:

- Members are attracted to the team's purpose.
- Members share similar values, needs and interests.
- Members fulfil for each other important interpersonal needs, such as affection (acknowledging each other's point of view), inclusion (allowing each member to play a role in activities) and control (allowing each member to determine certain actions pertinent to the member's role).

Individuals participate in teams through the roles they play in them. Researchers have formulated different classifications of the role structure of teams. Two commonly used models are the Task-Maintenance Classification and the Belbin Inventory of Team Roles.

The Task-Maintenance Classification divides team roles into two main categories: task roles and maintenance roles. Task roles represent the actions members must take to accomplish specific goals, and include the roles of 'information giver', 'information seeker', 'expediter' and 'analyzer'. Maintenance roles represent the types of behaviour that each member must exhibit to keep the group functioning smoothly, and include the positive roles of 'supporter', 'harmonizer', 'gatekeeper', and the negative roles of 'aggressor', 'joker', 'withdrawer' and 'monopolizer'.

It should be emphasized that all these roles are inclusive, in the sense that each member can play one or more roles within one team. The roles are defined in terms of what the team members do in response to situations that arise in the team interaction, not in terms of who the team members are, as in personality characteristics. Consider each role in more detail.

Task Roles

- The information giver: This role entails providing content for discussion. Because the function of a team is most often to discuss or analyze and work with information, this role is the foundation of the team; usually all members play this role, unless one member is specifically assigned to present information from sources that s/he has researched. Information givers need to be well-prepared by having consulted various sources and having thought about the issue carefully before participating in a meeting. In business settings, the more objective and evidence-supported a team member's opinion is, the more this member's information giving role is appreciated and effective in influencing the team.

- The information seeker: This role entails asking for more information or clarifications on an issue. Information seekers protect the team from reaching a decision before all sides have been considered, by eliciting more details and explanations on the issue. Again, in many teams, more than one person may assume the role of information seeker.
- The expediter: This role entails keeping the team on track. Although digressions are sometimes useful in enlarging the scope of an issue or brainstorming alternative viewpoints, they are just as often a hindrance to the smooth functioning of team dynamics. The expediters help the group stick to the agenda, by asking for relevance.
- The analyzer: This role entails analyzing the issue in depth by probing both information content and line of reasoning. Analyzers point out that the group has skipped a point, passed over a point too lightly or not considered pertinent information. Analyzers are important in acknowledging and addressing the complexity of an issue. Methods of analyzers include asking questions that test the data presented, and asking for definitions and alternative viewpoints.

Maintenance Roles

- The supporter: The supporter recognizes the contribution of team members and shows appreciation for their input. Supporters' methods are usually encouraging comments, or non-verbal cues, such as a smile or a nod.
- The harmonizer: The harmonizer attempts to resolve conflict by reducing tension and straightening out misunderstandings and disagreements. This person tries to cool down high emotions by introducing objectivity in the discussion and mediating between hostile or opposing sides.
- The gatekeeper: From the point of view of the consumer or client, gatekeepers generally have a bad reputation as those that prevent access to a desired location, person or object. For example, the secretary through whom we have to pass to reach the company president is a gatekeeper. In broadcasting, programming managers are gatekeepers in selecting the programs we watch or listen to, thereby channelling and restricting our options. From the point of view of management or team dynamics, however, gatekeepers are significant in monitoring that all eligible parties have equal access to a decision making process, and in keeping communication channels between different parties open. In meetings, for instance, gatekeepers keep in check those who tend to dominate, and encourage those that are reluctant to contribute to be more forthcoming.
- The aggressor: Aggressors produce conflict in a group by constantly or inordinately criticizing others' opinions or behaviour, and by making personal attacks

when they do not agree on a point. One way to counteract aggressors is to take them aside and describe to them what they are doing, and the effect it is having on team dynamics.

- The joker: Jokers produce conflict by ridiculing or playing down others' opinions or behaviour, or by making complex topics look light-hearted when in fact they need to be taken seriously. Humour is a positive factor in team dynamics helping members to keep their spirits up and see the optimistic side of things. However, if humour is inappropriate, inconsiderate or offensive, it needs to be kept in check to avoid irritation or resentment. Like with aggressors, the best way to deal with jokers is to make them aware of what they are doing.
- The withdrawer: Withdrawers refuse to contribute to the team, usually out of lack of interest, lack of confidence, or inadequate preparation. Some ways to deal with withdrawers include asking them questions, finding out what they are good at and making sure that they are given the opportunity to contribute in that area, and acknowledging their positive contributions.
- The monopolizer: Monopolizers dominate discussions by voicing an opinion about everything said, and interrupting or not allowing others to make a contribution. In some cases monopolizers try to impress the team with their skills or knowledge; in other cases, they try to compensate for a lack of confidence by asking too many (often irrelevant) questions, or trying to answer every question to prove their competence. When they are genuinely knowledgeable, monopolizers can be beneficial because they help to direct the group. When they get disruptive or intimidating, however, they should be interrupted and others drawn into the discussion.

The second model we examine here is the one formulated by communication researcher Meredith Belbin. Belbin constructed a typology of roles of participants in team interactions – the Belbin Inventory. In this, he distinguished nine team roles:

- The Plant: These are 'ideas people', innovators and inventors, who provide the foundations from which major developments emerge. They are often eccentric, working alone, and approaching problems in an unconventional way. Although clever and competent, these roles are not good at social communication. As their function is often to generate proposals and solve complex problems, they are needed in the initial stages of a project or when a project is failing to progress. One plant in a team is usually enough, since plants tend not to be co-operative but focus more on reinforcing their own ideas and challenging each other.
- The Resource Investigator: These are good at communicating, both within and outside the group, negotiating, and exploring links with different contacts. They are generally not a source of original ideas, but are adept at picking up and exploiting other people's ideas. They have a practical inclination, which gives

them the skill to find out what is available and how it can be used. Resource investigators are inquisitive and ready to see new possibilities, but they need to remain stimulated and part of an approving team. Their function in a team is to explore and report back on ideas, developments and resources outside their group.

- The Monitor Evaluator: These are the 'down to earth' contributors, whose main function is to analyze and evaluate information. They tend to have a high critical thinking ability and capacity for shrewd judgments. They also need a good eye for objectively evaluating the advantages and disadvantages of a situation. A team with a plant and a resource investigator but no monitor evaluator would be at a serious disadvantage, because it is the monitor evaluator that steers the group in practical ways, and helps the members reach hard decisions.
- The Coordinator: These are distinguished by their ability to encourage others to work towards shared goals. Coordinators need to be trusting and confident, since they have to delegate duties. They need to detect individual talents and use them productively in the pursuit of shared goals. They should have the ability to manage people and command respect. In teams that have diverse skills and characteristics, coordinators are very important because they can bring together the team's different features for more harmonious and effective cooperation.
- The Shaper: These have a directive function and perform the duties of leaders in the team. They tend to be highly motivated with a strong sense of achievement and energy drive. They have a winner's mentality, and, although they are resourceful in overcoming obstacles, they can also exhibit strong emotional reactions to disappointment and frustration. They do not delve on the maintenance tasks of the group, aiming instead at achieving their objectives and those of the group. They generate action and thrive under pressure, so they can enthuse the members of a team and can be useful in teams where political complications tend to slow the pace. They are well-suited to change, and do not hesitate to take unpopular decisions. As their name suggests, they forge a shape on group discussions and activities, and are the most effective members in guaranteeing positive action.
- The Team Worker: These are the most supportive members of a team. Their skills include flexibility, tact, intuition and sensitivity. They are good listeners and are generally popular in the team. The major problem of team workers is indecisiveness: they tend to leave important decisions to others. Their role is to prevent interpersonal conflict within the team and thus allow members to function effectively. They complement shapers, who are not inclined to consider the team cohesion. The presence of team workers in a team improves morale and co-operation.

- The Implementer: These are disciplined and practical. Although they can be inflexible, they are systematic, which makes them work for the group's interests. They tend to be reliable and apply themselves to the problem at hand. Implementers tend to do what needs to be done, and they have an eye for relevance.
- The Completer-Finisher: These are able to follow-through with projects, and tend to start only what they can finish. Typically, they do not require external stimuli but are self-sufficient and self-motivated. They tend to be intolerant of those who lack perseverance, or exhibit a casual attitude to the project. They tend not to delegate, preferring to complete tasks by themselves, and they generally complete projects by set deadlines.
- The Specialist: These have expert knowledge and technical skills in a specific area. They tend to be self-sufficient, lacking interest in others' work. They maintain professional standards and are keen to further knowledge in their field. In a team, specialists provide the knowledge base and command support because they know more about their field than other members, so they are often called upon to make decisions based on their experience. In some teams, every member is a specialist in his/her own fields. In this case, each member combines this role with another role to maintain cohesion.

As was noted also with the previous model, these roles are not always exclusive, and an individual can play more than one in a single group, depending on the situation. Individual characteristics, such as 'personality traits', do play a part in the allocation of roles. However, it is mostly the demands of the project, and contextual factors, such as the hierarchy of the organization, its values, etc, as well as practical concerns, such as time and money, which have the final say in who plays what role.

Collaboration

Apart from the leader's role, which is usually assigned, the above described team roles typify individual practices that take place in meetings and discussions. They describe forms of behaviour, usually reflected in language but also in non-verbal communication, that can be exhibited by any team member. Another aspect of teamwork is the formally implemented system for duty allocation, negotiation, delegation of duties, monitoring of progress and feedback; in other words, methods of collaboration.

Three types of collaboration that are commonly used in business and industry contexts are the sequential, the functional and the mix-and-match.

Sequential Collaboration

In this type, each department/section in a company, or person in a group for smaller projects, is assigned a specific, non-overlapping, responsibility in the project. For example, in a software company, three departments are sometimes involved in producing the user documentation:

- Software specialists assemble the material;
- Communication specialists are in charge of word processing and designing; and
- The art and printing department is responsible for publishing the documentation.

In this case, each department must finish its job before passing the material to another department for the next stage.

The sequential type of collaboration can be effective at times, especially when the work of each segment is specialized and each stage is self-sufficient. However, projects completed sequentially take longer than when other methods are employed, and a project manager is often necessary to coordinate the project and to ensure that deadlines are kept, all parties understand requirements, and transitions from one stage to the next are smooth.

Functional Collaboration

This type is organised according to the skills or job function of the members. All stages of a project are undertaken concurrently, and all parties can monitor procedures at each stage. For example, a four-person team carrying out a user documentation project for software might be organised as follows:

- A manager schedules and conducts meetings, assists team members, issues progress reports to management, solves problems by proposing alternatives, and generally coordinates efforts to keep the project on schedule.
- A researcher collects data, conducts interviews, searches the literature, administers tests, gathers and classifies information, and then prepares notes on the work.
- A writer/editor receives the researcher's notes, prepares outlines and drafts, and circulates them for corrections and revisions.
- A graphics expert obtains and prepares all visuals, specifying why, how, and where visuals should be placed and designing the document layout. He or she might even suggest that visuals replace certain sections of text.

All parties work on the project at the same time, and interact regularly through meetings and e-mail communication.

Mix and Match Collaboration

In this type of collaboration, team members agree on shared objectives, and then work independently on separate sections of the project by undertaking all tasks. The team members meet at specified times to compare their work and choose the best samples from each other's work. This approach is constructive in smaller scale projects, when team members have similar skills but cannot meet regularly.

A different version of this approach occurs when all members share the same interactive software and can work on the same project concurrently, each contributing according to their own skills which may or may not overlap. Continuing our software documentation example, a mix and match type of collaboration could mean that members from the engineering, communication and art departments have the same software installed in their computers and work on the same documentation project at the same time, without waiting for one department to finish their tasks before passing the project to another department. This would most likely cut costs and reduce time, compared with the sequential model, but it would necessitate that all members work cooperatively, and that project milestones and outcomes are very clearly set out and agreed by all in advance (to reduce the risk of 'you're treading on my toes' symptom).

Conflict

Conflict is embedded in human relations. It arises when there is incompatibility of orientation between individuals or groups, and it can form in such situations as when people form incompatible goals and behaviours, when resources have to be allocated, and when decisions have to be made. Conflict is associated with:

- Value: underlying values are different. This is arguably the most important and serious type of conflict because values are entrenched in social interaction and behaviour, and are very difficult to change.
- Interests: what promotes one's self-interest opposes another's. For example, when two colleagues compete for the same promotion inevitably some degree of conflict will arise.
- Policy: existing regulations do not reflect current needs. This often manifests in cases where conflict leads to employees' strikes or group protests. This is what happens, for example, when prices increase but salaries remain static, leading to a strike, or when women have achieved breakthroughs in social equality but legislation regulating gender issues remains at a primitive level, leading to demonstrations, or ground breaking legal proceedings. Policy is very closely aligned with value.
- Goals: there is controversy or disagreement about where a project is going. In a project, for example, some members may think the goal is to produce routine results, whereas others may want to produce a radical breakthrough.
- Method: there is controversy or disagreement about how to arrive at the desired outcome. Such conflict may arise when one side has low uncertainty avoidance,

and therefore is more optimistic about the future, while the other side has high uncertainty avoidance and wants more control over a situation, leading them to choose high-risk methods (such as war over negotiation, for instance).

Managed properly, conflict can result in growth because it allows for different points of view to be aired and considered. Managed badly, it can be destructive and costly – in resources and relationships. Groups can suffer from two opposite evils: too little conflict, and too much conflict. A little conflict can be a good thing for change and rejuvenation of outmoded structures and beliefs. A lot of conflict, however, can destroy a project and in serious cases even lead to costly lawsuits and official investigations.

Avoiding Conflict: The Groupthink Syndrome

Sometimes people think that avoiding conflict at all costs is the best course of action in order to maintain harmony within a group or organisation. This attitude can often lead to a 'sweeping things under the carpet' approach, where serious differences in policy or value are politely ignored until they burst out violently and destructively. Yale sociologist Irving Janis studied such cases where wrong decisions are made about important matters because the interested parties did not consider options that were outside their established framework. He referred to misplaced conformity or agreement within a group as 'Groupthink' ('group' being for him a collectivity of individuals working together as decision-makers in large organizations).

Janis examined a number of 'fiascoes', historical cases where groups made ineffective decisions because they strived to reach consensus without taking into account possible risks or alternatives. In these cases he observed certain common features pointing to three categories and eight symptoms of group behaviour. These constitute the Groupthink syndrome, described in the table below:

Table: Groupthink

Type I: Overestimations of the group	
• Belief in being invincible	• The group believes it is invincible, which may lead to excessive optimism and unnecessary risk-taking.
• Belief in inherent morality	• Group members believe that their decisions are inherently moral, and brush away thoughts of unethical behaviour by assuming that they cannot do anything wrong.
Type II: Closed-mindedness	
• Attempts to rationalise about all issues	• Group members explain away warnings or threats.
• Stereotyping	• The group stereotypes opponents as being too evil, stupid, or too weak to take seriously.

Type III: Pressures towards uniformity	
• Self-censorship	• Group members with doubts censor themselves to preserve the appearance of consent.
• Belief in unanimity	• The group believes there is unanimity on an issue because nobody raises an objection.
• Direct pressure	• Group members apply direct pressure to conform to anyone who tries to question the status quo within the group.
• Imposing mind-guards	• Just as bodyguards protect from physical harm, so some group members set themselves as censors or gatekeepers in order to prevent challenging or threatening information available outside the group from appearing before the group.

Janis' findings supported his hypothesis that 'whenever a policy-making group displays most of the symptoms of groupthink, we can expect to find that the group also displays symptoms of defective decision-making'. Major signals indicating that a faulty decision-making process is at play include:

- The group has not fully considered alternatives.
- The group has not clearly examined objectives.
- The group has not taken into account the possible risks of their decision.
- The group has not re-evaluated alternatives that it rejected at a previous stage of the process.
- The group has not conducted a comprehensive information search, and may therefore be ignorant of important issues.
- The group has shown prejudice or bias in evaluating the information at hand.
- The group has not worked out what to do in an emergency or if their decision proves ineffective.

Assessing Conflict: The Thomas-Kilman Conflict Mode Instrument

Individuals react differently to conflict. In fact, different reactions are necessary to deal with different forms of conflict, different contexts, etc. An influential method of assessing these reactions to conflict was formulated by Kenneth Thomas and Ralph Kilmann, and is known as the Thomas-Kilmann Conflict Mode Instrument.

Thomas and Kilmann examined individual reactions in situations involving conflict and described their behaviour using two axes, 1) assertiveness, the extended to which the individual attempts to satisfy his/her interests, and 2) cooperativeness, the extent to which the individual attempts to satisfy the other person's interests. They then used these axes to define five modes, or methods, of dealing with conflicts: competing, collaborating, compromising, avoiding and accommodating. No mode is better or worse than another per se; rather, each mode is appropriate in certain situations but inappropriate in others, and successful conflict management depends on knowing which to choose and when. Here are some more details on each mode.

- Competing: This mode is assertive and uncooperative. The person pursues his/her own concerns usually at the other person's expense, using whatever power seems appropriate towards this end. Competing may mean standing up for one's rights, defending a position one believes is correct, or simply trying to win. Cases where competing would be appropriate include:
    - In emergency situations where decisive action is required.
    - When unpopular courses of action need to be implemented.
    - As a safeguard when non-competitive behaviour is exploited.
- Accommodating: This is the opposite of competing – unassertive and cooperative. The person sacrifices his/her own concerns to satisfy the concerns of the other person. This includes selfless generosity or charity, obeying a command when one would prefer not to, or yielding to another's point of view. Cases where accommodating would be appropriate include:
    - When one realizes one is wrong.
    - When the issue is not important to one but important to the other person.
    - When continued competition would damage one's cause; for example, when one's opinion is outnumbered by the opposite view.
    - When preserving harmony is especially important.
- Avoiding: This mode is unassertive and uncooperative. The person does not pursue his/her concerns directly nor does s/he yield to the other person. Rather s/he does not address the conflict. This might take the form of diplomatically side-stepping an issue, postponing an issue until a better time, or simply withdrawing from a threatening situation. Cases where avoiding would be appropriate include:
    - When an issue is not as important as others at one time.
    - When there is no chance to satisfy one's concerns; for example, in cases of low power or when confronted by a situation where one's sphere of influence is diminished.
    - When the costs of confronting a conflict outweigh the benefits of resolving it.

    - When the situation involves high risk and more information is important in assessing the advantages of a decision.
    - When the issue is symptomatic of a more fundamental issue.

- Collaborating: This is the opposite of avoiding – assertive and cooperative. The person attempts to work with another person to find a solution that satisfies the concerns of both. It attempts to identify the underlying concerns of both parties and to find an alternative that meets both sets of concerns. This includes exploring a disagreement to learn from each other's insights, resolving some condition that would otherwise have the two parties competing for resources, or confronting each other and trying to find a solution to a problem. Cases where collaborating would be appropriate include:
    - When the concerns of both parties are too important to be compromised.
    - When the objective is to learn by understanding the views of others.
    - To gain commitment from others by incorporating their concerns in a decision.
- Compromising: This is intermediate to assertiveness and cooperativeness. The person attempts to find an expedient, mutually acceptable solution that satisfies both parties. It includes addressing an issue more directly than avoiding, but not exploring this issue in as much depth as collaborating. It could mean exchanging concessions or seeking a middle ground. Cases where compromising is appropriate include:
    - When the goals are not worth the effort of the potential disruption involved in being more assertive.
    - When two opponents are equally committed and equally strong.
    - When there is time pressure and an expedient solution must be reached.

Conflict in Teams

Some teams are highly effective, while others never seem to get off the ground. When teams are not working well, it can be a very serious matter, costing the organisation money and time. While the reasons that make a team unproductive are not fixed or universal, there are some guidelines regarding what could not be working right that can be used to clarify the situation:

- The team may be lacking the required specialist skills to tackle a project expertly and confidently.
- The team may be lacking one or more vital roles.

- Members may feel their personal skills are not appreciated and they may lose motivation (often the result of weak leadership or bad management).
- The team may feel their efforts will not be supported by authorities and funding agencies, especially if they are working under budget constraints and/or on obscure or unpopular projects.
- A conflict of values or expectations may exist where some team members may expect different results from the project or the team may be expecting different results from the management.
- The brief describing the objectives and scope of a project may be unclear, leading to confusion.
- Personal conflicts may hinder the achievement of goals. This is especially true of competitive environments where people are not accustomed to working cooperatively.

Managing Conflict in Teams

As it probably has become clear from the preceding discussion, managing conflict is no easy matter. In most aspects of interpersonal communication, contextual factors, such as the setting of the interaction, the background of the participants and the nature of the interaction, are important in pointing to the most appropriate reactions, and conflict management is no exception to this. However, as regards teamwork, which has been our main focus in the last two sections, a general process for managing conflict involves five steps:

- Define the problem:

  The definition of the problem is the most important step in finding a solution. In many cases there is low morale and a lack of commitment by team members because there is a problem that has not been voiced or made conscious within the group dynamics. An effective method of discussing the problem that caused this conflict is to describe it in writing. Each conflicting side should describe their perspective on the matter as clearly and as objectively as possible, avoiding 'I said / he said' type criticism. It is also important to avoid generalizations, such as 'they', 'always', 'never', etc, and to determine if the reaction is proportional to the situation. In describing the issue, consider if it had objective grounds to escalate into conflict, or if it is likely to have been caused by misunderstanding. Also examine the history of the situation and the participants: Are there leftover emotions, grudges from a previous event?

- Analyze the problem:

  Once the group agrees on the nature of the problem, the next step is to analyze it in terms of size, causes and criteria of evaluation. At this stage, it is important not to succumb to the temptation of listing possible solutions before having analyzed the problem thoroughly. Before answering the question 'what can be done to solve the conflict', team members should answer 'why is this a conflict?' and 'for whom is it a conflict?'

- Generate possible solutions:

  Brainstorming is usually an effective way to generate ideas that could lead to the resolution of the conflict. At this stage, evaluation or nitpicking criticism of ideas should be avoided, and team members should produce as many possible solutions as they can.

- Evaluate and test the various solutions:

  After the brainstorming stage, each possible resolution should be examined to ascertain its merits and drawbacks. Factors to consider carefully include if the solutions are likely to work, if they are fair to all, and if they can be implemented easily. This should eliminate the solutions that are not worthwhile and leave a reduced number of options.

- Choose a mutually acceptable solution:

  From the reduced number of possible solutions the one that seems to be the most effective can be chosen for a trial period. The best way to articulate this would be, once again, in writing. At times choosing an option is a risky act, with no guarantees that the selected solution will work. However, if the decision was reached by (relative) consensus (while avoiding the traps of Groupthink), all the parties involved will be responsible for testing it and providing feedback.

Effective Listening

Effective listening contributes enormously to group dynamics and conflict resolution. In interpersonal communication, poor listening skills are at fault in many, if not most, cases of misunderstanding.

When working with others, much of the communication that takes place when suggesting, instructing, requesting, criticising, praising and negotiating is non-verbal. Listening actively by making a physical and mental effort to understand what someone else is saying engages the whole body, not just ears.

It is a way of communicating that signifies:

- You hear what you are feeling
- You understand how you see things now
- You are interested and concerned

- You understand where you are
- You do not wish to judge you or change you.

Here are seven tips for active listening:

- Stop talking – don't be afraid of silence: Many people talk too much because they feel uncomfortable with silence. However, you can't listen if you are talking.
- Remove noise as much possible: 'Noise' is used in the communications sense of distractions to the unhindered transmission of the message. Therefore, it refers not only to external factors such as street noise, but also other factors, such as excessive heat or cold, and distracting mannerisms. Common distracting mannerisms include clicking pens, shuffling papers, checking clothing or fingernails, and gazing around the room. If you need to talk to a team member or colleague about something serious, it is advisable to arrange a meeting in pleasant and relaxed surroundings.
- Ask open questions: which begin with the 5Ws and 1H: what, when, why, where, who and how. This helps to keep the conversation on the topic and to obtain as much information as possible on it. When people answer W and H questions they have to reply in full sentences, and so their replies are more factual than they would be if the questions were of the 'Do you' type, which elicits, simpler 'yes-no' answers.
- Be supportive: Let the other person know that you want to know what he or she is talking about. It is well attested that most people will talk if they get attention and interest from the listener. Sensing indifference or impatience discourages a constructive response.
- Respond to feelings: If the situation at hand has an emotional investment by one or all the participants, it is best to acknowledge this. Hidden or 'bottled' feelings may cloud or sabotage the information you require.
- Summarise to check mutual understanding: A summary ensures that both parties have the same understanding of what has been said, and helps to create closure to an issue or topic of discussion. In business, for example, a summary is formalised in a Memorandum of Understanding listing the points that have been agreed upon in a previous discussion.

Information Management

'Information management' refers broadly to the systematic and deliberate accessing and organizing of the knowledge that all the members of a company possess. The concept behind information management is that tapping into available (but sometimes hidden) mental resources and skills can lead to reaping substantial benefits. The value of information management practices has been aptly captured by an often quoted remark by Lew Platt, former Chief Executive Officer of Hewlett-Packard: 'If Hewlett-Packard knew what it knows, we'd be three times as profitable'.

Several examples have been documented to support the positive effect of information management initiatives. For example, IBM held a brainstorming session with all its employees, in May 2001, called World Jam. This produced about 6000 ideas suggested by approximately 52,000 employees. The ideas were recorded in an online archive that can be accessed by staff. Also, a British company set up an interactive voicemail system, called 'what's hot and what's not'. Employees contributed short news items about customers, technology and products, and these could be accessed on cell phones by all company staff. Finally, Xerox employees who encounter a problem that is not mentioned in product documentation can enter a description and analysis of this problem in a database called Eureka. This database can be accessed by Xerox representatives worldwide and provides valuable assistance in dealing swiftly with product glitches.

Such initiatives have fuelled an interest in the general nature of information and knowledge, and in how knowledge is communicated in business settings. A useful model for analyzing the processes involved in knowledge acquisition was formulated by Takeuchi and Nonaka. This has a spiral pattern, going through four sequences, Socialisation – Externalisation – Combination – Internalisation (SECI). This model is based on a distinction between explicit knowledge, that is, knowledge that exists in the public domain, or the external world, and tacit knowledge, that is, knowledge that belongs to particular specialist groups or individuals. The model encompasses the following phases involved in knowledge acquisition:

1. Socialisation (tacit-to-tacit): This is what happens when those involved in a project do not have enough insider or specialist knowledge to accomplish the task and need training to acquire this knowledge. An example would be software engineers designing a new program aimed to monitor the heart and general health condition of mountain climbers. Unless the engineers are mountain climbers themselves, they would not be aware of such vital information as clothing, occupational habits and body movements of climbers; and lack of such knowledge would hinder them from designing equipment that would be effective in being portable and in recording accurate data on the health of the climbers. What the engineers would have to do, therefore, would be to obtain information from climbers through interviews, observations, etc. This would be a case of socialisation: a systematic transfer of knowledge by means of interviewing, observation, on-the-job-training, coaching and mentoring.
2. Externalisation (tacit-to-explicit): In this second phase, what starts off as peripheral data becomes central in solving a problem or dealing with an issue. Continuing the above example, having obtained the necessary information from mountain climbers, the engineers are faced with the problem of what material

to use for containing their software. They need something light enough to be carried around unobtrusively while at the same time strong enough to withstand extreme changes in temperature (when the users are climbing mountains in very hot or freezing climates). To solve thc problem they build virtual simulations and experiment with different materials, they brainstorm ideas, they connect with colleagues in a different department of the company who have worked on similar projects in the past, and they form hypotheses, which they then test. All this activity represents the externalization phase of the acquisition of knowledge. From the data they gather during this process, the engineers are able to determine the appropriate material to encase their software.

3. Combination (explicit to explicit): In this stage, the knowledge acquired during the previous phases is put to practice, tried out and publicized to allow for revision and integration. The software engineers in our example have now created their software and are combining the new knowledge they have created with the knowledge that already exists. They write an article for a specialist journal and present a paper at a conference, describing what they have accomplished and how this differs from or is similar to other software in related areas. More importantly, they present their product to the mountain climbers who will be using it, and make a trial experiment. They take on board suggestions and criticisms for consideration. This activity represents the combination phase of the acquisition of knowledge.

4. Intrernalisation (explicit-to-tacit): This final phase of the SECI sequence completes the cycle. The knowledge gained in the previous phases through interaction with others becomes specialist knowledge. The engineers have established an evaluation plan, which will help them to get feedback from the practical applications of their product (this could take the form, say, of meeting twice yearly with the group of mountain climbers over the next two years). Since the product is now in the market, the marketing section of the company have also established an interactive database to obtain feedback from users and retailers. This activity represents the internalisation stage of the acquisition of knowledge.

Information management has evolved since the mid-90s in line with technological developments, mainly because computer technology has allowed new ways of information retrieval, allocation and storage. Databases that store information from across an organization at a central place, Intranet sites and blogs to which a large number of individuals can contribute are all examples of information management schemes.

Quality Indicators of Information

Information management, its functioning and effectiveness, is also dependent on the quality of information collected. Gathering and classifying a large amount of information is not enough, or even appropriate, to make this information effective, usable or credible. Evaluating the quality of information, therefore becomes key. Organizational analyst Harold Wilensky proposed a useful model for evaluating information that has been constructively used by researchers since its formulation. In this model, Wilenski distinguishes six criteria for high-quality information: clarity, timeliness, reliability, validity, depth, and diversity.

- Clarity: Information must be easily understandable by its intended receivers; also enough information must be given to allow receivers to interpret it within a meaningful context. Clarity is defined from the point of view of the receiver, so audience analysis assumes an important role. In the Challenger example, engineers could have tried to make specialist concepts clear to non-specialist receivers in order to better convey the urgent nature of the situation.
- Timeliness: Information must be available when needed, and must be kept up to date. For example, in areas afflicted by earthquakes, the government must have enough information about how to handle such a natural disaster before an earthquake actually occurs, and must receive updates of this information as new scientific findings become available.
- Reliability: Information must be accurate, unambiguous and consistent so that those that use it to take action will not be faced with contradictory or vague directives and regulations. Recording sources, double-checking and revising data are important tasks for ensuring reliability.
- Validity: Information must be unbiased and closely reflect existing conditions. For example, when statistical analyses are conducted, it is important to ensure the sample population was not selected deliberately to favour particular conclusions that represent the interests of certain groups. Recording sources (e.g. stating where the statistics came from), and justifying hypotheses and conclusions are important tasks in ensuring validity.
- Depth: Information must be comprehensive, taking into account all relevant facts, issues and options about the situation. Although this is of course very important in making the information effective, at the same time care must also be taken not to include too much information, as this may result in overload. The challenge here is to gather comprehensive information while maintaining time limits, so that the information is not out dated by the time it is communicated.
- Diversity: Information must come from a variety of sources and include different viewpoints and angles. This indicator too must be used with care, keeping in mind that not all sources of information are equally credible or valid. Often trying to gather as much information as possible about a topic can lead to scope creep, where a project becomes expanded out of proportion with its initial objectives. Therefore, a balanced approach to information collection should be sought.

Project Management

A project in business and industry consists of a series of activities leading to one major goal or purpose. 'Project management' refers to the planning necessary to complete a major project on time, within budget, according to specifications, and with the consultation and consent of all relevant parties. Projects tend to be undertaken by a 'project team', a group of people responsible for managing a project. Projects usually begin with a proposal and end with a completed outcome, and a final report showing how the initial goals were reached or not. During the progress of a project, the team is generally required to submit progress reports at specified times (such as monthly or bi - monthly), in order to keep management informed of what has been achieved and what still remains to be done.

Components of Effective Project Management

A project is carefully defined as the first step. Aspects of project definition include:

- Problem definition: is the project attempting to solve a problem? For whom is this a problem? How is the problem defined?
- Scope: what issues or topics will the project cover? How much detail will it provide? What are the parameters that project team members have to work within?
- Outcome: what will be the result of the project? For example, if a computer system is being developed, what functions should it perform and to what standard?
- Resources: what advantages do the team have in undertaking the project? Are they highly skilled? Do they have a large budget? Do they have adequate time to complete all the tasks? Is up-to-date technology available to them?
- Constraints: is the budget modest? Is the staff limited, in numbers or in knowledge? Are there tight deadlines? Is there a lack of appropriate technology?
- Risks: what are the possible dangers of the project and what can be done to minimize them?
- Planning: Each step in the process is planned before further action is taken.

Tasks (activities representing one step towards the completion of a project) undertaken in the planning stage include:

- Identifying the steps required to complete the project
- Listing the priorities: What should be done first, second, third?
- Identifying dependent and independent tasks: Which tasks need to be put aside while other tasks are being completed? Which tasks are urgent, and which may

be delayed without damaging the project? Project Managers usually divide tasks into three categories:

- A critical task must be completed on time for the entire project to be completed on time.
- A milestone is an event that signifies the accomplishment of a series of tasks during a project. A milestone often signals the ending of a stage or section in the development of the project.
- A deliverable is a concrete object produced at a specific stages in the project (and usually delivered to a manager of client). Deliverables are used in some types of project management, like, for example, software design and engineering. For example, the systems requirements report, produced near the beginning of the project and describing what the projected software will achieve, is a deliverable.

- Creating a timeline for task completion and allocating roles to project team members.

Direction: Each project is directed according to a line of responsibility. Project managers are responsible for monitoring and controlling progress and activities. Members of the project team report to managers, who in turn report to upper level management and clients. Team members who are able to meet all the requirements of the project at a minimum cost and on time are highly valued.

Two particular dangers to watch out for in project management are known as scope creep and feature creep. Both of these can lead to delays, incomplete projects and conflicts within the project team.

Scope creep is exemplified by the tendency of stakeholders to expect more and more from the outcome of the project as the project progresses. For example, businesses and users might expect increasing functionality and performance from a computer system as the process of developing the system unfolds.

Feature creep refers to the tendency to add more and more features and details to the expected product of the project without bearing in mind that the incorporation of these features will take extra time and money. The type of project determines what kind of feature creep may exist. In software design, for example, feature creep leads to the uncontrolled addition of technical features to the software under development. In a personal project, such as writing a university assignment, feature creep might refer to the tendency to obsessively perfect the details rather than the major requirements of the assignment.

Feedback in Project Management

Team projects need to be monitored to ensure they are progressing satisfactorily. Communication among team members is essential in appraising the development of the allocated tasks, solving disputes and coming up with alternative courses of action when necessary. Unfortunately, feedback is not an easy matter. Personal concerns often cloud objective assessment of a situation, and projects are obstructed because of communication breakdown and individual idiosyncrasy of team members. Communication experts tend to concur on some general guidelines for giving and receiving feedback.

When giving feedback:

- Feedback should not be personal. All critical comments should be focused on behaviour within a professional context, not on personal aspects.
- Positive remarks should be included, and specific examples that are relevant to the project aims should be given.
- Feedback should be given soon after the particular situation, but at a time when it is likely to be received well. In many cases, if a problematic situation is allowed to continue for a long period, it might be very difficult to correct it later.
- Feedback should come in small doses and should focus on the main points. Commenting on everything that may be unacceptable in a situation can be counterproductive and may be perceived as hostile.
- In oral feedback, body language and tone of voice should be consistent with verbal comments. For example, praise should be accompanied by appropriate eye contact and tone of voice.

When receiving feedback:

- Time should be given between the feedback and the response. Impulsive responses are often not well thought out and, therefore, inappropriate. Care should also be taken to avoid defensive responses:
    - Diverting: "you think that many would say..."
    - Explaining: "That's because..."
    - Rejecting: "Yes, but..."
    - Discounting: "Gee, I didn't think you'd take this so seriously..."
    - Intellectualising: "The premises of your argument are conditional on..."
    - Attacking: "Who are you to make such comments..."
    - Whining: "If only I had more time, you'd..."
- It is important to understand clearly what the feedback is about and to ask for explanations when the feedback is unclear.

- It is also important, in cases where criticism is excessive and expectations unfairly demanding, to indicate that the point has been taken and no further comment is necessary ('enough is enough').

References

- Organizational-theory-and-behaviour: universityofcalicut.info, Retrieved 10 February, 2019
- Business-communication, directions-of-business-communication-explained, business-communication: yourarticlelibrary.com, Retrieved 18 April, 2019
- Oral-communication: managementstudyguide.com, Retrieved 19 January, 2019
- Written-communication: managementstudyguide.com, Retrieved 7 August, 2019
- Non-verbal-communication: managementstudyguide.com, Retrieved 6 May, 2019
- Communication: its.caltech.edu, Retrieved 4 March, 2019

4

Leadership in Organizations

Leadership in a group involves creating a vision and then influencing, motivating and transforming others in order to achieve that vision. Some of the different processes which are associated with leadership are assessment of the organization or business, development of strategy and integrated management of business performance. All these diverse principles of leadership have been carefully analyzed in this chapter.

Leader and its Characteristics

The ability to create a vision and influence, motivate, inspire and transform others to achieve certain goals towards that vision is known as leadership."

Leadership is the specific set of skills and attributes which can be acquired through learning.

Leader: A Leader is a person who guides others and motivates them to achieve specific goals to accomplish his vision.

Difference between Managers and Leaders:

Basis for Comparison	Manager	Leader
Position and Status	Managers are appointed personnel at official positions.	Any person can be a leader no matter what his position and status is.
Way of thinking	Controlled mindset	Out of the box thinking
Focus	Goal-oriented	People-oriented
Aim	Achieving targets	Accomplishing their vision
Objective	Getting the work done	Bringing some change
Tools	Power and control	Trust and honesty
Originality	Replica of one another, all doing the same thing	Original and individual personality
Attitude	Accept the existing situation and works accordingly	Challenge the existing situation and work to change the same
Perspective	Short term	Long term

Qualities of a Good Leader

A Good Leader has following qualities:

- Proactive
- Ability to Inspire
- Clear Vision
- Good Communication Skills
- Confident
- Self-Driven
- Decision Maker
- Responsible
- Learner
- Patient Listener
- Commitment
- Never Give Up Attitude
- Trustworthy.

Leadership Process

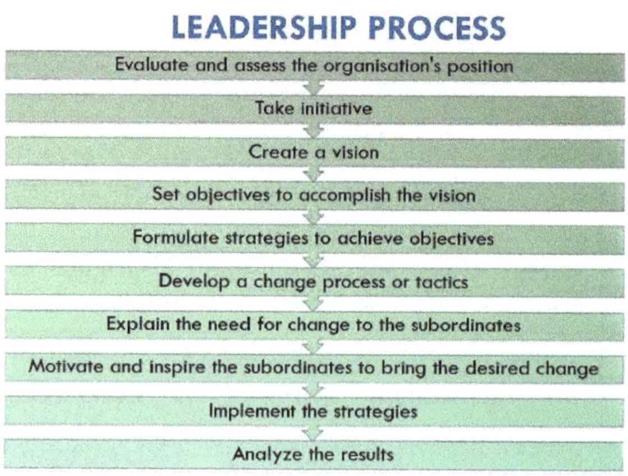

1. Evaluate and assess the organisation's position
2. Take initiative
3. Create a vision
4. Set objectives to accomplish the vision
5. Formulate strategies to achieve objectives
6. Develop a change process or tactics
7. Explain the need for change to the employees
8. Motivate and inspire the employees to bring the desired change
9. Implement the strategies
10. Analyze the results.

Leadership Styles

1. Supportive Leadership: Leaders are more attentive towards the welfare and individual needs of the subordinates.
2. Directive Leadership: Leaders establish the standards of performance for the subordinates and expect them to adhere to the rules and regulations. They provide complete guidance to the subordinates.
3. Achievement-oriented Leadership: Leaders usually set challenging goals for the subordinates, expecting their constant improvement in performance. They have confidence that the subordinates will perform excellently.

4. Participative or Democratic Leadership: Leaders invite opinions and suggestions from the subordinates while making decisions.
5. Autocratic or Authoritative Leadership: Leaders have the complete hold over the subordinates and do not entertain opinions, suggestions, questions and complains. They take all the decisions solely without the participation of subordinates.
6. Strategic Leadership: Strategic leaders frame a set of strategies towards their vision and motivate subordinates to accomplish that vision.
7. Charismatic Leadership: Charismatic Leader has an extraordinary and powerful personality and acts as a role model for his followers who follow him blindly.
8. Laissez-faire or Delegative Leadership: Leaders are lenient and assign authority and responsibility to the subordinates. The subordinates are free to work as they like to and take their own decisions with the minimal interference of the management. Laissez-faire is one of the least effective styles of leadership.
9. Transformational Leadership: Transformational Leaders initiates a revolutionary change in the behaviour, perception and attitude of the subordinates. They motivate and inspire the subordinates to develop their own skills to perform better and ultimately accomplish the vision of the organisation.
10. Transactional Leadership: Transactional Leaders believe in motivating subordinates through rewards and incentives and discouraging them through punishments.
11. Coaching Leadership: A Coaching Leader is well experienced in his role and is focussed on the long-term growth of his subordinates.
12. Cross-cultural Leadership: In today's global scenario, Cross-cultural Leaders keep themselves updated and aware of the different cultures around the world, and uses this knowledge to lead culturally diverse teams.
13. Visionary Leadership: A Visionary Leader communicates his vision for the organisation to his followers and intellectually influences them to become self-driven towards the shared vision.
14. Bureaucratic Leadership: Bureaucratic leaders use their position to exercise power and strict control over the subordinates. The subordinates have to be in complete discipline and are promoted on the basis of their capability to comply with the rules and regulations of the organisation.

Behind the success of every organisation there lies an effective leadership. Leadership involves the exercise of influence by one person over others. Wherever there is an organised group of Leaders are people who do the right thing; managers are people who do things right. – Professor Warren G. Bennis.

Leadership is the art of getting someone else to do something you want done because he wants to do it. – Dwight D. Eisenhower.

Leadership can be defined as an interpersonal influence directed toward the achievement of goals. Three important parts of this definition are the terms interpersonal, influence and goal.

- Interpersonal means between persons and thus, a leader has more than one person or group to lead.
- Influence is the power to affect others.
- Goal is the end one attempts to attain.

Characteristics of Leadership

- Empathy: Creating a legitimate rapport with your staff makes it less likely that personal issues and resentment can creep in and derail the group. When your team knows that you are empathetic to their concerns, they will be more likely to work with you and share in your vision, rather than foster negative feelings.
- Consistency: Being a consistent leader will gain you respect and credibility, which is essential to getting buy-in from the group. By setting an example of fairness and credibility, the team will want to act the same way.
- Honesty: Another characteristic of leadership that lends itself to credibility. Those who are honest, especially about concerns, make it far more likely that obstacles will be addressed rather than avoided. Honesty also allows for better assessment and growth.
- Direction: Having the vision to break out of the norm and aim for great things then the wherewithal to set the steps necessary to get there is an essential characteristic of good leadership. By seeing what can be and managing the goals on how to get there, a good leader can create impressive change.
- Communication: Effective communication helps keep he team working on the right projects with the right attitude. If you communicate effectively about expectations, issues and advice, your staff will be more likely to react and meet your goals.
- Flexibility: Not every problem demands the same solution. By being flexible to new ideas and open-minded enough to consider them, you increase the likelihood that you will find the best possible answer. You will set a good example for your team and reward good ideas.
- Conviction: A strong vision and the willingness to see it through is one of the most important characterizes of leadership. The leader who believes in the mission and works toward it will be an inspiration and a resource to their followers.

Factors of Leadership

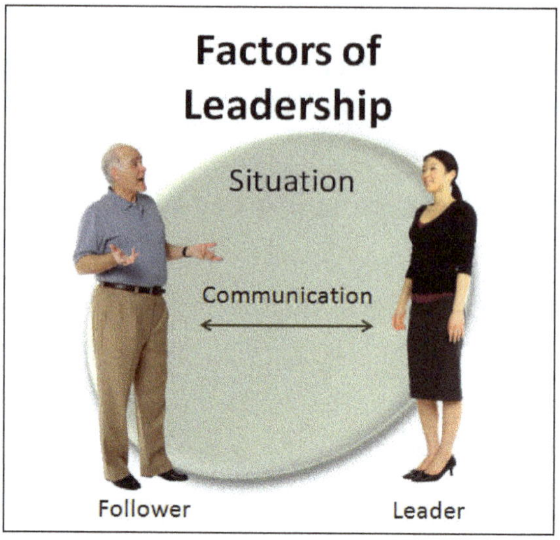

Leaders are people who are able to think and act creatively in abnormal situations and who set out to influence the ations, beliefs and feelings of others. There are four major factors in leadership.

1. Leader: Leader must have an honest understanding about himself, what he know, and what he can do. Also, note that it is the followers, not the leader or someone else who determines if the leader is successful. If they do not trust or lack confidence in their leader, then they will be uninspired. To be successful you have to convince your followers, not yourself or your superiors, that you are worthy of being followed.

2. Followers: Different people require different styles of leadership. For example, a new employee requires more supervision than an experienced employee does. A person who lacks motivation requires a different approach than one with a high degree of motivation. You must know your people! The fundamental starting point is having a good understanding of human nature, such as needs, emotions, and motivation. You must come to know your employees' be, know, and do attributes.

3. Communication: Leadership is possible only through two-way communication. Much of it is nonverbal. For instance, when you "set the example," that communicates to your people that you would not ask them to perform anything that you would not be willing to do. What and how you communicate either builds or harms the relationship between you and your followers.

4. Situation: All situations are different. What you do in one situation will not always work in another. Leader must use his judgment to decide the best course of action and the leadership style needed for each situation. For example, you

may need to confront an employee for inappropriate behaviour, but if the confrontation is too late or too early, too harsh or too weak, then the results may prove ineffective.

Qualities of a Successful Leader

Leadership is the ability to influence the behaviour of a group of individuals in a particular pattern. A leader should possess certain qualities which is helpful to influence the group for achieving the best results from individuals. Leadership traits can be divided in to two.

They are personal traits and management traits:

- Personal traits:
    - Intelligence
    - Self confidence
    - Foresight and vision
    - Initiative
    - Sound physique
    - Dynamic personality
    - Objectivity
    - Empathy
    - Responsibility
    - Emotional stability
    - Tact.
- Managerial Traits:
    - Technical knowledge
    - Organising ability
    - Ability to deal with people.

Importance of Leadership

Leadership plays an important role in making organisation successful. All organisations require leaders to lead the organisation. Leaders are able to build a team for achievement of organisational objectives. Without a good leader, organisation cannot function efficiently and effectively.

The importance of good leadership are following:

- Motivating employees
- Better utilisation of human resources
- Creating confidence
- Promoting the spirit of co-ordination
- Builds morale
- Directing group activity
- Develops good human relations
- Helps to fulfil social responsibilities.

Leadership Styles

From Mahatma Gandhi and Winston Churchill, to Martin Luther King and Steve Jobs, there can be as many ways to lead people as there are leaders. Fortunately, business-people and psychologists have developed useful frameworks that describe the main ways that people lead.

Lewin's Leadership Styles

Psychologist Kurt Lewin's developed his framework in the 1930s, and it provided the foundation of many of the approaches that followed afterwards. He argued that there are three major styles of leadership:

- Autocratic leaders make decisions without consulting their team members, even if their input would be useful. This can be appropriate when you need to make decisions quickly, when there's no need for team input, and when team agreement isn't necessary for a successful outcome. However, this style can be demoralizing, and it can lead to high levels of absenteeism and staff turnover. There are three types of autocratic leaders:
    - Strict autocrat – who follows autocratic style in a very strict sense. He influences subordinates through negative motivation like criticing subordinates', imposing penalty etc.
    - Benevolent autocrat – leader influences his subordinates through positive motivation. He uses reward and incentives in directing his subordinates towards these organisational goals.

- ◦ Manipulative autocrat – the autocrat leader tries to make the subordinate to feel that they are actually participating in decision making even though he had already take a decision.

- Democratic leaders - make the final decisions, but they include team members in the decision-making process. They encourage creativity, and people are often highly engaged in projects and decisions. As a result, team members tend to have high job satisfaction and high productivity. This is not always an effective style to use, though, when you need to make a quick decision.
- Laissez-faire or free rein - leaders give their team members a lot of freedom in how they do their work, and how they set their deadlines. They provide support with resources and advice if needed, but otherwise they don't get involved. This autonomy can lead to high job satisfaction, but it can be damaging if team members don't manage their time well, or if they don't have the knowledge, skills, or self-motivation to do their work effectively. (Laissezfaire leadership can also occur when managers don't have control over their work and their people.)
- Paternalistic leaderships - under this style leader assumes that his function is paternal or fatherly. Their relationship is same as father and family. The leader guides and protects his subordinates as members of his family. As the head of the family, the leader provides good working conditions and fringe benefits to his subordinates.

Leadership and Management

These are two notions that are often used interchangeably. Leadership and management must go hand in hand. They are not the same thing. But they are necessarily linked, and complementary. Any effort to separate the two is likely to cause more problems than it solves.

- The manager is a copy; the leader is an original.
- The manager maintains; the leader develops.
- The manager focuses on systems and structure; the leader focuses on people.
- The manager relies on control; the leader inspires trust.
- The manager has a short-range view; the leader has a long-range perspective.
- The manager asks how and when; the leader asks what and why.
- The manager has his or her eye always on the bottom line; the leader's eye is on the horizon.
- The manager imitates; the leader originates.

- The manager accepts the status quo; the leader challenges it.
- The manager is the classic good soldier; the leader is his or her own person.
- The manager administers; the leader innovates.
- The manager does things right; the leader does the right thing.

Perhaps there was a time when the calling of the manager and that of the leader could be separated. A foreman in an industrial area factory probably didn't have to give much thought to what he was producing or to the people who were producing it. His or her job was to follow orders, organize the work, assign the right people to the necessary tasks, coordinate the results, and ensure the job got done as ordered. The focus was on efficiency.

But in the new economy, where value comes increasingly from the knowledge of people, and where workers are no longer undifferentiated cogs in an industrial machine, management and leadership are not easily separated. People look to their managers, not just to assign them a task, but to define for them a purpose. And managers must organize workers, not just to maximize efficiency, but to nurture skills, develop talent and inspire results.

The late management guru Peter Drucker was one of the first to recognize this truth, as he was to recognize so many other management truths. He identified the emergence of the "knowledge worker," and the profound differences that would cause in the way business was organized.

Leadership Theories

An organisation has the greatest chance f being successful when all of the employees work toward achieving its goals. Since leadership involves the exercise of influence by one person over others, the quality of leadership exhibited by supervisors is a critical determinant of organisational success. Thus, supervisors study leadership in order to influence the actions of employees towards the achievement of the goals of the organisation.

Effective leadership is a function of the characteristics of the leader, the style of leadership, the characteristics of the followers and the situation exists in the organisation. The leadership theories can be categorised as follows:

- Trait theories
- Behavioural theories
- Contingency theories
- Transformational theories

Trait Theories of Leadership

The trait model of leadership is based on the characteristics of many leaders - both successful and unsuccessful - and is used to predict leadership effectiveness. The resulting lists of traits are then compared to those of potential leaders to assess their likelihood of success or failure.

Scholars taking the trait approach attempted to identify physiological (appearance, height, and weight), demographic (age, education and socioeconomic background), personality, self- confidence, and aggressiveness), intellective (intelligence, decisiveness, judgment, and knowledge), task-related (achievement drive, initiative, and persistence), and social characteristics (sociability and cooperativeness) with leader emergence and leader effectiveness.

Successful leaders definitely have interests, abilities, and personality traits that are different from those of the less effective leaders. Through many researchers conducted in the last three decades of the 20th century, a set of core traits of successful leaders have been identified. These traits are not responsible solely to identify whether a person will be a successful leader or not, but they are essentially seen as preconditions that endow people with leadership potential.

Among the core traits identified are:

- Achievement drive: High level of effort, high levels of ambition, energy and initiative.
- Leadership motivation: an intense desire to lead others to reach shared goals.
- Honesty and integrity: trustworthy, reliable, and open.
- Self-confidence: Belief in one's self, ideas, and ability.
- Cognitive ability: Capable of exercising good judgment, strong analytical abilities, and conceptually skilled.
- Knowledge of business: Knowledge of industry and other technical matters.
- Emotional Maturity: well adjusted, does not suffer from severe psychological disorders.
- Others: charisma, creativity and flexibility.

Advantages of Trait Theory

- It is naturally pleasing theory.
- It is valid as lot of research has validated the foundation and basis of the theory.

- It serves as a yardstick against which the leadership traits of an individual can be assessed.
- It gives a detailed knowledge and understanding of the leader element in the leadership process.

Limitations of the Trait Theory

- There is bound to be some subjective judgment in determining who is regarded as a 'good' or 'successful' leader.
- The list of possible traits tends to be very long. More than 100 different traits of successful leaders in various leadership positions have been identified. These descriptions are simply generalities.
- There is also a disagreement over which traits are the most important for an effective leader.
- The model attempts to relate physical traits such as, height and weight, to effective leadership. Most of these factors relate to situational factors. For example, a minimum weight and height might be necessary to perform the tasks efficiently in a military leadership position. In business organizations, these are not the requirements to be an effective leader.
- The theory is very complex.

Implications of Trait Theory

The trait theory gives constructive information about leadership. It can be applied by people at all levels in all types of organizations. Managers can utilize the information from the theory to evaluate their position in the organization and to assess how their position can be made stronger in the organization. They can get an in-depth understanding of their identity and the way they will affect others in the organization. This theory makes the manager aware of their strengths and weaknesses and thus they get an understanding of how they can develop their leadership qualities.

The traits approach gives rise to questions: whether leaders are born or made; and whether leadership is an art or science. However, these are not mutually exclusive alternatives. Leadership may be something of an art; it still requires the application of special skills and techniques. Even if there are certain inborn qualities that make one a good leader, these natural talents need encouragement and development. A person is not born with self-confidence. Self- confidence is developed, honesty and integrity are a matter of personal choice, motivation to lead comes from within the individual, and the knowledge of business can be acquired. While cognitive ability has its origin partly in genes, it still needs to be developed. None of these ingredients are acquired overnight.

Behavioural Theories

Behavioural theories of leadership are classified as such because they focus on the study of specific behaviours of a leader. For behavioural theorists, a leader behaviour is the best predictor of his leadership influences and as a result, is the best determinant of his or her leadership success.

This behaviour-focused approach provides real marketing potential, as behaviours can be conditioned in a manner that one can have a specific response to specific stimuli. As a result, we have gone from the supposition that leaders are born, (Great Man Theory) through to the possibility that we can measure your leadership potential (Trait Theory) via psychometrics measurements and then to the point that anyone can be made a leader (Behavioural Theories) by teaching them the most appropriate behavioural response for any given situation. There are two important Behavioural studies:

Ohio State University

As leadership studies that were aimed at identifying the appropriate traits didn't yield any conclusive results, a group of people from Ohio State University developed a list of 150 statements from their generated responses that included 1,800 hundred statements. The list was designed to measure nine different behavioural leadership dimensions.

One of the primary purposes of the study was to identify common leadership behaviours. After compiling and analyzing the results, the study led to the conclusion that there were two groups of behaviours that were strongly correlated. These were defined as Consideration (People Oriented behavioural Leaders) and Initiating Structure (Task Oriented Leaders).

Task Oriented Leaders

The task concerned leaders are focusing their behaviours on the organizational structure, the operating procedures and they like to keep control. Task-oriented leaders are still concern with their staff motivation; however it's not their main concern. They will favour behaviours that are in line with:

- Initiating
- Organizing
- Clarifying
- Information Gathering.

People Oriented Leaders

The people oriented leaders are focusing their behaviours on ensuring that the inner needs of the people are satisfied. Thus they will seek to motivate their staff through emphasizing the human relation. People oriented leaders still focus on the task and the results; they just achieve them through different means. Leaders with a people focus will have behaviours that are in line with:

- Encouraging
- Observing
- Listening
- Coaching and Mentoring.

University of Michigan

Lead by the famous organizational psychologist, Dr. Rensis Likert, the leadership studies at the University of Michigan identified three characteristics of effective leadership; two of which were previously observed in studies that had been conducted at Ohio State University. The study showed that task and relationship-oriented behaviours weren't of major significance within the world of organizational psychology. However it was the third observation that introduced a new concept, one of participative leadership.

The Blake-Mouton Managerial Grid

The Blake-Mouton Managerial Grid was published in 1964, and it highlights the most appropriate style to use, based on concern for people and concern for production/tasks.

With a people-oriented style, focus is on organizing, supporting, and developing team members. This participatory style encourages good teamwork and creative collaboration.

With task-oriented leadership, focus is on getting the job done. We define the work and the roles required, put structures in place, and plan, organize, and monitor work.

According to this model, the best style to use is one that has both a high concern for people and a high concern for the task – it argues that you should aim for both, rather than trying to offset one against the other.

Understanding the Model

The Managerial Grid is based on two behavioural dimensions:

- Concern for People – This is the degree to which a leader considers the needs of team members, their interests, and areas of personal development when deciding how best to accomplish a task.
- Concern for Results – This is the degree to which a leader emphasizes concrete objectives, organizational efficiency and high productivity when deciding how best to accomplish a task.

Using the axis to plot leadership 'concerns for results' versus 'concerns for people', Blake and Mouton defined the following five leadership styles:

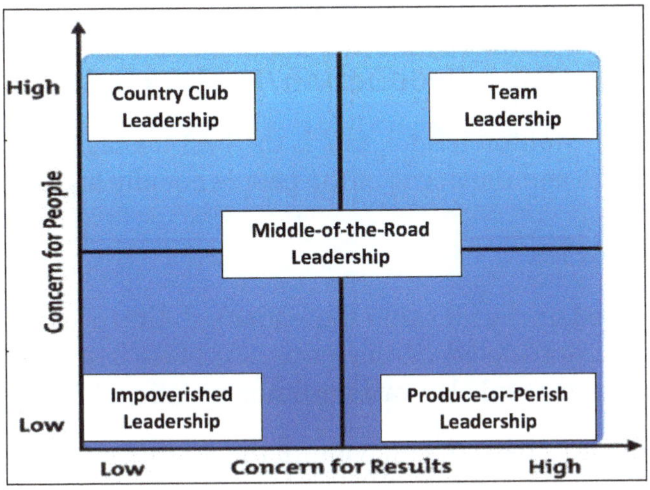

The Blake Mouton Managerial Grid.

Impoverished Management – Low Results/Low People

This leader is mostly ineffective. He/she has neither a high regard for creating systems for getting the job done, nor for creating a work environment that is satisfying and motivating. The result is disorganization, dissatisfaction and disharmony.

Country Club Management – High People/Low Results

This style of leader is most concerned about the needs and feelings of members of his/her team. These people operate under the assumption that as long as team members are happy and secure then they will work hard. What tends to result is a work environment that is very relaxed and fun but where production suffers due to lack of direction and control.

Authority-Compliance Management – High Results/Low People

Also known as Authoritarian or "Produce or Perish" Leaders, people in this category believe that employees are simply a means to an end. Employee needs are always secondary to the need for efficient and productive workplaces. This type of leader is very autocratic, has strict work rules, policies, and procedures, and views punishment as the most effective means to motivate employees.

Middle-of-the-Road Management – Medium Results/Medium People

This style seems to be a balance of the two competing concerns, and it may at first appear to be an ideal compromise. Therein lies the problem, though: When you compromise, you necessarily give away a bit of each concern, so that neither production nor people needs are fully met. Leaders who use this style settle for average performance and often believe that this is the most anyone can expect.

Team Leadership – High Production/High People

According to the Blake Mouton model, this is the best managerial style. These leaders stress production needs and the needs of the people equally highly.

Contingency Theories

These theories are based on the idea that the leader's ability to lead is a contingent upon various situational factors, including the leader's preferred style, the capabilities and behaviours of the followers and also various other situational factors.

Contingency theories are a class of behavioural theory that tells there is no best way of leading and that a leadership style that is effective in some situations may not be successful in others. The important contingency theories are:

Fiedler's Contingency Model

This theory was developed by Fred.E.Fiedler. This is the first comprehensive contingency theory of leadership. He believes that leader effectiveness depends upon bothe the leaders personality and the situation. Certain leaders are effective in one situation but not in others.

Least preferred Co-worker (LPC) Scale

Fiedler identified the a Least Preferred Co-Worker scoring for leaders by asking them first to think of a person with which they worked that they would like least to work with again, and then to score the person on a range of scales between positive factors (friendly, helpful, cheerful, etc.) and negative factors (unfriendly, unhelpful, gloomy, etc.). A high LPC leader generally scores the other person as positive and a low LPC leader scores them as negative.

High LPC leaders tend to have close and positive relationships and act in a supportive way, even prioritizing the relationship before the task. Low LPC leaders put the task first and will turn to relationships only when they are satisfied with how the work is going.

Three factors are then identified about the leader, member and the task, as follows:

- Leader-Member Relations: The extent to which the leader has the support and loyalties of followers and relations with them are friendly and cooperative.

- Task structure: The extent to which tasks are standardised, documented and controlled.
- Leader's Position-power: The extent to which the leader has authority to assess follower performance and give reward or punishment.

The best LPC approach depends on a combination of these three. Generally, a high LPC approach is best when leader-member relations are poor, except when the task is unstructured and the leader is weak, in which a low LPC style is better.

The leadership style of the leader, thus, fixed and measured by what he calls the least preferred co-worker (LPC) scale, an instrument for measuring an individual's leadership orientation. The LPC scale asks a leader to think of all the people with whom they have ever worked and then describe the person with whom they have worked least well, using a series of bipolar scales of 1 to 8, such as the following:

Unfriendly 1 2 3 4 5 6 7 8 Friendly

Uncooperative 1 2 3 4 5 6 7 8 Cooperative

Hostile 1 2 3 4 5 6 7 8 Supportive

.... 1 2 3 4 5 6 7 8 ....

Guarded 1 2 3 4 5 6 7 8 Open

A high LPC score suggests that the leader has a "human relations orientation", while a low LPC score indicates a "task orientation". Fiedler assumes that everybody's least preferred co-worker in fact is on average about equally unpleasant. But people who are indeed relationship motivated, tend to describe their least preferred co-workers in a more positive manner, e.g., more pleasant and more efficient. Therefore, they receive higher LPC scores. People who are task motivated, on the other hand, tend to rate their least preferred co-workers in a more negative manner. Therefore, they receive lower LPC scores. So, the Least Preferred Co-worker (LPC) scale is actually not about the least preferred worker at all, instead, it is about the person who takes the test; it is about that person's motivation type.

Situational Favourableness

According to Fiedler, the ability to control the group situation (the second component of the contingency model) is crucial for a leader. This is because only leaders with situational control can be confident that their orders and suggestions will be carried out by their followers. Leaders who are unable to assume control over the group situation cannot be sure that the members they are leading will execute their commands. Because situational control is critical to leadership efficacy.

The contingency theory allows for predicting the characteristics of the appropriate situations for effectiveness. Three situational components determine the favourableness of situational control:

1. Leader-Member Relations, referring to the degree of mutual trust, respect and confidence between the leader and the subordinates. When leader-member relations in the group are poor, the leader has to shift focus away from the group task in order to regulate behaviour and conflict within the group.
2. Task Structure, referring to the extent to which group tasks are clear and structured. When task structure is low (unstructured), group tasks are ambiguous, with no clear solution or correct approach to complete the goal. In contrast, when task structure is high (structured), the group goal is clear, unambiguous and straightforward: members have a clear idea about the how to approach and reach the goal.
3. Leader Position Power, referring to the power inherent in the leader's position itself.

When there is a good leader-member relation, a highly structured task, and high leader position power, the situation is considered a "favourable situation." Fiedler found that low-LPC leaders are more effective in extremely favourable or unfavourable situations, whereas high-LPC leaders perform best in situations with intermediate favourability.

Leaders in high positions of power have the ability to distribute resources among their members, meaning they can reward and punish their followers. Leaders in low position power cannot control resources to the same extent as leaders in high power, and so lack the same degree of situational control.

For example, the CEO of a business has high position power, because she is able to increase and reduce the salary that her employees receive. On the other hand, an office worker in this same business has low position power, because although they may be the leader on a new business deal, they cannot control the situation by rewarding or disciplining their colleagues with salary changes.

Leader-situation Match and Mismatch

Since personality is relatively stable though it can be changed, the contingency model suggests that improving effectiveness requires changing the situation to fit the leader. This is called "job engineering" or "job restructuring". The organization or the leader may increase or decrease task structure and position power, also training and group development may improve leader- member relations.

Examples:

1. Task-oriented leadership would be advisable in natural disaster, like a flood or fire. In an uncertain situation the leader-member relations are usually poor,

the task is unstructured, and the position power is weak. The one who emerges as a leader to direct the group's activity usually does not know subordinates personally. The task-oriented leader who gets things accomplished proves to be the most successful. If the leader is considerate (relationship-oriented), they may waste so much time in the disaster, that things get out of control and lives are lost.

2. Blue-collar workers generally want to know exactly what they are supposed to do. Therefore, their work environment is usually highly structured. The leader's position power is strong if management backs their decision. Finally, even though the leader may not be relationship-oriented, leader-member relations may be extremely strong if they can gain promotions and salary increases for subordinates. Under these situations the task-oriented style of leadership is preferred over the (considerate) relationship-oriented style.

Tri-Dimensional Leader Effectiveness Model

Depending on employee's competencies in their task areas and commitment to their tasks, leadership style should vary from one person to another. They classified most of the activities of leaders into the following two distinct behavioural dimensions.

1. Task behaviour: It is the extent to which leaders are likely to organise and define the roles of the members of their group and to explain what activities each is to do and when, where and how tasks are to be accomplished ; characterised by endeavouring to establish well defined patterns of organisation, channels of communication and ways of getting jobs accomplished.

   The leader engages in one way communication with the workers by telling what each worker is to do. The communication is characterised as one way because there is no chance for workers to give feedback to the leader.

2. Relationship behaviour: Relationship behaviour on the other hand is the extent to which leaders are likely to maintain personal relationships between themselves and members of their group by opening up channels of communication, providing socio emotional support, active listening, psychological strokes, and facilitating behaviours. In this case the leaders and workers engage in two ways communication. There are sufficient opportunities for feedback.

In order to understand a persons leadership style there must be a combination of task and relationship behaviour. They are directing/telling, coaching/selling, supporting/participating and delegating.

1. Directing/telling: it is known as high task low relationship leadership behaviours directing. When the follower cannot do the job and is not motivated,

then the leader takes a highly directive role, telling them what to do and without a great deal of concern for the relationship.

2. Coaching/selling: High task-High relationship leadership behaviour is referred to as coaching. Leaders still define roles and tasks, but seek ideas and suggestions from the follower. Decisions remain the leader's choice, but communication is much more two way.

3. Supporting/Participating - Low task-High relationship leadership behaviour is referred to as supporting. Leaders pass day to day decisions, such as task allocation and processes, to the follower. The leader facilitates and takes part in decisions, but control is with the follower. For people who have competence, but lack confidence or motivation does not need much direction because of their skills, but support is necessary to bolster their confidence and motivation.

4. Delegating: finally, low task - low relationship leadership behaviour is referred to as delegating. When the follower can do the job and is motivated to do it, then the leader can basically leave them to it, trusting them to get on with the job. The leader allows group members considerable autonomy in completing the task. In the tri dimensional model it shows that the effectiveness of leaders depends on how appropriate their leadership style is to the situation in which they operate. The added effectiveness dimension also attempts to integrate the concepts of leader style with situation demands of a specific environment. So where the style is appropriate to a given situation it will be deemed effective, and where it is not appropriate it will be concluded ineffective.

Leader Member Exchange Theory [Lmx]

Leader-Member Exchange Theory, also called LMX or Vertical Dyad Linkage Theory, describes how leaders in groups maintain their position through a series of tacit exchange agreements with their members.

In-group and out-group

In particular, leaders often have a special relationship with an inner circle of trusted lieutenants, assistants and advisors, to whom they give high levels of responsibility, decision influence, and access to resources. This in-group pay for their position. They work harder, are more committed to task objectives, and share more administrative duties. They are also expected to be fully committed and loyal to their leader. The out-group, on the other hand, are given low levels of choice or influence.

This also puts constraints upon the leader. They have to nurture the relationship with their inner circle whilst balancing giving them power with ensuring they do not have enough to strike out on their own.

The LMX Process

These relationships, if they are going to happen, start very soon after a person joins the group and follow three stages:

1. Role taking: The member joins the team and the leader assesses their abilities and talents. Based on this, the leader may offer them opportunities to demonstrate their capabilities.

   Another key factor in this stage is the discovery by both parties of how the other likes to be respected.

2. Role making: In the second phase, the leader and member take part in an unstructured and informal negotiation whereby a role is created for the member and the often-tacit promise of benefit and power in return for dedication and loyalty takes place.

   Trust-building is very important in this stage, and any felt betrayal, especially by the leader, can result in the member being relegated to the out-group.

   This negotiation includes relationship factors as well as pure work-related ones, and a member who is similar to the leader in various ways is more likely to succeed. This perhaps explains why mixed gender relationships regularly are less successful than same-gender ones (it also affects the seeking of respect in the first stage). The same effect also applies to cultural and racial differences.

3. Routinization: In this phase, a pattern of on-going social exchange between the leader and the member becomes established.

Success Factors

Successful members are thus similar in many ways to the leader (which perhaps explains why many senior teams are all white, male, middle-class and middle-aged). They work hard at building and sustaining trust and respect.

To help this, they are empathetic, patient, reasonable, sensitive, and are good at seeing the viewpoint of other people (especially the leader). Aggression, sarcasm and an ego-centric view are keys to the out-group wash-room.

The overall quality of the LMX relationship varies with several factors. Curiously, it is better when the challenge of the job is extremely high or extremely low. The size of the group, financial resource availability and the overall workload are also important.

Onwards and Upwards

The principle works upwards as well. The leader also gains power by being a member of their manager's inner circle, which then can then share on downwards. People at the bottom of an organization with unusual power may get it from an unbroken chain of circles up to the hierarchy.

The principle works upwards as well. The leader also gains power by being a member of their manager's inner circle, which then can then share on downwards. People at the bottom of an organization with unusual power may get it from an unbroken chain of circles up to the hierarchy.

Path Goal Theory

The path–goal theory, also known as the path–goal theory of leader effectiveness or the path–goal model, is a leadership theory developed by Robert House, an Ohio State University graduate, in 1971 and revised in 1996. The theory states that a leader's behaviour is contingent to the satisfaction, motivation and performance of her or his subordinates. The revised version also argues that the leader engages in behaviours that complement subordinate's abilities and compensate for deficiencies.

The path–goal model can be classified as a Transaction leadership theory. According to the first of all theory, the manager's job is viewed as guiding workers to choose the best paths to reach their goals, as well as the organizational goals. The theory argues that leaders will have to engage in different types of leadership behaviour depending on the nature and the demands of a particular situation. It is the leader's job to assist followers in attaining goals and to provide the direction and support needed to ensure that their goals are compatible with the organization's goals.

A leader's behaviour is acceptable to subordinates when viewed as a source of satisfaction, and motivational when need satisfaction is contingent on performance, and the leader facilitates, coaches, and rewards effective performance. The original path-goal theory identifies achievement-oriented, directive, participative, and supportive leader behaviours:

1. The directive path-goal clarifying leader behaviour refers to situations where the leader lets followers know what is expected of them and tells them how to perform their tasks. The theory argues that this behaviour has the most positive effect when the subordinates' role and task demands are ambiguous and intrinsically satisfying.

2. The achievement-oriented leader behaviour refers to situations where the leader sets challenging goals for followers, expects them to perform at their highest level, and shows confidence in their ability to meet this expectation. Occupations in which the achievement motive was most predominant were technical jobs, sales persons, scientists, engineers, and entrepreneurs.

3. The participative leader behaviour involves leaders consulting with followers and asking for their suggestions before making a decision. This behaviour is predominant when subordinates are highly personally involved in their work.

4. The supportive leader behaviour is directed towards the satisfaction of subordinates needs and preferences. The leader shows concern for the followers' psychological well-being. This behaviour is especially needed in situations in which tasks or relationships are psychologically or physically distressing.

Path–goal theory assumes that leaders are flexible and that they can change their style, as situations require. The theory proposes two contingency variables, such as environment and follower characteristics, that moderate the leader behaviour-outcome relationship.

Environment is outside the control of the follower-task structure, authority system, and work group. Environmental factors determine the type of leader behaviour required if the follower outcomes are to be maximized. Follower characteristics are the locus of control, experience, and perceived ability. Personal characteristics of subordinates determine how the environment and leader are interpreted. Effective leaders clarify the path to help their followers achieve goals and make the journey easier by reducing roadblocks and pitfalls. Research demonstrates that employee performance and satisfaction are positively influenced when the leader compensates for the shortcomings in either the employee or the work setting. This theory is useful because it reminds leaders that their central purpose as a leader is to help subordinates define and reach their goals in an efficient manner.

Leader-Participation Model

The Vroom-Yetton-Jago model or Leader- Participation Model is a contingency approach to group decision making that is designed specifically to help leaders select the best approach to making decisions. The model identifies different ways a decision can be made by considering the degree of follower participation. It proposes a method for leaders to select the right approach to making a decision in a given set of circumstances.

The Vroom-Yetton-Jago model defines five different decision approaches that a leader can use. In order of participation from least to most, these are:

1. AI – Autocratic Type 1: Decisions are made completely by the leader. Leaders make the decision on their own with whatever information is available.

2. AII – Autocratic Type 2: The decision is still made by the leader alone, but the leader collects information from the followers. Followers play no other role in the decision- making process.

3. CI – Consultative Type 1: The leader seeks input from select followers individually based on their relevant knowledge. Followers do not meet each other, and the leader's decision may or may not reflect followers' influence.

4. CII – Consultative Type 2: Similar to CI, except the leader shares the problem with relevant followers as a group and seeks their ideas and suggestions. The followers are involved in the decision, but the leader still makes the decision.

5. GII – Group-based Type 2: The entire group works through the problem with the leader. A decision is made by the followers in collaboration with the leader. In a GII decision, leaders are not at liberty to make a decision on their own.

Recent Approaches to Leadership Theories

1. Transformational Leadership: The leadership frameworks discussed so far are all useful in different situations, however, in business, "transformational leadership" is often the most effective style to use.

   Transformational leaders have integrity and high emotional intelligence. They motivate people with a shared vision of the future, and they communicate well. They're also typically self-aware, authentic, empathetic, and humble.

   Transformational leaders inspire their team members because they expect the best from everyone, and they hold themselves accountable for their actions. They set clear goals, and they have good conflict-resolution skills. This leads to high productivity and engagement.

   However, leadership is not a "one size fits all" thing; often, you must adapt your approach to fit the situation. This is why it's useful to develop a thorough understanding of other leadership frameworks and styles; after all, the more approaches you're familiar with, the more flexible you can be.

2. Charismatic Leadership: Charismatic leadership resembles transformational leadership: both types of leaders inspire and motivate their team members.

   The difference lies in their intent. Transformational leaders want to transform their teams and organizations, while leaders who rely on charisma often focus on themselves and their own ambitions, and they may not want to change anything.

   Charismatic leaders might believe that they can do no wrong, even when others warn them about the path that they're on.

3. Transactional Leadership: This style starts with the idea that team members agree to obey their leader when they accept a job. The "transaction" usually involves the organization paying team members in return for their effort and compliance on a short-term task. The leader has a right to "punish" team members if their work doesn't meet an appropriate standard.

   Transactional leadership is present in many business leadership situations, and it does offer some benefits. For example, it clarifies everyone's roles and responsibilities. And, because transactional leadership judges team members on performance, people who are ambitious or who are motivated by external rewards including compensation often thrive.

The downside of this style is that, on its own, it can be chilling and amoral, and it can lead to high staff turnover. It also has serious limitations for knowledge-based or creative work.

As a result, team members can often do little to improve their job satisfaction.

4. Transformational Leadership: According to Hodgetts and Luttans, transformational leaders are visionary agents with a mission who are capable of motivating their followers to accept new goals and new ways of doing things. Over the last 30 years, transformational leadership has become one of the most prominent theories of organizational behaviour. Transformational leadership has been defined by the ability of the leader to create a shared vision and a strong identification with team members that is based on more than just rewarding completion of project activities. Through this shared vision, the transformational leader is then able to mobilize commitment and transcendent performance of both the individual and the project as a whole. Such leaders are said to show charisma, as a means of motivating others to integrate into the collective vision, and a strong consideration of and support for individual team member needs.

   In contrast to leadership based on individual gain and the exchange of rewards for effort, transformational leaders direct and inspire employee effort by raising their awareness of the importance of organizational values and outcomes. In doing so, such leaders activate the higher-order needs of their employees and encourage them to transcend their own self-interest for the sake of the organization and its clientele.

   Research not only has validated the existence of transformational leadership but also consistently has linked the practice of these transformational leadership behaviours with employee performance and satisfaction. Transformational leaders use idealized influence, inspiration and motivation, intellectual stimulation and individualized consideration to achieve superior results.

Leadership Substitutes

Leadership substitutes is one of the more recent theories on leadership. Although not many studies have been done so far to test them, these theories suggest certain different and interesting ways of looking at leadership.

The concept of substitutes for leadership was developed because leadership models and theories do not account for situation s in which leadership is not needed. They simply try to specify what kind of a leader behaviour is appropriate. The substitutes concept, however identifies situations in which leader behaviours are neutralised or replaced by characteristics of the subordinate, the task, and the organisation.

Under certain circumstances, leaders and leadership become unnecessary because they are no longer necessary for employees high performance and satisfaction.

Factors that can substitute for leadership include the following:

- Certain individual characteristics, including ability, knowledge, experience, training, independence, and indifference toward organisational rewards.
- Certain task characters, including routineness, high structure, frequent feedback, and intrinsic satisfaction.
- Certain organisation characteristics, including clear plans and goals, rules and procedures, cohesive work groups, rigid reward structure, and physical distance between leader and subordinates.

The distinction between maintenance focus and task focus is pertinent also when it comes to leadership of a team. Maintenance-focused leaders tend to pay attention to the cohesion of the group, ensuring that it remains harmonious while working towards team objectives. They are good at resolving conflict, and can delegate and supervise effectively. Such leaders, however, may be ineffective in some situations, such as when there is strong opposition within the group. Task-focused leaders, on the other hand, are focused on achieving objectives whatever the cost and they can drive change through resistance. They are not too concerned about cohesion or harmonious cooperation, focusing, instead, on achieving results. Their directive skills work best with subordinates rather than equals, and, generally, leading self-motivated people is not their strong point.

Regardless of whether their focus is to maintain cohesion or to initiate tasks, effective team leaders share certain characteristics. According to Qubein, these common characteristics are:

- They value people: they acknowledge the importance and contribution of others.
- They listen actively: they make an effort to understand the needs and desires of others.
- They are tactful: they criticize sparingly, constructively and diplomatically.
- They give credit: they praise others and their contributions publicly.
- They are consistent: they control their personal moods, and are fair in their exchanges with others.
- They admit mistakes: they take the blame for errors they committed.
- They have a sense of humour: they maintain a pleasant disposition and pleasant manner.
- They set a good example: they follow their own regulations.

Like other managers, team leaders can exhibit styles of direction with varying degrees of dominance or control. These styles vary from contexts where the leader enforces his/her decision on team members, to the opposite extreme where the leader listens to all parties and allows for unlimited individual initiative. In many cases the leader's powers and responsibilities are inscribed in the organization's management structure, but, as in most facets of human behaviour, they also depend on individual leader's interpretation of this structure. According to the leadership continuum model first proposed by R Tannebaum and W. H. Schmidt, leadership strategies range from autocratic to laissez-faire, and comprise several steps in-between. The leadership continuum is shown in the following diagram.

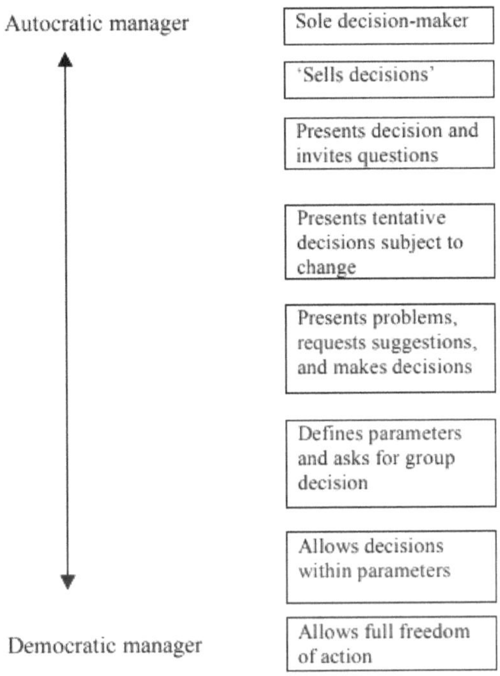

Leadership continuum.

Leadership Process

The leadership role often changes significantly in a High Performance organization. This is true for executives and supervisors alike. All too often, leaders consider changes to High Performance as a technique or program which others must implement, but fail to realize the extent to which they must be personally involved and change themselves.

Since High Performance is a way of thinking about and managing the business, the transformation process begins by helping senior leadership define not only what they should be doing in the organization, but how they should go about doing it.

The Leadership Process includes five essential steps:

Step 1: Leadership Orientation and Commitment

Leadership orientation and commitment is normally a one to two-day orientation session in which key leaders from the organization learn about High Performance. In this session participants go through an organization simulation to experience the difference between traditional and High Performance work systems. As they learn and discuss principles of High Performance, they will learn about the transformation process, explore the level of trust within the organization, and identify change needs driving their organization.

Step 2: Assessment of the Business and Organization

The purpose of this step is to complete a comprehensive assessment of the organization, creating a common understanding of the current state of the business. Key leadership, with a cross-section of people from the organization, analyzes a business case study to learn how to use the Transformation Model as a framework for organization analysis. Then, applying the Transformation Model to their own organization, they systematically analyze seven key elements: current results; the business environment; the current strategy; current core processes, current structure; and coordination and development systems.

Following their analysis, they summarize key issues to address and identify organization strengths, weaknesses, and alignment issues. Armed with comprehensive assessment data, they can develop a list of change initiatives for improving the organization and moving toward High Performance. The assessment process can be modularized into half-day sessions spread over a nine to ten week period, or it can be accomplished more quickly in a single three-day session. This step often surfaces significant problems within the organization, creating a sense of direction and momentum for needed changes. Every participant will come away from this dynamic session with a greater sense of responsibility, know-how, and enthusiasm for making the business succeed.

Step 3: Development of Strategy and Vision

In step three, key leaders develop and/or adjust the business strategy and direction of the organization. During this process they review their strategy and vision based on current business realities, refocusing and redefining their strategy to fit marketplace and competitive demands.

Specifically they will accomplish the following during the process:

1. Understand the demands of the current business environment.
2. Forecast the future business situation.

3. Clarify a mission that motivates and inspires.
4. Identify the principles by which people will conduct themselves.
5. Define future customers and how they will deliver value to them.
6. Identify core competencies needed to succeed in the long run.
7. Create a long-term business focus and identify anchors that distinguish them from competitors.
8. Set short-term performance goals.
9. Identify performance initiatives and establish a master plan to implement the strategy.

The strategy development process often requires several in-depth exploration and discussion sessions which may be accomplished over a period of weeks or months, depending on the size, motivation, and complexity of the organization. Clearly, the process must be tailored to the individual needs of each organization. We are confident that senior leadership will emerge from the strategy development sessions being very clear about their strategy and united in their commitment to implement it throughout the organization.

Step 4: Chartering the Change Process

During this step, senior leadership determines the need for organization redesign to address organization weaknesses and alignment issues identified during assessment. They create a design charter, outlining the expected outcomes and the scope and parameters of the redesign process. They assign resources, establish time frames, and identify a design team to participate in and guide in-depth process analysis and redesign of the organization as necessary. They also determine the scope of the development process, identifying leadership training, employee orientation, team development, technical skills development, interpersonal skills development, and other projected training and development needs. These plans are factored in with strategic initiatives and change opportunities identified during strategy development and assessment to create an overall change plan. The charter is then shared with employees to communicate the need for change and explain how the transformation process will work throughout the organization.

Step 5: Integrated Management of Business Performance

Management of business performance, especially in today's complex and rapidly changing environment, can be extremely challenging. Consequently, management behavior can be short-term and crisis-oriented. Managers and supervisors alike often react to demands which seem urgent, but may only be symptoms of deeper causes related to flawed processes or systems. A further problem is that work may be segmented into functional areas, promoting poor communication, turf battles, lack of problem ownership, and general inefficiency. In step five, Integrated Management of Business Performance, leaders develop a common plan and establish management processes to proactively manage the short and long-term performance of the business. One of the first tasks here is to help leaders begin to work as a team as they share responsibility for the overall management of the enterprise.

During assessment, the organization identified key results areas and current performance in those areas. During strategy development, the leaders identified ideal key results areas, how they will measure them, and what their goals are. Armed with this data, the leadership team outlines a process for how they will monitor, track, and integrate performance throughout the organization on an on-going basis, including common initiatives, clear expectations, and consistent performance metrics. This may lead them into discussion or readjustment of recognition, reward, or performance management systems as well.

Power and Politics in Organizations

Organizations are organized bodies of persons or systems. They are neither the rational, harmonious entities celebrated in managerial theory nor the arenas of apocalyptic class conflict projected by Marxists. Rather, it may be argued, a more suitable notion lies somewhere between these two, a concept of organizations as politically negotiated orders. Survival in any organization is a political act. Thus, organizational life is dominated by political interactions. Politics in organizations involve the tactical use of power to retain or obtain control of real symbolic resources. Organizational structures are emergent entities. They are the result of the conscious political decisions of particular actors and interest groups.

The comparative studies of organizations by sociologists in the last three to four decades have, for the most part, adopted an apolitical view of organizations. This view point may be attributed to a narrow interpretation of Max Weber's approach to organizations. Sociologists have spent a disproportionate amount of time trying to prove or disprove the plausibility of Weber's ideal construct of bureaucracy. It is safe to say that Weber remains the most cited organizational theorist; however, the narrowness of his impact is best exemplified by the fact that the pages of his work most frequently cited by organizational researchers are those few where he presents his ideal typical model of the organization.

While it is true that Weber specified some of the primary dimensions of organizational structure, it is also true that he viewed organizational structure as emerging from the conscious political decisions of interest groups within or outside the organization. For Weber, organizations are not simply rationally determined systems of interdependent structures. They are also systems in which political tension among interest groups can emerge and re-emerge.

Bacharach observes that students working within the structural tradition of Blau and Schoenherr have been guided by two assumptions that inhibit the development of a political interpretation of intra organizational dynamics. First, they have tended to cast organizations as normatively integrated systems, thereby ignoring political conflicts and other tensions. Secondly, they tend to view the organization as a holistic entity, and this view overlooks such organizational sub-units as interest groups and coalitions, which are crucial to the development of a political perspective of intra- organizational behaviours. In other words, organizations are not inherently apolitical. Rather, such a characterization may be an artefact of a given theoretical perspective, especially one that emphasizes normative integration and maintenance of the total organization.

From the work of Dahrendor, it is clear that three groups appear to be critical to the development of a political analysis of organizations:

a) Work groups: This may be based on departmental differences, differences in departmental work activity, or differences prescribed by the organizational hierarchy.

b) Interest groups: This may be defined as groups of actors who are aware of the commonality of their goals and commonality of their fate beyond simply their interdependence with regard to the conduct of work.

c) Coalition: A coalition may be defined as grouping of interest groups who are committed to achieving a common goal. They are based on the joint action of two or more interest groups against other interest groups.

From the above, a political analysis must be concerned mainly with the nature of power across groupings in the organization and the specification of tactics and countertactics that groups employ.

In emphasizing work groups, interest groups, and coalitions as units of analysis, it is believed that individuals become political in groups, and that groups are capable of effecting and often do effect organizational structure. In the same vein, if organizations are to be understood as political systems, we must come to grips with how, when and why groups mobilize power. Thus, let us now explore the subject of power more deeply.

Power

Definitions of Power

Like many other words in English language, power has no single definition. A few definitions of power are stated below:

- "Power is the ability to employ force and mobilize resources, energy and information on behalf of a preferred goal" – Gbadamosi.

- "Power is the probability that a person can carry out his or her own will despite resistance" – Max Weber.
- "Power is the ability of persons as groups to impose their will on others despite resistance through deterrence either in the form of withholding regularly supplied rewards or in the form of punishment inasmuch as the former, as well as the latter, constitutes in effect negative sanction" – Blan.
- "Power is defined as a force that results in behaviour that would not have occurred if the forces had not been present" – Mechanic.
- "Power is the ability of one person or group of persons to influence the behaviour of others, that is, to change the probabilities that others will respond in certain ways to specified stimuli" – Kaplan.
- "Power is a capacity that 'A' has to influence the behaviour of 'B' to do things he or she would not otherwise do" – Obisi.

From the different definitions of power given above, it is quite evident that sanctions are an inherent aspect of a power relationship. Though the specific ways in which the sanctions are manifested in a relationship vary with the social setting, sanction can be treated in terms of two probability dimensions on a formal level:

- The probability using sanctions and
- The probability of successful sanctions.

Notwithstanding the specific content, power can be partially portrayed in terms of these formal probabilities.

Subjective Nature of Power

Power is the ability a person has to influence another. The extent of this power is, however, determined, to a large extent, by the perception of the term power by the person at whom the power is directed. It may be more important what a person thinks a superior officer's power is than what in reality it is. Managers may take advantage of this phenomenon by pretending they have more power than they actually have, that is, by bluffing. If a manger's bluffing succeeds, the effect is exactly the same as if the one bluffing actually possessed the formal power. Thus, power is a delicate phenomenon. This is because of the influence of subjective factors, including ethical and moral considerations.

Uses of Power

Power, when acquired, is meant to be used to achieve some purpose(s). Appropriate use of power leads to the achievement of desired goals and objectives. Ineffective use of power or failure to use power when the need arises has been described as the major cause of defective functioning of a system. This is possible among inexperienced managers and those who lack self-confidence. They tend to avoid using power, preferring to pass problems with difficult employees and the like to others.

The organizational consequences of not using power appropriately become increasingly pronounced toward the top of an organization because in hierarchical systems abdications of authority have effects all the way down the line. Yet, trying to use power that one does not have (because of legal constraints, for instance) can be equally detrimental. This is true because managerial actions with regards to employees may be reversed by labour relations, board decisions (where it exists), the courts, arbitrators and the power of public pressure at considerable cost to the company. Thus, judicious and effective use of power is one of the most difficult lessons a manager has to learn.

Bases and Sources of Power

Bases of Power

There is a need to make a distinction between BASES of power and SOURCES of power. This distinction has important implications for the authority-influence contrast. In dealing with the bases of power, we are interested in what parties control that enables them to manipulate the behaviour of others. In referring to the sources of power we are speaking of how parties come to control the bases of power.

French and Raven distinguish six major bases of power. They include:

a) Coercion – This implies the threat of decreasing another's outcomes. The holder can apply punishment or sanction;

b) Expertise – This is formal or specialized knowledge about particular issues or activities with an organization. The person with expertise has the status of an expert and thus is likely to be accurate;

c) Rewards – This implies the promise of increasing the outcomes of the employer. The holder of this can give or withhold something desired;

d) Legitimacy – The holder of this power is viewed as right in terms of the values of the one influenced; this is tantamount to authority. Authority is power based on rights of control and concomitant obligations to obey;

e) Referent Power – This is more interpersonal in nature than legitimacy. It means power based on identification with another. This is exemplified by the power of charismatic leaders who elicit deference and are accorded credibility by others. The individual influenced desires to model his/her behaviour to the source of influence; and

f) Information - This consists of the access or opportunity actors have to gain information about the inner workings of the organization or about the relation of the organization to the environment. This information may or may not be related to the actor's level in the hierarchy of authority in the organization.

Given the contrast of bases and sources of power, Etzioni provides a somewhat better starting point. Unlike French and Raven, Etzioni appears to maintain a consistent focus on the bases of power. He identifies three forms of power, each relying on a different type of sanction:

- Coercive Power: rests on the ability to apply the threat of physical sanction.
- Remunerative Power: based on the control of material resources and reward, and
- Normative Power: based on the control of symbolic rewards.

An additional basis for power needs to be added to Etzoni's three. In an organizational setting, access to information, that is, knowledge, also becomes a basis of power.

When an actor in an organization controls unique information and when that information is needed to make a decision, the actor has power (Pettigrew, 1973). Drawing on the Etzioni and the French and Raven schemes, we can identify four primary bases of power:

- Coercive
- Remunerative
- Normative and
- Knowledge.

The coercive base of power is the control of punishment; the remunerative base is the control of rewards; the normative base is the control of symbols; and the knowledge base is the control of information. Any power relationship in an organization can encompass all these bases, but each relationship may well be characterized by one of them rather than another.

Sources of Power

Having identified the primary bases of power, attention must now turn to the different Sources of power. There are about four main sources of power.

These include:

- Office or Structural Position: The office or structural position might provide a party access to various bases of power. Some positions might provide little information but substantial coercive resources, while others might give the occupant the capacity to manipulate symbols or mobilize internalized commitments to certain norms.

- Personal Characteristics: The most marked personal characteristic that is a source of power is charisma. As Weber (1947) indicates, the charismatic leader has power by virtue of extraordinary and often mystical characteristics. However, relevant personal characteristics might also include verbal skill, ability to argue effectively for positions, or even physical attributes (for example, a physical disability of a veteran espousing a prior anti-war position).
- Expertise: Expertise refers to the specialized information actors bring to the organization. It is typically based on activities outside the organization, for example, education. This is treated as a source of power, rather than a basis of power in French and Raven's terms, because it seems to be a means by which a party comes to control specialized information rather than the control itself.
- Opportunity: This particular source of power is embedded in the informal structure of the organization. The idea comes from Mechanic's (1962) analysis of the power of the lower levels in an organization (such as sectorial staff). The informal aspects of formal positions or informal positions that are not identified officially by the organization can provide an important source of power.

Authority and Power Relations

A manager may have the authority (right) to do something but may lack the power (ability) to do it. On the other side of the coin, one may have the power to do something, but may lack the authority to do it. Any of these two conditions describes an unstable organization. Failure to match power and authority adequately at all levels cause conflict in the organization. In extreme cases, this disequilibrium may lead to destruction of the organization, perhaps even to bloodshed. Obisi (1996) was at pain to point out how the Nigerian management fails to match power with authority. Inability to balance power with authority may lead to conflict and in extreme cases bring individuals and organizations to enormous pain.

One of the most important jobs of managers at all levels is to provide subordinates with equal authority and power. That is, the subordinate should, for organizational stability, have means (power) equal to their right (authority) to do the things necessary to accomplish their part of the organization's objectives.

When power and authority for a given person or position are roughly matched, we have a condition we may call legitimate power or workable authority. Achieving a state of legitimate power or workable authority at all levels in the organization is a goal toward which managers should strive.

Relationship of Sources, Bases and Types of Power

So far, two types of power (authority and influence), four bases of power, and four sources of power have been identified. The table below presents the relationship among these aspects of power and it enables us to relate the sources and bases to the authority-influence distinction. It could be argued that all the bases of power could be generated from each source in a given context.

Table: Relationship of Sources, bases and Types of Power.

	Source	Type	Bases
a.	Structure	Authority	Coercion Remunerative Normative Knowledge
b.	Personality	Influence	Normative Knowledge
c.	Expertise	Influence	Normative Knowledge
d.	Opportunity	Influence	Coercion Knowledge

The table above helps to illustrate some of the contrasts between authority and influence. First, authority and influence rely on different sources of power. Authority is based mainly on structural sources of power, whereas influence can be grounded in any of the other sources. Second, the relevance of the four bases of power depends on the power source, and this also has significant implications for the authority-influence contrast. In a given structural context, one or more of the power bases may be constrained or limited by the structure, but on a general theoretical level authority implies all four bases of power. On the whole, all four bases of power should characterize authority relations.

Flow of Power

The treatment of dimensions of authority implies that authority as a form of power is mainly unidirectional. This means that it typically flows from the top or higher levels downward. That is, it applies solely to superior-subordinate relationships and deals with the power of superiors over subordinates. However, the treatment of power implies that subordinates can also exercise power, and that power is actually multidirectional. Influence, of course, is the multidirectional aspect of power. It is the mode of power that both gives subordinates the capability of manipulating superiors and gives superiors the capability of getting more from their subordinates than is specified in the formal role obligations.

The literature of organizations stresses the authority aspect of power. This is reflected in the long-standing concern with centralization and decentralization. Viewed from this literature, power flows down from the top of the organization. Power is something allocated by a higher echelon to a lower echelon in the hierarchy of the organization. This unidirectional and managerial view of power is an integral element of rationalistic consensual models of organizations. The major gap in this approach is the failure to consider that power may also be taken by the lower echelon. The organizational literature places emphasis on power given by the top while neglecting the possibility that subordinates will take power beyond that given to them in the organizational structure. This additional side of power – the taking of power – must be a central concern of the political model of organizations. Individuals and subgroups within organizations are not passive recipients awaiting the downward trickle of power but rather active participants mobilizing power for their own ends. Thus, a political approach to organizations implies a multidirectional image of power, and this means an emphasis on influence apart from, as well as in the context of, the authority structure.

Organizational Politics

The term politics is derived from the Greek word "politics" meaning a city or state. It was originally used by Aristotle (384-322) in his book politics to mean the affairs of Greek city or state. In his view, man is a political animal who by interacting with another or more persons produces a relationship called political. Lasswell writes that politics is essentially the struggle for positions of power and influence by which those who succeed in monopolizing such positions in society are able to make decisions that affect the lives of every citizen within the country. By implication, politics can be practiced by all persons in both governments and organizations with the objective to struggle for power, influence, conflict, bargaining, reconciliation, resolution and consensus. Thus, there are two types of politics, namely: state politics and organizational politics. Here, we will concentrate mainly on organizational politics.

Organizational politics relates to behaviours that are outside those in which the organization has taken a specific position for or against, the behaviors are intended to obtain selfish and individual ends that are opposed to the ends of others in the organization. Organizational politics may focus on the goals of groups as well as individuals and they may well involve behaviours that are harmful to the organization as a whole. They appear to be inevitable but at the same time there are wide variations from organization to organization. Ethical issues often come to the fore and bargaining is an important consideration in organizational politics.

Organizational politics create very ambivalent responses because people look at the whole process both negatively and positively, depending on the particular perspective they have in mind. However, those who are successful in organizational politics tend to be viewed positively perhaps because they are successful competitors in other respects as well.

Recent research works unfold that political matters of this kind are a frequent topic of conversation and that the most frequent issues are interdepartmental coordination, delegation of authority, and promotions or transfers. A common concern is the promotion of a less competent person based on favouritism. Inherent in this and many others politicized situations are the influencing of performance evaluations, positively for oneself and negatively for competitors, and the influencing of authority allocations, as between one work union and another or between supervisor and subordinate.

It is important to explain that organizational politics become more prevalent and more important for the individual at each higher level of management as the competition becomes rougher. The following table suggests that tactics used also change with management level and the kinds of people who are effective politicians are somewhat different. There is enough evidence that strategic decisions at the levels of the organizations may well be influenced politically. For example, new company location may be influenced by the desires of top people regarding where they would like to live or visit. It appears that such a reason may influence the location of a company's headquarter. In Nigeria, such desires have influenced the location of many projects which today turned out to be white elephant projects, all in attempt to satisfy certain interest.

Table: Ranking of tactics and characteristics of good politicians frequency of mention.

Tactical Approaches	Chief Executive Officers	High-level Staff Manager	First Level Supervisors
Attacking or blaming others; scape gloating	1	2	3
Withholding, distorting overwhelming	2	1	2
information			
Developing base of support for one's idea	3	4	7
Creating a favourable image; Impression management	4	3	1
Developing strong allies and forming power coalitions	5	7	5
Praising others; ingratiating one-self with others.	6.5 } *tie*	6	4
Associating with influential people	6.5	5	8

Table: Frequently noted characteristics of good politicians.

Sensitive	Sensitive	Competent
Articulate	Articulate	Popular
Ambitious	Ambitious	
Aggressive		
Intelligent	Socially adapt	Devious
Organization man	Competent, Self-confident, Logical	

Political Tactics

The above table provides an idea of the types of political tactics widely used. All the approaches are among the most frequently used but there are notable differences among them. Interestingly, attacking or blaming others is noted by at least 50 per cent of the managers in all three categories; competition is clearly a prime force in organizational politics. Furthermore, a number of the approaches involve establishing a strong bargaining position.

Some Suggested Political Tactics

The following are some of the political tactics proposed to achieve a competitive advantage. These tactics have their origin in practical experience:

- Expert influence over the time and place of your bargaining efforts so that these conditions are selected to support your goals. In many cases, it is advisable to bargain in your home territory.
- It is a desirable bargaining tactic to disguise your true interests for as long as possible; to be overly eager for a given outcome may leave you at a district disadvantage with regard to other related considerations.
- Shoot for the moon initially so that you can then settle for less but do not use this tactic too often with the same person.
- Identify any weaknesses that adversaries may have and continually work on and publicize them.
- Where the opposition consists of a loosely assembled coalition try to point out the differences within the coalition and any common interests you have with each member, thus attempting to divide and conquer.
- Establish alliances with superiors, peers, and subordinates so that when needed they can be counted to be on your side.
- Select subordinates who are not only competent but reliable, dependable and, above all else, loyal.
- Do not get yourself in a position of relying on an adversary's expertise: if you are not knowledgeable in an area, secure your own expert and take steps to establish his or her credibility.
- Do not injure another person who is or might well be in a position to take revenge.
- Do not do anything to alienate or anger former colleagues when leaving a position; bridges that have been burned may be needed unexpectedly.

- If a proposal developed by an adversary is unattractive but cannot be thwarted immediately, attempt to refer it to a committee to delay it and widen the bargaining area.
- If the outcome is uncertain, it is often desirable to support the aggressive efforts of someone else rather than take the lead oneself. That way, it may be easier to get the ship early if it happens to sink. - In dealing with an adversary, try to leave the door open so that communication is not closed off and differences can still be resolved if necessary.
- Avoid dealing in personalities, never attack the adversary personally and focus on real facts and issues. Choose when and under what circumstances a vote should be used to settle an issue. Let matters go to a vote for resolution only when you know you have a majority.

In the same vein, the questionnaire model can be used to explain the nature of organizational politics. This model is contained in the table below and it is presented here not because it represents a well-researched standardized measure but the questions provide a further indication of what we see in the organization. The questionnaire is normally scored by giving one point for each "mostly agree" answer. It takes a score of sixteen or more to conclude that a strong inclination toward playing politics exists.

Organizational Climates

Ever wonder why we form groups and organizations? Organizations exist to meet certain needs and achieve definite purposes.

The success of any organization can be measured by asking to what extent they have achieved their purpose. Organizations have at least two easily identifiable sets of needs, namely, task needs and people needs.

Task needs present the function of the work done by the organization. A school, for example, needs adequate supplies and materials, properly trained personnel, appropriate physical facilities, sufficient funds to operate, input from parents and community agencies, and strategies for putting programmes into action.

People needs occur simply because people work within organizations. People bring with them needs for belonging, achievement, recognition self-worth, identity, integrity, as well as others such as financial security. Through the interaction between individuals within organizations, to some extent, they find their people-needs met.

Any broad effort directed toward improving an organization's success must necessarily focus on:

- Increasing the efficiency of the organization's task activities, i.e., better meeting the task needs and

- Maximizing the possibility for human growth within the organization, such as better ways to meet people needs.

When speaking of improving the effectiveness of the organization, it seems useful to break down these concerns into parts, treating human growth and development as different from the task of the organization. People working alone or in collaboration with others can carry out the myriad of tasks of organizations. Every effective organization has needs that they meet by performing certain tasks, as well as those they meet by developing human relationships.

Concept of Climate

Individuals have moods and feelings. So do organizations, and this is called climate. Outsiders often feel or sense the climate better than the group itself. They may experience the climate as peaceful, angry, charged, tense, vigorous, or fast paced. People immersed in a group have difficulty in sensing the group's climate. If the group climate is one of threat and attack, individuals sense their own reaction of fear, or of desire to withdraw, even though they may not understand the climate.

The group climate is the predominant feeling tone of a group (i.e., the quality of their being together). Individuals sense the climate through their own emotional reactions. For a group to diagnose or name its own climate, each individual has to report and share his/her observation of the group's behaviour. If everyone openly and honestly reports these observations the group can look at the pooled observations for patterns of group behaviour. From this composite they can make a statement of the group's climate. For example, in a group of ten, if three people say they observed people arguing, three report they observed people interrupting each other, four report that they saw people withdraw by non-participation while others involved themselves in a tug-of-war with feelings such as resentment and hurt, they can label the group as a high-threat climate arising from hurtful or angry competition.

Group Aspiration

At the same time, a group may have or be able to develop common aspirations about what it wants its climate to be. Just as individuals have values that provide an ideal about what they want to be, groups can do the same out of common, shared values that create motivation for improving their climate.

If the members of the group can share their observations of each other's behaviour, reflect together and label the group climate, they learn that they share a sense of dissatisfaction. Upon reflection, group members may indicate that they would like a climate in which they feel safer, more secure, and more able to express themselves without attacking others or being attacked. This group aspires at that point to a climate characterized by mutual support.

Norms or Operative Values

According to D'Souza, to change the group's climate, the groups norms (or operative values) must change. Norms are implicit ground rules that a group operates by. Members individually conform and seldom deviate from these norms impulsively or unilaterally without receiving a negative or coercive response from the group.

In a group, an implicit norm says, "displays of emotion are a sign of weakness". In that atmosphere, individuals will rarely show emotion. If they do, the group will attempt to control the emotion (tune it down, explain it away, or show open disapproval) or withdraw from the individual until he/she has regained control. The group does this by such things as changing the subject of discussion, silence, no one shows any response, group members break eye contact with the emotional individual, or people leave the room.

D'Souza further states that people rarely identify this operative value directly. If members observed that each time a point of difference or disagreement arose between two group members, the remainder of the group anxiously rushed in to change the subject, to assure the two people their view points were not in conflict and that they really meant the same thing, or that the difference was only a sanantic problem, then observers can infer that a powerful norm in this group demanded that the members cover up, avoid, or harmonize differences at all cost.

In this instance, group members share an operative unconsciously or by implicit mutual expectations.

Changing Climate by Changing Norms

According to D'Souza, groups can change climates by:

1. Identifying the present climate.
2. Developing a common desire for a new one.
3. Identifying the operative values in the group that generate the less desirable climate. Groups do this by:
    i. Having each individual report observed behaviour, and looking for behavioural patterns, and
    ii. Inferring the norm or common expectation that underlies the pattern.
4. This makes the norm reach a level of consciousness so that the group can reflect and choose to change it. In this way, the group begins to gain control of its climate.
5. The group introduces the behaviours they want to change or they specify the new norms and expectations they want to create, and

6. Groups do not change climates simply by sharing, developing awareness, and holding common desires. Individuals must change their behaviour towards other members and group events for the climate to change. Unless people change their own behaviour, the group climate cannot improve.

Ethics and Legitimacy

Whether a certain type of political behaviour can be viewed as ethical must be judged against some model or criterion. Behaviour may be evaluated in terms of the utilitarian model (the greatest good for the greatest number), the right model (an individual right should not be violated) or the justice model (there should be fair and equitable distribution of benefits and burdens). Ideally, all three models should be applied and behaviour should meet all three tests to be considered ethical. Yet, there are cases where conflicts occur or information is limited so that it is not entirely clear what is ethical.

A somewhat different consideration is whether the behaviour involved is considered within or outside the organization's normal and acceptable range. Where certain political behaviours are viewed as illegitimate, severe sanctions may be brought to bear against those who engage in them.

Types of Political Behaviour

The table below provides a way of looking at political behaviors and method of distinguishing between what is likely to be considered legitimate and illegitimate activities.

Pattern of Political Behaviour in Organizations

	Internal to the organization		External to the organization	
Direction or political behavior	Legitimate behavior	Illegitimate behavior	Legitimate behavior	Illegitimate behavior
Vertical (up) and down the hierarchy	Direct voice complain to supervisor	Sabotage symbiotic protests mutinies Riots	Law/suits against the firm	Whistle blowing to the public regarding organization
	By-passing claim of command obstructionism so that policies are not implemented			
	Coalition formation exchange of favours reprisals			
Horizontal (across) the hierarchy		Physical threats from another organization outside professional activity	Talks with counterpart from another organization outside professional activity	A defection to competitor organization and duplicity such as spying.

Remedies of Negative Impact of Organizational Power and Politics

Negative power and politics within the organization as earlier pointed out do not augur well for the growth and productivity of the organization. The question, therefore, is how can management minimize the negative impact of power and politics? The view is here held that bargaining and communication can be used to speed up the rate of organizational cooperation. Bernard (1968) accepted this view by formulating his principles of organizational communication system for maintaining formal authority.

Bernard's Principles of Organizational Communication Systems for Maintaining Formal Authority:

Premises

1. Communication has presumption of authority when it originates at sources of organization information, communication center – better than individual sources.
2. Some people have superior ability. Their knowledge and understanding regardless of position command respect. This is the authority of leadership.

Accordingly

When the authority of leadership is combined with the authority of position, people who have an established connection with an organization generally will grant authority, accepting orders far outside the zone of indifference.

Principles

1. Channels of communication should be definitely known.
2. Objective authority requires a definite formal channel of communication to every member of an organization.
3. The line of communication must be as direct or short as possible.
4. The complete line of communication must be used.
5. The competence of the persons serving as communication centers, that is, officers, supervisory heads, etc. must be adequate and
6. Every communication should be authenticated. The person communicating must be known actually to occupy the position of authority concerned, that is, it is within its authority and it actually is an authorized communication from his office.

Thus, if adequate communication process is applied, conflicts and frictions that will develop into power tussle and organizational politics will be diminished.

References

- Leadership: businessjargons.com, Retrieved 1 March, 2019
- Organizational-theory-and-behaviour: universityofcalicut.info, Retrieved 12 August, 2019
- Communication: its.caltech.edu, Retrieved 8 January, 2019
- Leadership-process: centerod.com, Retrieved 7 April, 2019
- The-Influence-of-Power-and-Politics-in-Organizations: hrmars.com, Retrieved 26 February, 2019

5

Organizational Structure and Systems

The system which details the manner in which specific activities of an organization are directed and divided is known as organizational structure. The process through which the different elements of an organization are arranged into an efficient structure is known as departmentalization. The topics elaborated in this chapter will help in gaining a better perspective about the different aspects of organizational structure and systems.

Structure and Design of an Organizational System

When two or more people work together to achieve a group result, it is an organization. After the objectives of an organization are established, the functions that must be performed are determined. Personnel requirements are assessed and the physical resources needed to accomplish the objectives determined. These elements must then be coordinated into a structural design that will help achieve the objectives. Finally, appropriate responsibilities are assigned.

Determining the functions to be performed involves consideration of division of labour; this is usually accomplished by a process of departmentalization.

Departmentalization

Grouping related functions into manageable units to achieve the objectives of the enterprise in the most efficient and effective manner is departmentalization. A variety of means can be utilized for this purpose. The primary forms of departmentalization are by function, process, product, market, customer, geographic area, and even matrix (also called project organization). In many organizations, a combination of these forms is used.

Function

Perhaps the oldest and most common method of grouping related functions is by specialized function, such as marketing, finance, and production (or operations). Sometimes this form of departmentalization may create problems if individuals with specialized functions become more concerned with their own specialized area than with the overall business. An example of departmentalization by function appears in figure.

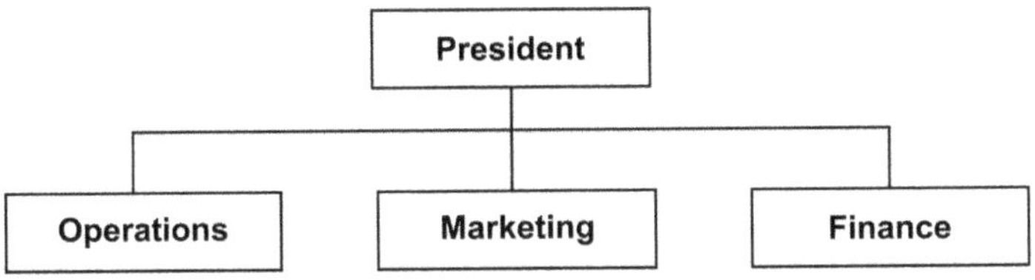

Departmentalization by function.

Process

Departmentalization can also take place by process. This type of departmentalization, often exists in manufacturing companies. Departmentalization in manufacturing companies.

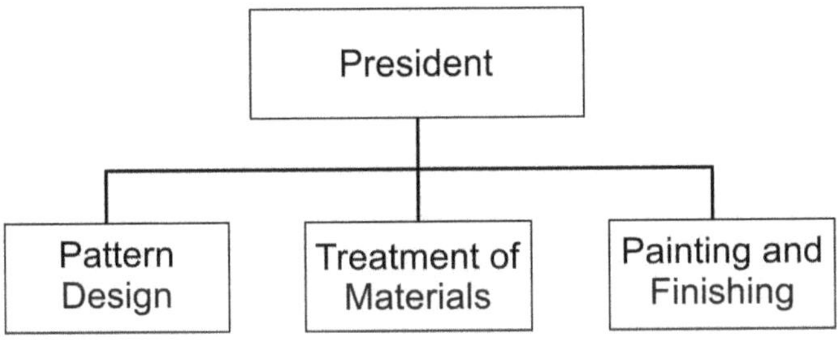

Departmentalization in manufacturing companies.

Product

Whenever specialized knowledge of certain products or services is needed, departmentalization by product may be best. This usually occurs in large diversified companies. Departmentalization by product.

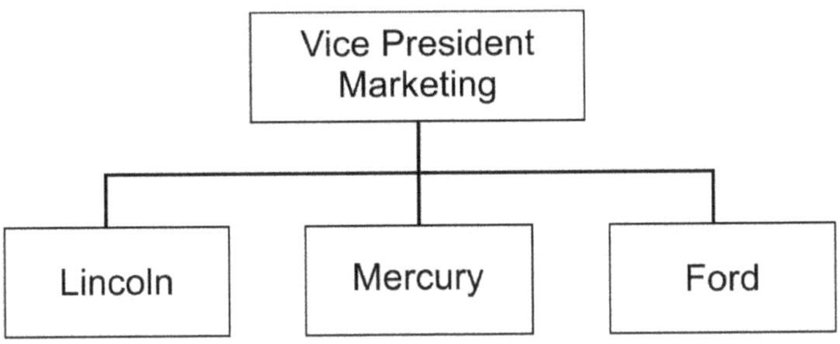

Departmentalization by product.

Market

When a need exists to provide better service to different types of markets, departmentalization by market may be the appropriate form.

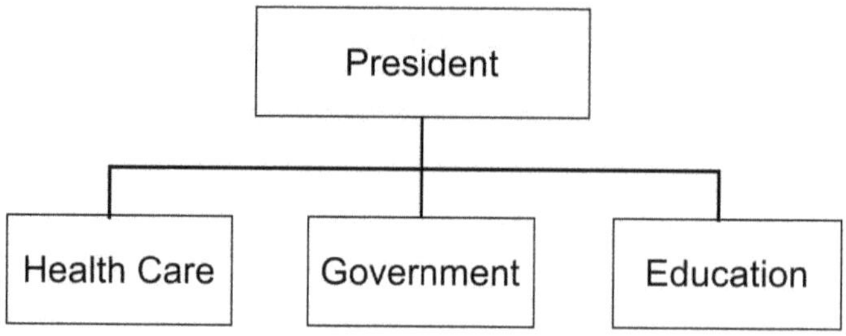

Market form of departmentalization.

Customer

Sometimes key or major customers warrant departmentalization by customer. This is often the case in banks.

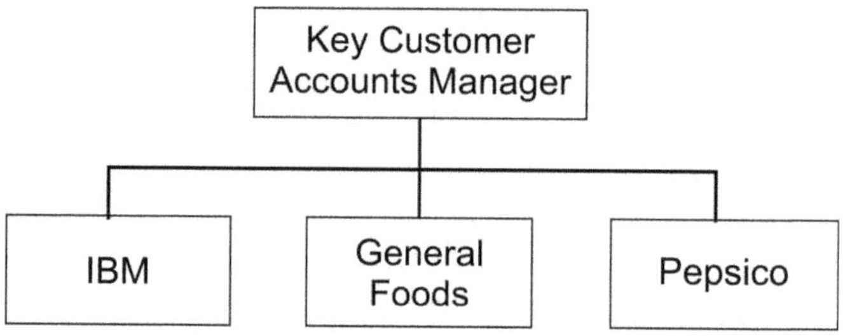

Departmentalization by customer.

Geographic Area

When organizations are spread throughout the world or have territories in many parts of a country, departmentalization by geographic area may provide better service to customers and be more cost effective.

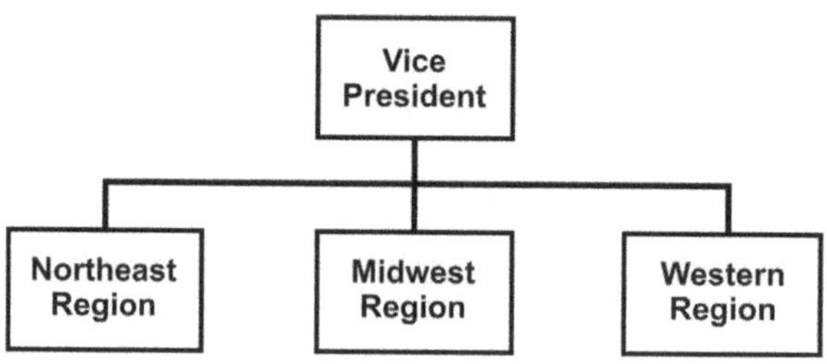

Departmentalization by geographic area.

Matrix (Project Organization)

Departmentalization by matrix, or project, has received considerable use in recent years, particularly in such industries as aerospace (e.g., NASA). In this method, personnel with different backgrounds and experiences that bear on the project are assembled and given the specific project to be accomplished within a certain time period. When the project is completed, these specialized personnel return to their regular work assignments. An example of this form is illustrated in Figure which often takes the shape of a diamond.

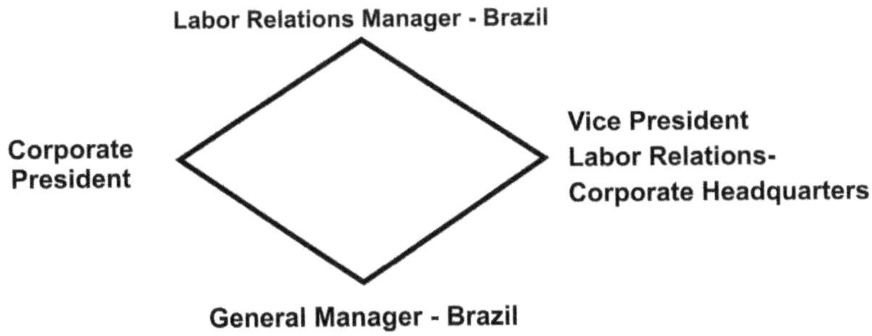

Departmentalization by matrix.

Combination Approach

Many organizations, particularly large, physically dispersed and diversified organizations, utilize several different forms of departmentalization. Figure is an organizational chart showing the use of several forms of departmentalization.

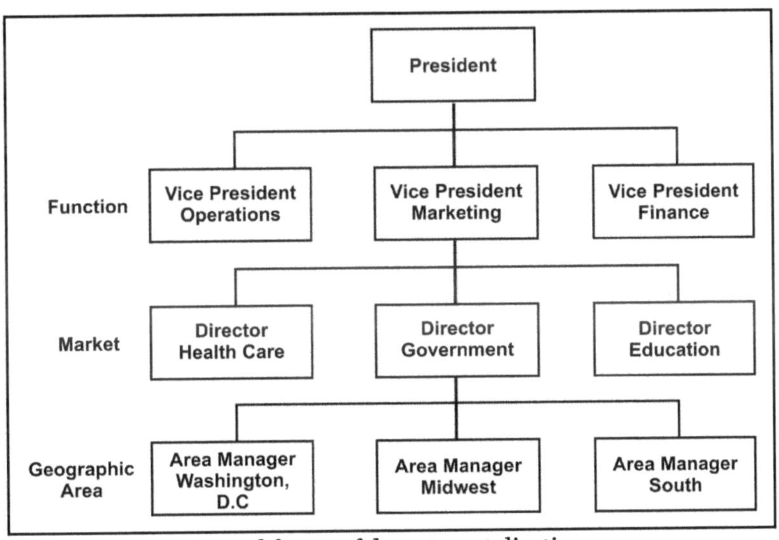

Several forms of departmentalization.

Determining the functions to be performed in an organization involves consideration of division of labour; this is usually accomplished by a process of departmentalization. The primary forms of departmentalization are by function, process, product, market, customer, geographical area, matrix (project) or some combination of these forms.

Delegation the Art of Managing

As shown earlier, the process of managing begins with the establishment of objectives. Once the objectives have been established, the functions that must be accomplished are considered. Then the work to be performed or the responsibilities to be assigned are determined. This means it is necessary to know the personnel and physical resources needed to accomplish the objectives of the enterprise. Thus, when the functions, personnel, and other resources are grouped together by some means of departmentalization into a logical framework or organizational structure, the process of delegation begins.

Delegation is the process that makes management possible. Why? Because management is the process of getting results accomplished through others.

Delegation Process, Authority and Accountability

At the moment a job becomes too complex, too diverse, or too voluminous for one person, the need for delegation arises. In its simplest form, imagine the sole administrator with objectives and with no time to accomplish them. Means allowing, the manager can create a new job, hire an employee, and assign the accomplishment of the objectives to the new employee.

To meet these responsibilities, the new employee must also have the authority to achieve them. Thus, authority is delegated along with the responsibility. The manager, however, is still ultimately responsible. By assigning some of his or her responsibilities, the manager transfers or creates accountability. If the employee does not exercise the responsibility properly, the manager can always withdraw the authority. Delegation without control is abdication.

In practice, the process of management works in conjunction with the process of delegation. Since management is the process of getting results through others, delegation facilitates that process by assigning responsibilities, delegating authority, and exacting accountability by employees.

The delegation process works as follows. The manager has certain defined objectives (i.e., results) to accomplish at the end of the budget period. He or she assigns the responsibilities (i.e., duties to be performed) to key employees, along with the commensurate authority to go with those responsibilities. Thus, the accomplishment of the assigned responsibilities should equal the defined objectives.

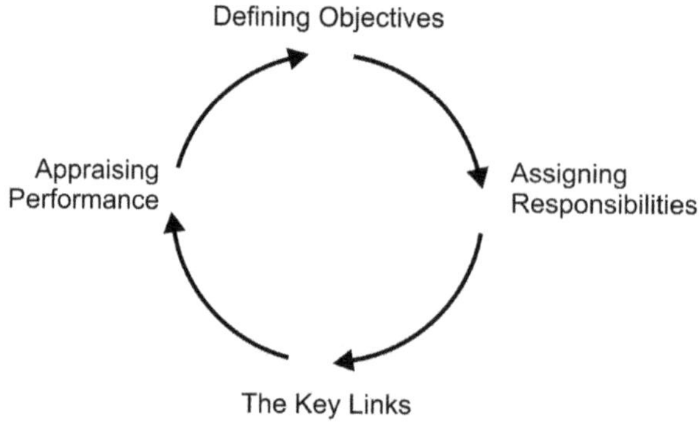

The manager then develops standards of performance with each key employee (i.e., the conditions that should exist when a job is done well). These standards should be developed mutually to be effective. In essence, these standards of performance become the accountability of each employee for the budget period. The successful accomplishment of the standards of performance should equal the assigned responsibilities. The process continues with the appraisal of key subordinates rated against the agreed-upon standards of performance and closes with evaluation and feedback to the beginning of the next budget cycle, when the process begins all over again.

Risks in Delegation

The sheer volume of management responsibilities necessitates delegation. There is somewhat of a paradox in this situation, however, because delegation involves taking risks. Among the risks of delegation are loss of control, reverse delegation, and even loss of a job.

Loss of Control

In giving over authority to another, the manager loses some control over the proper completion of a project. The manager who has lived by the adage "If you want it done right, do it yourself" may find it difficult to delegate tasks for which he or she will ultimately be held accountable.

The key to successful delegation is assigning the right responsibilities to the right person. Of course, one never knows who the right persons are until one meets and works with them, but it must realistically be assumed that a given organization, department, or section employs at least some competent, willing, and responsible individuals. This assumption does not address itself to the fact that it is nearly impossible today for the manager to be technically superior to all employees. A staff that is not utilized effectively because of a manager's failure to delegate is a major loss to an organization, a waste of human resources.

Reverse Delegation

An important consideration for the manager who tries to do everybody's job is that he or she does so at the expense of the job for which he was hired--managing. An interesting analogy that underscores the value of delegation for management's sake is the "monkey-on-the-back" analogy, which claims that managers spend far more time with their employees than they even faintly realize. This habit occurs especially when a problem is brought to the manager's attention. In encounters with employees, the manager's use of simple phrases, such as "send me a memo on that," or "let me think about that and I'll let you know," or "just let me know what I can do," causes the "monkey" (problem) to jump onto the manager's back.

The manager assumes the responsibility for handling the task that was delegated to the employee in the first place, and when the employee reaches an impasse, the manager takes the next step. This is reverse delegation, and many employees are adept at it. Naturally, there will be situations in which the next step is justified, but unless the manager wants endless lines at the office door, he or she should avoid the casual and repeated use of those phrases that permit employee problems to ride on the manager's back. In fact, this principle of delegation is that accountability to a superior cannot be delegated.

A solution to this problem is to encourage initiative in employees. Employees should not have to wait until told to do something; nor should they have to ask. They should practice the completion of assigned tasks. By keeping the responsibility where it belongs, the manager will increase discretionary time to manage and can still handle system-imposed tasks. To develop initiative in employees early is one of the ways to develop a new generation of capable managers.

Loss of Job

The foregoing discussion brings to mind another risk in delegation from management's viewpoint. Is it possible to delegate one's self right out of a job? Suppose a subordinate develops so much initiative that he or she becomes superior to the boss. This is a threatening problem for the manager. The employee would be very happy if his or her development resulted in promotion, but what if the promotion means the manager's job?

Consensus among theorists suggests that the employee should be given the opportunity to perform to as high a level of responsibility as possible if this improves the group's performance. The manager should then endeavour to reward that person accordingly, even if it means helping that person to land a better lob outside the organization. To neglect and waste the talents of any individual is as criminal as the misuse of company funds or equipment.

In practice, we have all heard stories from individuals who feel more competent dim their managers. Thus it would seem that the best safeguard a manager has in preserving his or her position is to be a good manager and to prepare for his or her own advancement.

Techniques of Delegation

The art of delegation often depends on a given situation. Plans change and people differ, but this does not imply that the employee should have to be notified on a daily basis of what is needed. Nor does it imply that there are not some generally accepted techniques that can facilitate the process of delegation, as discussed below. More suggestions are detailed in the list of do's and don'ts.

Responsibilities and Authority

A clear definition of responsibilities and the authority to accomplish them constitute the foundation of the art of delegation. Whenever possible, these responsibilities should be stated in writing. The employee should also have a good idea of how the job fits into the total picture and why it is important. The manager should also encourage questions and be completely approachable. This practice, in combination with exhibiting confidence and trust by allowing subordinates to pursue goals without undue reporting, constant checking, and other exaggerated forms of control, will create a supportive climate and help to build an effective working relationship.

Performance Rating

Once the employee understands the job, that person should be made aware of how performance will be measured. This step in the management process has already been mentioned.

By and large, and within reason, managers receive the type and level of job performance they expect or informally accept over a period of time. In fact, low expectations tend to breed low performance and the opposite is true of high expectations. The failure to confront lower than desired levels of performance is tantamount to acknowledging them as acceptable; high expectations mean setting challenging but achievable goals. The focus should be on results that are motivating and attainable.

The manager should establish a system for setting objectives and set up a procedure for periodically reporting progress toward these objectives. Consideration of less-experienced employees demands more frequent consultation and, possibly, reporting. The manager who is committed to delegating authority should avoid switching back and forth in delegation, thereby causing only confusion and stagnation among employees.

Awareness of Limitations

It may seem self-evident, but delegation cannot be used when the individual does not welcome additional responsibility. Knowing who wants greater responsibility or promotion is as important as knowing who is qualified for a job. It is often difficult for successful executives, who owe their success to a driving desire for greater responsibility and recognition, to understand others who seem to lack that motivation.

In essence, the manager-employee relationship is one of interdependence. A major goal of delegation is to reduce dependence on the manager, but the manager incurs a certain responsibility to the employee in delegation. The manager is responsible for helping the assistant discover how best to develop his or her abilities in order to meet future responsibilities.

Managers can develop employees through the art of delegation and should practice this art judiciously. With effective delegation, a manager can multiply his or her effectiveness and, through others, achieve the results expected.

Parity of Authority and Responsibility

An important principle of organization as well as management is that authority should equal responsibility. This principle is known as the parity of authority and responsibility and ensures that work will be performed with a minimum amount of frustration on the part of personnel. By not delegating authority equal to responsibility, a manager will create employee dissatisfaction and generally waste energies and resources.

Scalar Principle

This concept is generally referred to as the chain of command. It means that there should be a clear definition of authority in the organization and that this authority flows, one link at a time, through the chain of command from the top to the bottom of the organization. Communication in the organization is through channels. Following this principle generally results in clarification of relationships, less confusion, and improved decision-making.

Delegation is the process that makes management possible because management is the process of getting results accomplished through others. Understanding the process of delegation involves employing the principles of responsibility, authority, and accountability, as well as understanding the concept of the chain of command (scalar principle).

Delegation Do's and Don'ts

Do's

- Delegate as simply and directly as possible. Give precise instructions.
- Illustrate how each delegation applies to organizational goals.
- Mutually develop standards of performance.
- Clarify expected results.
- Anticipate the questions your employees may have, and answer them in order.
- Discuss recurring problems.
- Seek employee ideas about how to do the job.
- Accentuate the positive rather than the negative. Be supportive. Exhibit trust.
- Recognize superior performance.
- Keep your promises.

Don'ts

- Do not threaten your staff. Effective delegation depends more on leadership skills than on position power.

- Do not assume a condescending attitude.
- Do not merely give answers. Show an employee how to do something and why it is done that way.
- Do not overreact to problems. Refrain from criticizing an employee in front of others.
- Avoid excessive checks on progress.

Centralization versus Decentralization

The issues of centralization and decentralization involve the principle of delegation of authority. When a limited amount of authority is delegated in an organization, it is usually characterized as centralized. When a significant amount of authority is delegated to lower levels in the organization, the business is characterized as decentralized. Centralization and decentralization are opposites, and there are different degrees of each. In a highly centralized organization, employees at lower levels have a limited range of decision-making authority. The scope of authority to make decisions in decentralized organizations, by way of contrast, is very broad for lower level employees.

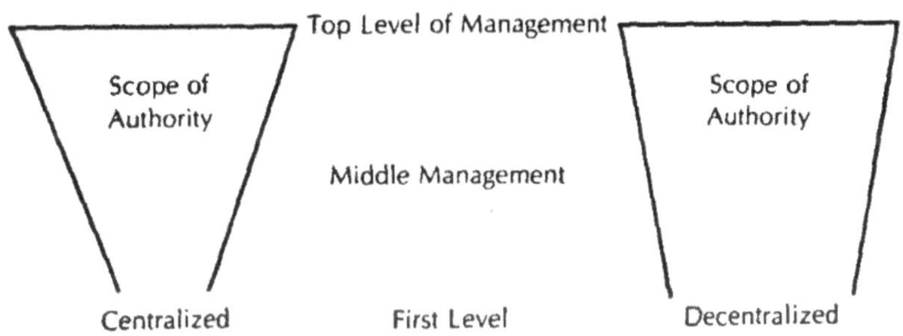

One cannot classify all forms of centralization as effective or ineffective. The same applies to decentralization. Each form has its advantages and disadvantages and is affected by a number of factors. For example, the size and complexity of the enterprise can affect the delegation of authority. If an organization is very large and diversified, the limitations of expertise will generally lead to decentralization of authority to the heads of these different businesses. if speed and adaptability to change are characteristic of the business, it tends toward decentralization. Geographic dispersion also favours decentralization of authority. On the other hand, some organizations have excellent and speedy communications systems that tend to favour the centralization of authority. In situations in which adequate personnel are unavailable, the organization tends to centralized authority.

Advantages of Centralization

- Closer control of operations.
- Uniformity of policies, practices, and procedures.

- Better use of centralized, specialized experts.

Advantages of Decentralization

- Faster decision-making without resort to higher level consultation.
- Excellent training experience for promotion to higher level management.
- Decisions better adapted to local conditions.

The issues of centralization and decentralization involve the principle of delegation of authority. In centralization, a limited amount of authority is delegated; in decentralization, a significant amount of authority is delegated to lower levels. Each form has its advantages and disadvantages and is affected by a number of factors, such as size of organization and the amount of geographic dispersion.

Organizational Structures

The primary formal relationships for organizing, as discussed earlier, are responsibility, authority, and accountability. They enable us to bring together functions, people, and other resources for the purpose of achieving objectives. The framework for organizing these formal relationships is known as the organizational structure. It provides the means for clarifying and communicating the lines of responsibility, authority, and accountability.

Major Types of Organizational Structure

Although there are a number of variations of organizational structure, we shall discuss line and staff organizations and committee organization here.

Line Organization

The line organization is the simplest organizational structure. It is the "doing" organization, in that the work of all organizational units is directly involved in producing and marketing the organization's goods and services. There are direct vertical links between the different levels of the scalar chain. Since there is a clear authority structure, this form of organization promotes greater decision-making and is simple in form to understand.

On the other hand, managers may be overburdened when they have too many duties.

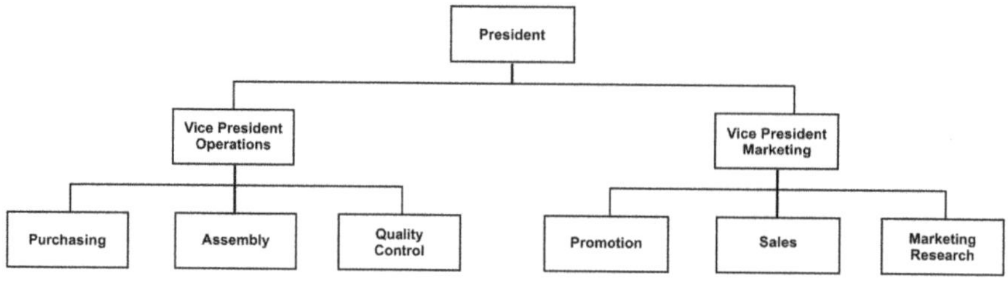

Simple line organization

Line and Staff Organization

When staff specialists are added to a line organization to "advise; "serve;" or "support" the line in some manner, we have a line and staff organization. These specialists contribute to the effectiveness and efficiency of the organization. Their authority is generally limited to making recommendation to the line organization. Sometimes this creates conflict. However, such conflict can be reduced by having staff specialists obtain some line experience, which will tend to make them better understand the problems facing the line managers they support. Such functions as human resources management and research and development are typical staff functions.

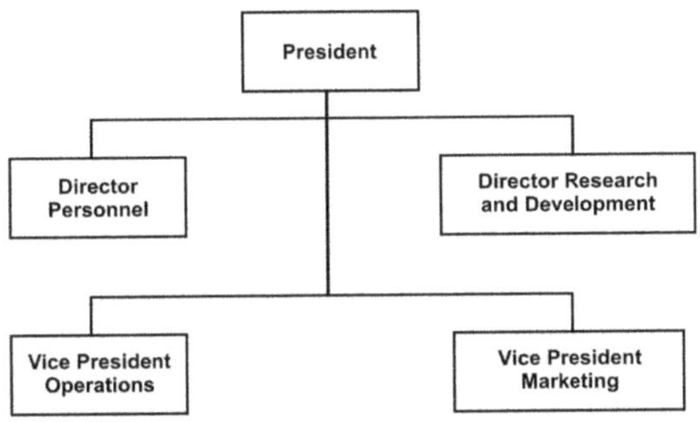

Committee Organization

When a group of people is formally appointed to consider or decide certain matters, this type of structure is a committee. Committees can be permanent (standing) or temporary and usually supplement line and staff functions. Sometimes ad hoc or temporary committees are set up to deal with a specific problem. Once this committee makes its recommendations, it is dissolved. On the other hand, permanent committees usually act in an advisory capacity to certain organizational units or managers. For example, committees are used to a large extent in universities. They may report to a dean or department chair. Certain committees, called plural committees, have the authority to order, not only to recommend. These committees are usually reserved for a very high level, such as the board of directors. An example is an executive committee of the board for compensation or for succession planning.

Although committees have a number of advantages, they also have a number of disadvantages, particularly being excessively time consuming. Hence they should be managed effectively.

Organizational Structure and Environment and Technology

Most studies that have been conducted on the relationship between organizational structure and the environment have concluded that the best organizational structure is contingent to some degree on the conditions in the environment. Several studies have also shown a relationship between technology and structure. In fact, these researchers even suggest that technology itself determines structure. These studies and others have led to a contingency approach to organizational structure.

Contingency Approach

This approach indicates that the most appropriate organizational structure depends not only on the organizational objectives but also on the situation, which includes the environment, the technology employed, the rate and pace of change, the managerial style, the size of the organization, and other dynamic forces.

Creating and Maintaining Organization Culture

Where do cultures come from? Understanding this question is important in understanding how they can be changed. An organization's culture is shaped as the organization faces external and internal challenges and learns how to deal with them. When the organization's way of doing business provides a successful adaptation to environmental challenges and ensures success, those values are retained. These values and ways of doing business are taught to new members as the way to do business.

The factors that are most important in the creation of an organization's culture include founders' values, preferences, and industry demands.

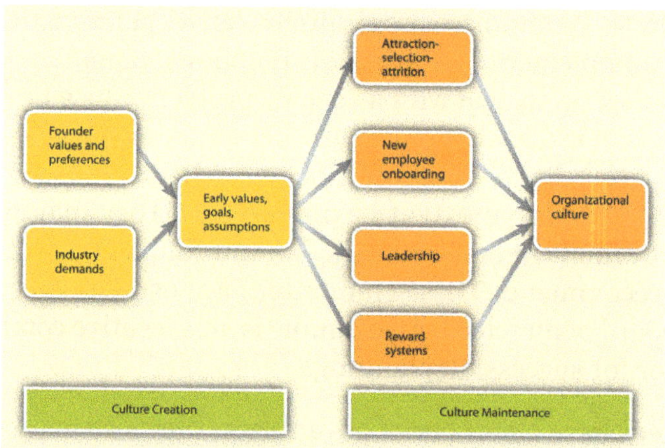

Model Describing How Cultures Are Created and Maintained.

Founder Values

A company's culture, particularly during its early years, is inevitably tied to the personality, background, and values of its founder or founders, as well as their vision for the future of the organization. When entrepreneurs establish their own businesses, the way they want to do business determines the organization's rules, the structure set up in the company, and the people they hire to work with them.

Founder values become part of the corporate culture to the degree to which they help the company be successful.

Industry Demands

While founders undoubtedly exert a powerful influence over corporate cultures, the industry characteristics also play a role. Companies within the same industry can sometimes have widely differing cultures. At the same time, the industry characteristics and demands act as a force to create similarities among organizational cultures. For example, despite some differences, many companies in the insurance and banking industries are stable and rule-oriented, many companies in the high-tech industry have innovative cultures, and those in non-profit industry may be people-oriented. If the industry is one with a large number of regulatory requirements—for example, banking, health care, and high-reliability (such as nuclear power plant) industries—then we might expect the presence of a large number of rules and regulations, a bureaucratic company structure, and a stable culture. The industry influence over culture is also important to know because this shows that it may not be possible to imitate the culture of a company in a different industry, even though it may seem admirable to outsiders.

Way to Maintain Culture of the Company

As a company matures, its cultural values are refined and strengthened. The early values of a company's culture exert influence over its future values. It is possible to think of organizational culture as an organism that protects itself from external forces. Organizational culture determines what types of people are hired by an organization and what types of people are left out. Moreover, once new employees are hired, the company assimilates new employees and teaches them the way things are done in the organization. We call these processes attraction-selection-attrition and onboarding processes. We will also examine the role of leaders and reward systems in shaping and maintaining an organization's culture.

Attraction-Selection-Attrition

Organizational culture is maintained through a process known as attraction-selection-attrition (ASA). First, employees are attracted to organizations where they will fit in. Someone who has a competitive nature may feel comfortable in and may prefer to work in a company where interpersonal competition is the norm. Others may prefer to work in a team-oriented workplace. Research shows that employees with different personality traits find different cultures attractive. For example, out of the Big Five personality traits, employees who demonstrate neurotic personalities were less likely to be attracted to innovative cultures, whereas those who had openness to experience were more likely to be attracted to innovative cultures.

Of course, this process is imperfect, and value similarity is only one reason a candidate might be attracted to a company. There may be other, more powerful attractions such as good benefits. At this point in the process, the second component of the ASA framework prevents them from getting in: selection. Just as candidates are looking for places where they will fit in, companies are also looking for people who will fit into their current corporate culture. Many companies are hiring people for fit with their culture, as opposed to fit with a certain job. By introducing the candidate to several future co-workers and learning what these co-workers think of the candidate, it becomes easier to assess the level of fit.

Even after a company selects people for person-organization fit, there may be new employees who do not fit in. Some candidates may be skilful in impressing recruiters and signal high levels of culture fit even though they do not necessarily share the company's values. In any event, the organization is eventually going to eliminate candidates eventually who do not fit in through attrition. Attrition refers to the natural process where the candidates who do not fit in will leave the company. Research indicates that person-organization misfit is one of the important reasons for employee turnover.

Because of the ASA process, the company attracts, selects, and retains people who share its core values, whereas those people who are different in core values will be excluded from the organization either during the hiring process or later on through naturally occurring turnover. Thus, organizational culture will act as a self-defending organism where intrusive elements are kept out. Supporting the existence of such self-protective mechanisms, research shows that organizations demonstrate a certain level of homogeneity regarding personalities and values of organizational members.

New Employee Onboarding

Another way in which an organization's values, norms, and behavioral patterns are transmitted to employees is through onboarding (also referred to as the organizational socialization process). Onboarding refers to the process through which new employees learn the attitudes, knowledge, skills, and behaviors required to function effectively within an organization. If an organization can successfully socialize new employees into becoming organizational insiders, new employees will feel accepted by their peers and confident regarding their ability to perform; they will also understand and share the assumptions, norms, and values that are part of the organization's culture. This understanding and confidence in turn translate into more effective new employees who perform better and have higher job satisfaction, stronger organizational commitment, and longer tenure within the company. Organizations engage in different activities to facilitate onboarding, such as implementing orientation programs or matching new employees with mentors.

What can Employees do during Onboarding?

New employees who are proactive, seek feedback, and build strong relationships tend to be more successful than those who do not. For example, feedback seeking helps new employees. Especially on a first job, a new employee can make mistakes or gaffes and may find it hard to understand and interpret the ambiguous reactions of co-workers. By actively seeking feedback, new employees may find out sooner rather than later any behaviors that need to be changed and gain a better understanding of whether their behavior fits with the company culture and expectations.

Relationship building or networking (a facet of the organizing function) is another important behavior new employees may demonstrate. Particularly when a company does not have a systematic approach to onboarding, it becomes more important for new employees to facilitate their own onboarding by actively building relationships. According to one estimate, 35% of managers who start a new job fail in the new job and either voluntarily leave or are fired within one and a half years. Of these, over 60% report not being able to form effective relationships with colleagues as the primary reason for this failure.

What can Organizations do during Onboarding?

Many organizations, take a more structured and systematic approach to new employee onboarding, while others follow a “sink or swim” approach where new employees struggle to figure out what is expected of them and what the norms are.

A formal orientation program indoctrinates new employees to the company culture, as well as introducing them to their new jobs and colleagues. An orientation program has a role in making new employees feel welcome in addition to imparting information that may help them be successful in their new jobs. Many large organizations have formal orientation programs consisting of lectures, videotapes, and written material, while some may follow more informal approaches. According to one estimate, most orientations last anywhere from one to five days, and some companies are currently switching to a computer-based orientation. Research shows that formal orientation programs are helpful in teaching employees about the goals and history of the company, as well as communicating the power structure. Moreover, these programs may also help with a new employee’s integration to the team. However, these benefits may not be realized to the same extent in computer-based orientations. In fact, compared to those taking part in a regular, face-to-face orientation, those undergoing a computer-based orientation were shown to have lower understanding of their job and the company, indicating that different formats of orientations may not substitute for each other.

What can Organizational Insiders do during Onboarding?

One of the most important ways in which organizations can help new employees adjust to a company and a new job is through organizational insiders—namely, supervisors, co-workers, and mentors. Leaders have a key influence over onboarding and the information and support they provide determine how quickly employees learn about the company politics and culture, while coworker influence determines the degree to which employees adjust to their teams. Mentors can be crucial to helping new employees adjust by teaching them the ropes of their jobs and how the company really operates. A mentor is a trusted person who provides an employee with advice and support regarding career-related matters. Although a mentor can be any employee or manager who has insights that are valuable to the new employee, mentors tend to be relatively more experienced than their protégés. Mentoring can occur naturally between two interested individuals or organizations can facilitate this process by having formal mentoring programs. These programs may successfully bring together mentors and protégés who would not come together otherwise.

Research indicates that the existence of these programs does not guarantee their success, and there are certain program characteristics that may make these programs more effective. For example, when mentors and protégés feel that they had input in the mentor-protégé matching process, they tend to be more satisfied with the arrangement. Moreover, when mentors receive training beforehand, the outcomes of the program tend to be more positive. Because mentors may help new employees interpret and understand the company's culture, organizations may benefit from selecting mentors who personify the company's values. Thus, organizations may need to design these programs carefully to increase their chance of success.

Leadership

Leaders are instrumental in creating and changing an organization's culture. There is a direct correspondence between the leader's style and an organization's culture. For example, when leaders motivate employees through inspiration, corporate culture tends to be more supportive and people-oriented. When leaders motivate by making rewards contingent on performance, the corporate culture tended to be more performance-oriented and competitive. In these and many other ways, what leaders do directly influences the cultures of their organizations. This is a key point for managers to consider as they carry out their leading P-O-L-C function.

Part of the leader's influence over culture is through role modelling. Many studies have suggested that leader behavior, the consistency between organizational policy and leader actions, and leader role modelling determine the degree to which the organization's culture emphasizes ethics. The leader's own behaviors will signal to individuals what is acceptable behavior and what is unacceptable. In an organization in which high-level managers make the effort to involve others in decision making and seek opinions of others, a team-oriented culture is more likely to evolve. By acting as role models, leaders send signals to the organization about the norms and values that are expected to guide the actions of its members.

Leaders also shape culture by their reactions to the actions of others around them. For example, do they praise a job well done or do they praise a favoured employee regardless of what was accomplished? How do they react when someone admits to making an honest mistake? What are their priorities? In meetings, what types of questions do they ask? Do they want to know what caused accidents so that they can be prevented, or do they seem more concerned about how much money was lost because of an accident? Do they seem outraged when an employee is disrespectful to a co-worker, or does their reaction depend on whether they like the harasser? Through their day-to-day actions, leaders shape and maintain an organization's culture.

Reward Systems

Finally, the company culture is shaped by the type of reward systems used in the organization and the kinds of behaviors and outcomes it chooses to reward and punish. One relevant element of the reward system is whether the organization rewards behaviors or results. Some companies have reward systems that emphasize intangible elements of performance as well as more easily observable metrics. In these companies, supervisors and peers may evaluate an employee's performance by assessing the person's behaviors as well as the results. In such companies, we may expect a culture that is relatively people - or team-oriented, and employees act as part of a family. However, in companies in which goal achievement is the sole criterion for reward, there is a focus on measuring only the results without much regard to the process. In these companies, we might observe outcome-oriented and competitive cultures. Whether the organization rewards performance or seniority would also make a difference in culture. When promotions are based on seniority, it would be difficult to establish a culture of outcome orientation. Finally, the types of behaviors that are rewarded or ignored set the tone for the culture. Which behaviors are rewarded, which ones are punished, and which are ignored will determine how a company's culture evolves. A reward system is one tool managers can wield when undertaking the controlling function.

Signs of Organizational Culture

How do you find out about a company's culture? We emphasized earlier that culture influences the way members of the organization think, behave, and interact with one another. Thus, one way of finding out about a company's culture is by observing employees or interviewing them. At the same time, culture manifests itself in some visible aspects of the organization's environment.

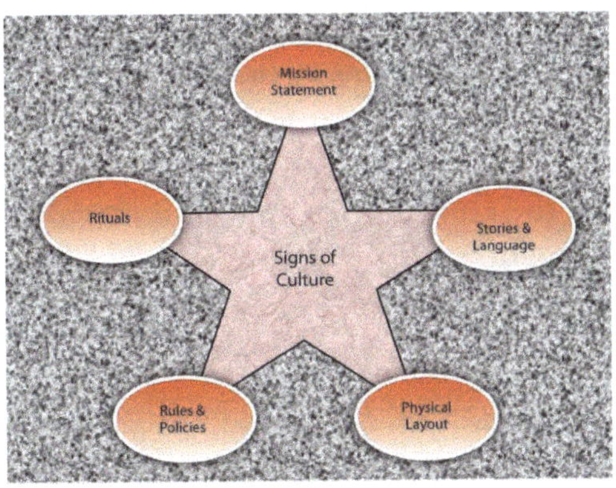

Visual Eleme nts of Culture.

Mission Statement

A mission statement is a statement of purpose, describing who the company is and what it does. It serves an important function for organizations as part of the first facet of the planning P-O-L-C function. But, while many companies have mission statements, they do not always reflect the company's values and its purpose. An effective mission statement is well known by employees, is transmitted to all employees starting from their first day at work, and influences employee behavior.

Some mission statements reflect who the company wants to be as opposed to who they actually are. If the mission statement does not affect employee behavior on a day-to-day basis, it has little usefulness as a tool for understanding the company's culture.

A mission statement that is taken seriously and widely communicated may provide insights into the corporate culture.

Rituals

Tradition is important at Mary Kay Cosmetics. Pink Cadillacs are given to top performers at large annual events.

Rituals refer to repetitive activities within an organization that have symbolic meaning. Usually rituals have their roots in the history of a company's culture. They create camaraderie and a sense of belonging among employees. They also serve to teach employees corporate values and create identification with the organization. During this ritual, employees feel a connection to the company culture and its values such as self-determination, willpower, and enthusiasm.

Rules and Policies

Another way in which an observer may find out about a company's culture is to examine its rules and policies. Companies create rules to determine acceptable and unacceptable behavior and, thus, the rules that exist in a company will signal the type of values it has. Policies about issues such as decision making, human resources, and employee privacy reveal what the company values and emphasizes. For example, a company that has a policy such as "all pricing decisions of merchandise will be made at corporate headquarters" is likely to have a centralized culture that is hierarchical, as opposed to decentralized and empowering. The presence or absence of policies on sensitive issues such as English-only rules, bullying and unfair treatment of others, workplace surveillance, open-door policies, sexual harassment, workplace romances, and corporate social responsibility all provide pieces of the puzzle that make up a company's culture. This highlights how interrelated the P-O-L-C functions are in practice. Through rules and policies, the controlling function affects the organization's culture, a facet of organizing.

Physical Layout

A company's building, layout of employee offices, and other workspaces communicate important messages about a company's culture.

The layout of the office space also is a strong indicator of a company's culture. A company that has an open layout where high-level managers interact with employees may have a culture of team orientation and egalitarianism, whereas a company where most high-level managers have their own floor may indicate a higher level of hierarchy. The degree to which playfulness, humour, and fun are part of a company's culture may be indicated in the office environment. A casual observation of their work environment sends the message that employees who work there see their work as fun.

Stories and Language

Perhaps the most colourful and effective way in which organizations communicate their culture to new employees and organizational members is through the skill-full use of stories. A story can highlight a critical event an organization faced and the organization's response to it, or a heroic effort of a single employee illustrating the company's values. The stories usually engage employee emotions and generate employee identification with the company or the heroes of the tale. A compelling story may be a key mechanism through which managers motivate employees by giving their behavior direction and by energizing them toward a certain goal. Moreover, stories shared with new employees communicate the company's history, its values and priorities, and create a bond between the new employee and the organization.

Language is another way to identify an organization's culture. Companies often have their own acronyms and buzzwords that are clear to them and help set apart organizational insiders from outsiders. In business, this code is known as jargon. Jargon is the language of specialized terms used by a group or profession. Every profession, trade, and organization has its own specialized terms.

Organizational Change and Development

The partial or total adaption of a new idea, concept or behaviour by organisational members is referred to as organisational change. Little wonder, Yang, Zhuo, & Yu, argues that changing the vision and mission statements, organisational strategy, organisational cultures, organisational structure, system, techniques of production and leadership style are some of the targets of organisational change. It arises as a result of pressures from the external environment and the need for internal alignment of structural defects.

From a broader perspective, change refers to a system of continuous transformation that take place in one or more organisational domain such as organisational technology, structure and human resources.

From a broader perspective, change refers to a system of continuous transformation that take place in one or more organisational domain such as organisational technology, structure and human resources.

Organisational change usually originate from discrepancies noticed from environmental dynamism, which takes the form of series of activities that support the process of improvement in the capabilities of individuals and groups that work in organisations.

Organisational change is a consequence of changes in the business activities as well as the outcome of managerial perception, choice and action.

In the opinion of Kotter and Schlesinger, organisational change implies or means the same thing as organisational transformation. However, change implementation is a more rigorous activity than it is often being perceived Szabla that is why it is estimated that two thirds of all organisational change effort does not succeed. According to Bennebroek Gravenhorst, Werkman, and Boonstra, despite this growing attention given to organisational change effort, more than 50 percent of all change initiative still does not succeed.

The goals of organisational change are very many, but they major ones centers on performance

Improvement. prevention or elimination of organisational crisis, and capacity to withstand competition and environment turbulence.

Therefore, all prospective change program must be supported by effective communication process for the following reasons: To convince the employees on the need for change, to enable individuals to appreciate the positive impact that the change will have on them, if successfully implemented, to identify any structural loophole in the change process, and to keep open the channels of communication as the plan progresses.

This change effort is often referred to as planned change. However, this type of change effort has its own draw-back, which according to some authors, is too much emphasis is incremental change, which makes is unreliable in situation that requires rapid approach to institutional and transformational change.

Cummings and Worley note that it is because of the multi-faceted nature of organisational change that the concept is viewed from a number of different perspectives, using multiplicity of models and theories, which sometimes are conflicting.

For the fact that organisations are political systems, so many change efforts in organisations are not initiated to further the interest of the organisation, in terms of better process or output, rather to benefit their own people or individuals. The same is true when you look at an organisation as a fragmentary system of distinct units each pursuing conflicting goals.

The same way we talk about organisational learning: Organisations don't learn, it is the individuals in the organisation that learn. Work teams, groups and organisations don't change, but the individuals in the work group, groups and organisations change. Organisations can only change if and only if members change their attitudes, behaviour and dispositions.

Types of Change

Changes has been classified in some many different ways by different authors using different perspectives, for instance Gersick, defines his classification as gradual or revolutionary; Dunphy and Stace, classify change as either incremental or transformational; Levy classify organisational change as either of 1st degree or 2nd degree, while Miller and Friesen, based their classification on either evolutionary or revolutionary. In all of the classifications, a major point that is common to all the classifications is about the magnitude of the change. Gradual, evolutionary, incremental and 1st degree all have to do with changes that come in bits or departmental or unit changes, while revolutionary, transformational and 2nd degree have to do with big changes that is holistic and involved all strategic units of an organisation.

Approaches to Managing Organisational Change

To succeed and survive in our present highly competitive and continuously evolving business terrain, an understanding of sound management approach of change is imperative. Interestingly, Robbins and Judge identify four main approaches to managing organisational change.

Kurt Lewin Model of Change

Kurt Lewin is the "founding father of change management, with his unfreeze–change–refreeze or 'changing as three steps' (CATS) regarded as the fundamental or 'classic' approach to, or classic 'paradigm' for managing organisational change". His model is based on premises that before introducing a change into an organisation, the individuals in the organisation must be prepared for the change, there must be motivated to change and there must be an established and integrated mechanism for bringing about the change in behaviours of all the organisational members.

Unfreezing the status quo: This involves recognizing the need for a change and improvement. According to Marquis and Huston, "during this stage change agents and all those involved in leading the process of change source for information required to solve the identified problem or lapses". This step is very important because it requires that leaders and managers should educate and motivate their subordinate so that they can buy the idea of change. It is very important to state at this point that any change process initiative involves two divergent types of forces. It is therefore necessary at this stage to identify the driving force of the change as well as the restraining forces of change which is alternatively referred to as the benefits and costs of the change implementations.

Movement to a desired position: This involves the development of new behaviour and attitudes and the execution of the change program. This is a very critical stage and according to Change Management Coach, the following must be done to ensure a successful movement. "You must provide continuous education on the need for the change that is taking place, you must provide extensive support to staff especially those that are resistant, and you must maintain an undiluted flow of communication with your subordinate regarding the change process, especially the benefits to be derived".

Refreezing: This means "stabilizing a change intervention by striking a balance between the driving forces of change and the restraining forces through policies, procedures, structures and cultural norms. For this stage to be successful, two things must be noted here: "The employees must not be rushed, therefore, they must be given ample time to adapt to the new change, and there is need to emphasize the benefits of the change initiative".

One of the criticisms of the Lewin model is that it is broad and rather too abstract. Furthermore, Lewin's model assumed that organisations operate in a stable state, which to a great extent, is not true. Moreso, Kurt Lewin model appears to be only relevant for managing small-scale change projects, and did not take into cognizance the concept of viewing an organisational as a political system (Still on small or incremental change, Sorensen argues that organisations with strong cultures are very good when it comes to incremental changes, but they do not do well when it comes to radical changes. Furthermore, Child argues that "Lenin's postulations appear to be too rigid and his thinking of 'refreezing' cannot be applied in today's complex and dynamic world that requires more of fluidity than rigidity". However, several other authors like McAleese, Creed and Zutshi, have countered some of those criticisms. For instance, the above authors argue that "there has been an unparallel adaptation of Lewin's theoretical heritage is sufficiently robust to withstand the criticisms of the refreeze stage".

Kotter 8- Steps Change Model

Kotter and Cohen investigated the various issues and impediments that people encounter in the course of initiating organisational changes, and came to a logical conclusion that a change initiative can only be successful when individuals are able to change their cognitions and behaviour by sincerely talking to their hearts. It was on the basis of the above shortcomings that Kotter suggested the following eight steps plan for implementing organisational change. The idea behind his insight is that when there is a vision for the change process, there will be a reduction in the rate of errors; this will lead altogether to an increase in the rate of success.

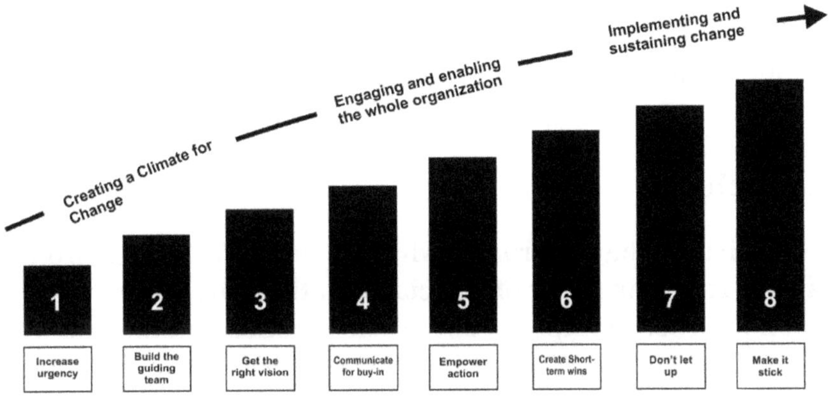

Kotter's 8-step change model.

From Kotter's 8 step change model figure, the first three steps (1, 2 and 3) focus is on creating an enabling environment for change to take place. Steps 4 to 6 focus on ensuring that all organisational members are actively involved in the process of change. The last two steps-7 and 8- (never giving up and making it stick) is all about ensuring the stability and sustenance of the change.

It is always a common phenomenon for organisational leaders to rush into a change program without having a clear conviction of what the impetus for the change is. More often than not, most organisational leaders erroneously assume that they can use the direct influence of their personality drive change and change related processes. Therefore, rather than communicating and aligning with those people that will implement the change, they singlehandedly plan the process and expect the subordinates to just follow. It is on the basis of the above that a guiding coalition becomes imperative, more so, since no individual has all the knowledge, skills and abilities that is required to bring about successful organisational change. However, all is not too well with Kotter's model of change.

The major weaknesses of Kotter's model is that the model appears to be too mechanistic, it is mostly applicable to large organisations and finally, it is not capable of sustaining a change program or any major transformation agenda. In the opinion of O'Keefe Kotter's model for managing change has two major drawbacks as follows: Firstly,

Kotter assumes change to be a one-off activity, which must be carefully managed. Secondly, he projected the model in such a way that will make employees to be suspicious of the change and therefore lose trust and credibility, as leaders make changes without the other employees' own input. In other words, the model makes employees to be mere instruments of change. In another development, but flowing from the same direction, Lewin's approach has also been criticized on the basis that it has become obsolete because it is only applicable in a world where the business environment is stable. This criticism is understandable since at the time of Lewin postulation, the business and economic environment were relatively stable. Secondly the model assumes that change is an unusual phenomenon in an otherwise peaceful world. This happens to support the reactive approach who strongly believes that change occurs only when there is a shock in both external and internal environment of an organisation. However, this assumption is not realistic considering today's turbulent, chaotic and dynamic environment.

Action Research

This is a research based change process which is chosen after a rigorous data collection and analysis. It is "the study of a social situation carried out by those involved in that situation in order to improve both their practice and the quality of their understanding". It is a systematic means involving external resource person collaboration with some organisation members with the aim of diagnosing a problem and the development of an effective solution. From the two definitions above, it is evident that the major goals of action research is to provide a sound scientific methodology useful for managing planned organisational change process, and to produce practical knowledge that is useful to people in the everyday conduct of their lives. From a general perspective, "there are four main themes from most of the definitions of action research namely: empowerment of participants, collaboration through participation, acquisition of knowledge, and social change". From some review of literature, it is observed that action research is mostly used in educational and social research. We can rightly say that action research is not a holistic approach to managing organisational change. It is used to solve a specific organisational identified problem. Action research requires the "active involvement of the organisational change agent so as to identify, promote and evaluate the issues at hand and recommend practical solutions as the case may be". Generally, action research can be divided into three categories.

Classical action research views research as a way of testing tentative statement in a real world environment. Contemporary action research focuses on logical ideas of both individuals and group when undertaking research. Critical action research is a specific type of action research that adopts a deep-rooted approach with the objective of improvement performance. The ability of participants to actually perceive the need for a change and be willing to collaborate in the process of change is indeed one of the major characteristics of action research. When this is done, all stakeholders will perceive the change process and the outcome of the process to be meaningful, reliable and actionable. Just like a normal scientific research process, action research has five basic logical steps.

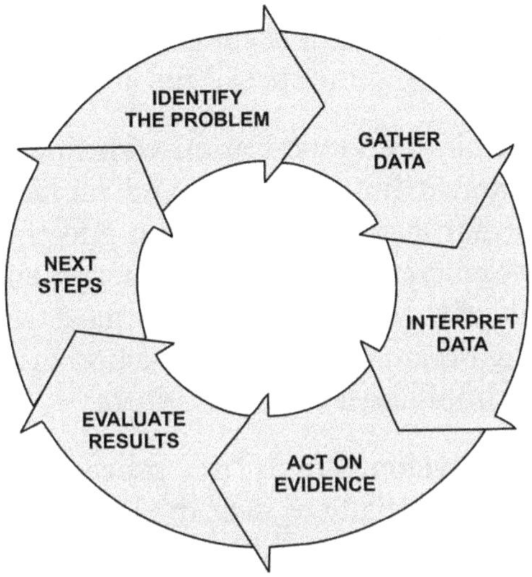

Action Research Cycle.

Action Research Process

- Problem identification: This involves interviews, reviews of opinions of the employees' records.
- Gathering of data: This is an attempt aimed at sourcing for the required set of data that is relevant to the study. Interpretation of data: Once data is gathered, the next thing is to analyse the data so that the data can now be in usable state. Once that is achieved, the analysed data is now interpreted for easy understanding by those who will utilize that data.
- Action: The change agent and the employees carry out the plans to remedy the problematic situation identified at the diagnosis stage.
- Evaluation: Initial data is used as a benchmark and evaluation is made to ascertain the success or otherwise of the change process.
- Next step: Thereafter the process continues because it is a never-ending process.

Organisational Development

"Organisational development refers to a special field involving well-trained people with expertise in facilitating successful organisational development interventions" to enhance improvement in organisations. It is a generic term used to describe various interventions strategies employed by organisations with the objective of increasing the capability of individuals and teams. Patching refers to OD as synonymous with management development, which he defines as activities having no direct physical impart on the organisation, but that its effectiveness lies in changing the behaviour of managers and employees. However, organisational development is a much broader scope than management development, since management development is aimed specifically at developing the competencies of organisational leaders in some specialized areas of knowledge.

Organisational development is "the organisation-wide application of behavioural science knowledge to the planned improvement, and reinforcement of the strategies, structures, and processes that lead to organisation effectiveness". One of the major goals of organisation development is to create an environment where organisations will be more open and more adaptive to learning in their quest to be learning organisations, because it is only a learning organisation that are action oriented towards learning by way of vitality and through imbibing a learning culture.

McLean views organisation development as "any process or activity, based on the behavioural sciences, that, either initially or over the long term, has the potential to develop in an organisational setting enhanced knowledge, expertise, productivity, satisfaction, income, interpersonal relationships, and other desired outcomes, whether for personal or group/team gain, or for the benefit of an organisation, community, nation, region, or, ultimately, the whole of humanity".

It is an "applied behavioural science approach to planned changes and development of an organisation because the emphasis on OD is more on improving organisation capabilities rather than the actual organisational processes and it is about large scale organisational change that is based on people's perception and behaviour".

Shvindina views organisational development as consistent with organisational transformations, which means the accumulation of organisational capabilities to solve organisational problem and to react to external challenges. Organisational development is not about restructuring or a reducing organisational layer, that is why Church defines OD by first outlining what he considers not being OD for instance, downsizing and process consolidation are not part of OD. He thereafter defines OD as a systematic organisational change. The idea here is that it is not every change that can be classified as organisational development.

Underlying Values in OD Interventions

- People should be treated with respect.
- There must be trust, openness and collaborative organisational climate.
- Less emphasis should be placed on hierarchical structures.
- Confrontation: Issues bothering on employees must be treated head-on.

- People that will be affected by the change must be included in the planning and execution of the change process.

Organisational Development Strategies/Techniques

- Sensitivity training: This is also called T-group: These are training groups that change behaviour and attitudes of employees though unstructured group interaction. Training is usually on process rather than on content.
- Survey feedback: This involves the use of questionnaire to illicit information from the employees. The interview is aimed at identifying the discrepancies among members perception, discussion follows and remedies are suggested. It is one of the human based processes OD intervention strategies aimed at enabling the employees to develop better understanding of their own and others behaviour for the purpose of improving interpersonal, intra-group, and inter-group relations.
- Process consultation: The aim of process consultation is to increase the value the relationships among individuals working in groups especially among students and teachers to achieve their common goals. It focuses on the context of interpersonal and group interactions rather than on what of the content.
- Team building: This involves a clear understanding of the mutual expectations from individuals, as well as the modalities of working with one another as collaborators in other to optimize the performance of each team member. It has to do with building a common value for the team, creating a strategic vision for the team, and crafting specific role for each team member.
- Appreciative inquiry: This intervention strategy seeks to identify the key organisational competencies with a view to developing those competencies so as to achieve individual and organisational improvements. Appreciative inquiry continuously emphasizes the positive since it first identifies the key competencies of an organisation, instead of looking for a problem to fix. Members, thereafter work on that key organisational strength with a view to improving performance. Naylor added role analysis, quality of work-life, and counselling as part of organisational development strategies.

Appreciative inquiry has no one specific guideline or procedure, however one of the oldest methods was the 4 principles of appreciative inquiry which states that inquiry into any social phenomena should be appreciative, collaborative, provocative, and applicable. Be that as it may, modern approaches have evolved over the years and one of the latest approaches is the 4 D model of appreciative inquiry created and popularized by Cooper rider, Whitney & Stavros). The 4D model is briefly explained below:

- Discovery: This is the period to think and reflect on the present state of the subject of inquiry.

- Dream stage: This stage is very important as it paints a better picture in the minds of the participants. At this state, participants are required to conceptualize an ideal situation that they all will aspire to experience.
- Design stage: At this stage, participants are asked to design an ideal organisation as conceptualized at the dream stage. Participants are encouraged to form groups or categories for the purpose of creating special projects.
- Destiny/Delivery stage: This stage was initially called delivery stage, until Cooper rider changed it to destiny when he discovered that delivery seem to be associated with traditional management change approach. This has brought about a lot of criticism from appreciative inquiry researchers.

According to Obie we all organisation development interventions or strategies that are rooted in the engineering, industrial psychology and in the applied fields of sociology and humanities are referred to as socio structural interventions. The following fall under the socio-structural interventions: Job enlargement; Job enrichment; Structural design; Downsizing; Re-engineering; Total quality management, and Work design. The purpose of which is to:

- Increase efficiency in work content, enhance task completion method, and building a mutual relationship among workers, and
- Reduce operational costs by replacing out-dated materials and equipment.

Benefits of Organisational Development Interventions

According to Hawai Pacific University, organisation that engages full organisational development program enjoys the following benefits: Continuous Improvement, effective communication, continuous employee development, quality products and services and increase in the organisations' bottom line. When stakeholders define the change and allow leaders to manage the change process, there is a high probability of a successful change process, but when leaders define the change and personally manage the change process, it often leads to failure. In the same way if stakeholders define the changes and allow staff to manage the change process, it will fail unless the leaders buy in to the outcome of the change process.

According to Rune the major cause of these failures has to do basic lack of a valid framework on change planning and implementation which make leaders to over-rely on inconsistent theories and models that lack empirical validation. It is as a result of this that the author argues that to have a successful OD intervention organisational leaders must be enthusiastic about improving the organisation's ability to adapt to environmental challenges. In order to improve their organisations, they must use both attitudinal and behavioural change processes that will increase the organisations ability to understand its vision, reduce the extent to which emotions influences group and organisational decisions making processes, procedures and actions, and as well, increase the organisation's capacity to achieve its potentials.

Permissions

All chapters in this book are published with permission under the Creative Commons Attribution Share Alike License or equivalent. Every chapter published in this book has been scrutinized by our experts. Their significance has been extensively debated. The topics covered herein carry significant information for a comprehensive understanding. They may even be implemented as practical applications or may be referred to as a beginning point for further studies.

We would like to thank the editorial team for lending their expertise to make the book truly unique. They have played a crucial role in the development of this book. Without their invaluable contributions this book wouldn't have been possible. They have made vital efforts to compile up to date information on the varied aspects of this subject to make this book a valuable addition to the collection of many professionals and students.

This book was conceptualized with the vision of imparting up-to-date and integrated information in this field. To ensure the same, a matchless editorial board was set up. Every individual on the board went through rigorous rounds of assessment to prove their worth. After which they invested a large part of their time researching and compiling the most relevant data for our readers.

The editorial board has been involved in producing this book since its inception. They have spent rigorous hours researching and exploring the diverse topics which have resulted in the successful publishing of this book. They have passed on their knowledge of decades through this book. To expedite this challenging task, the publisher supported the team at every step. A small team of assistant editors was also appointed to further simplify the editing procedure and attain best results for the readers.

Apart from the editorial board, the designing team has also invested a significant amount of their time in understanding the subject and creating the most relevant covers. They scrutinized every image to scout for the most suitable representation of the subject and create an appropriate cover for the book.

The publishing team has been an ardent support to the editorial, designing and production team. Their endless efforts to recruit the best for this project, has resulted in the accomplishment of this book. They are a veteran in the field of academics and their pool of knowledge is as vast as their experience in printing. Their expertise and guidance has proved useful at every step. Their uncompromising quality standards have made this book an exceptional effort. Their encouragement from time to time has been an inspiration for everyone.

The publisher and the editorial board hope that this book will prove to be a valuable piece of knowledge for students, practitioners and scholars across the globe.

Index

CPSIA information can be obtained
at www.ICGtesting.com
Printed in the USA
LVHW060908030122
707669LV00002B/400